John Updike
and the Cold War

John Updike and the Cold War

Drawing the Iron Curtain

D. Quentin Miller

UNIVERSITY OF MISSOURI PRESS

COLUMBIA AND LONDON

Copyright © 2001 by
The Curators of the University of Missouri
University of Missouri Press, Columbia, Missouri 65201
Printed and bound in the United States of America
All rights reserved
5 4 3 2 1   05 04 03 02 01

Cataloging-in-Publication data available from the Library of Congress

ISBN 0-8262-1328-6

⊗ This paper meets the requirements of the
American National Standard for Permanence of Paper
for Printed Library Materials, Z39.48, 1984.

Designer: Kristie Lee
Typesetter: The Composing Room of Michigan, Inc.
Printer and binder: The Maple-Vail Book Manufacturing Group
Typefaces: Garamond Book, Bodoni Heavy

Quotations from the following books written by John Updike are reprinted by permission of Alfred A. Knopf, a Division of Random House Inc., and Penguin UK: *Pigeon Feathers and Other Stories,* © 1962; *Couples,* © 1968; *Bech: A Book,* © 1970; *Picked-Up Pieces,* © 1975; *The Coup,* © 1978; *Hugging the Shore,* © 1983; *Odd Jobs,* © 1991; *Memories of the Ford Administration,* © 1992; *Collected Poems 1953–1993,* © 1993.

This book is dedicated to three people
whose love and support made it possible:
Robert Miller, Sylvia Miller,
and Julie Nash

Contents

Acknowledgments

I WOULD LIKE TO THANK Michael Meyer, Brenda Murphy, and Veronica Makowsky, all from the University of Connecticut, who guided me through the dissertation that led to this book with a tremendous amount of patience, insight, and encouragement. I would especially like to thank my wife, Julie Nash, who has read virtually every draft and revision and offered support and valuable criticism.

Thanks also to the research, scholarship, and creativity committee at Gustavus Adolphus College for providing me with a grant to study Updike's papers at the Houghton Library during the summer of 1997. I would also like to thank two research assistants from Gustavus, Kaethe Schwehn and Kate Krueger, who helped me track down sources and who kept my work in order. I am grateful to Michael Ronayne, Dean of the College of Arts and Sciences at Suffolk University, for helping to pay the permissions costs of Updike's publications.

I also want to thank Betty Falsey at the Houghton Library at Harvard for helping me with Updike's manuscripts and Leslie Morris for providing permission to quote from those sources.

Finally, I would like to thank John Updike for responding thoroughly, quickly, and generously to my questions over the years and for allowing me to quote from his papers at the Houghton.

Note on Citation

REFERENCES to Updike's books are in parentheses following the quotation; I have used the following abbreviations to designate the source:

A - *The Afterlife*

AP - *Assorted Prose*

Bech - *Bech: A Book*

Back - *Bech Is Back*

Bay - *Bech at Bay*

B - *Brazil*

Centaur - *The Centaur*

CP - *Collected Poems 1953 – 1993*

Coup - *The Coup*

C - *Couples*

HS - *Hugging the Shore*

IBL - *In the Beauty of the Lilies*

MFA - *Memories of the Ford Administration*

MS - *A Month of Sundays*

MM - *More Matter*

MW - *Museums and Women*

OJ - *Odd Jobs*

OF - *Of the Farm*

PP - *Picked-Up Pieces*

PF - *Pigeon Feathers*

TPF - *The Poorhouse Fair*

Rest - *Rabbit at Rest*

Rich - *Rabbit Is Rich*

Redux - *Rabbit Redux*

SC - *Self-Consciousness*

TFG - *Too Far to Go*

TET - *Toward the End of Time*

TM - *Trust Me*

WE - *The Witches of Eastwick*

John Updike
and the Cold War

Introduction

I'm a product of the nearly forty years of Cold War. So naturally
I've written about domestic, rather peaceable matters, while trying
always to elicit the violence and tension that does exist beneath the
surface of even the most peaceful-seeming life.

–John Updike, "An Interview with John Updike," 1988

DURING THE FIRST WEEK of August 1955, the month that John Updike launched his career as a writer for the *New Yorker,* a record-breaking
heat wave gripped New York City. Temperatures shot up so high that even
the *Times* carried front-page stories about sweltering New Yorkers trying
to protect themselves from the heat. As we look back at the lead stories
that week in the *Times,* we realize that the temperature of the Cold War
was a far more prominent concern than the hot weather; the tense headlines about strained U.S.-Soviet relationships, usually hinging upon the issue of the nuclear threat, are striking from a post–Cold War perspective.
The heat wave was news because it was different, but the Cold War was
news because it had to be: America's edgy relationship with the Soviet
Union was the very basis for national identity for nearly half a century,
from the end of World War II until the toppling of the Berlin Wall in 1989.
The acclaimed author, who described himself as "a helplessly 50's guy" in
1990, became a writer in the heart of this tense time in American history,
and now that it is possible to see the Cold War as a whole, it is also possible to see how it affected the trajectory of Updike's writing. Updike was
fourteen when the Cold War began, and his prolific writing career largely
overlaps with America's anti-Soviet identity quest. By studying Updike's

writing against the background of the flashpoints of Cold War history, it becomes evident that even the young writer of suburban domestic realism who initially worked to keep his writing free from overtly political content was profoundly affected by the early Cold War ideology that pervaded his world. He writes in 1995, "The thing about the Cold War was you ignored it if you could." My examination of Updike's writings has revealed that you couldn't, not if the subject of your fiction was the Cold War American in search of an identity.[1]

The way the Cold War affected Updike's writing is unique, partially because of his endurance and extraordinary output and partially because of his tireless experimentation. Other American writers fall more easily into subcategories within the broader "Cold War" category: the genre of international espionage fiction made famous by Tom Clancy and Ken Follett; McCarthy-era humanism including figures as diverse as Arthur Miller, Dorothy Parker, and Allen Ginsberg; or the paranoia school of postmodernism led by Don DeLillo and Thomas Pynchon. Yet the Cold War was pervasive in American culture and literature from the early 1950s onward, and it affected American life and letters in a variety of ways that are only apparent in retrospect. In his recent study *Flannery O'Connor and Cold War Culture,* Jon Lance Bacon has shown how even O'Connor—a writer traditionally associated with the American South and Catholicism—was profoundly affected by broad-reaching Cold War pressures such as political anxiety and the need to reexamine a national identity. Though Updike is also occasionally pigeonholed as a regional writer, a suburban writer, or a Protestant writer, he is more overtly concerned with chronicling America than is O'Connor. Joyce Carol Oates declares that "America without Updike to record it" is "unthinkable."[2] As Updike's writing career began, Cold War issues such as the threat of nuclear war, fear of Soviet aggression, and the position of America on the world stage were prominent concerns.

1. *New York Times* headlines from the week in August 1955 include: "Cultural Ties Parley Suspends with Soviet Union" (August 1); "[Soviet Premier] Bulganin Rejects Eisenhower Plan to Inspect Arms / Scorns Air Check / But Soviet Leader Calls President Sincere—Asks 'Cold War' End" (August 5); and "Curtain is Lifted By Soviet on Use of Atomic Energy" (August 8). Updike calls himself "a helplessly 50's guy" in "Why Rabbit Had to Go," *New York Times Book Review* (August 4, 1990): 24. The 1995 quote is from John Updike, letter to author, September 19, 1995.

2. Harold Bloom, ed., *John Updike,* 68.

Such issues, and more complicated versions of them, continued to haunt Updike's world as he went on to produce an unparalleled body of fiction, poetry, and literary reviews over the next forty years.

What makes Updike interesting as a Cold War writer is the fact that his characters, speakers, and narrators engage so deeply and complexly with their nation's identity as it evolves over the course of the post–World War II era. His writings reflect nothing less than the torturous growth of a wide-eyed, optimistic, self-assured, relatively unified nation in the 1950s into a jaded, cynical, self-doubting, fragmented, but mature nation in the 1990s. Updike's America is driven by the constant negotiation between what our nation hopes to be and what it actually is. The goal of the early Cold War was to preserve the 1950s American dream of prosperity, security, domestic harmony, and individual liberty. Such idealism clashed with the realism that became evident during the disruptive 1960s as Americans realized that nuclear weaponry provided a real threat to the existence of the world, competition with the Soviet Union occasionally meant that America must be aggressive, and fighting for democracy meant that you must occasionally fight a real war. American identity during and after the Cold War, according to Updike's fiction, is based on the clash between early Cold War optimism and late Cold War disillusionment. The zeitgeist of Updike's Cold War America is not paranoia, anticommunist hysteria, or anxiety, but rather nostalgia: a painful longing to return to the earlier, unfallen, innocent world of 1950s middle-class suburbia that no longer exists, and that only really ever existed in America's imagination.

I am speaking of the Cold War in its broadest sense: America's rivalry with the Soviet Union for global hegemony in the years between the end of World War II and the collapse of the Soviet empire in 1989. The nature of the war was military and economic, but especially ideological; as Tom Englehardt has argued in *The End of Victory Culture,* the Cold War was an attempt to repeat American history by retelling the familiar tale of the New World asserting its superiority over an established nation, and claiming itself worthy of the spoils of the modern world. By "Cold War" I mean only partially the actual foreign policy decisions and strategies that affected U.S.-Soviet relations from 1945 to 1990, when the Berlin Wall and all that it represented came crumbling down. I am more concerned in this study with the way in which those decisions and strategies affected middle-class Amer-

icans, who were the subjects of Updike's fiction, as well as his intended audience. American foreign policy trickled down to citizens during the Cold
War via newspaper headlines, radio, and the newest and most influential
member of the mass media, television. The rise of television culture paralleled the formation of a Cold War consensus. For example, two pivotal
events of the Cold War—the Vietnam War and the moon landing—were accessible to nearly all Americans by way of this new phenomenon. The general mood of Americans during the late 1960s took two forms: elation at
the grand achievement of the moon walk and discouragement at the suffering and destruction in Vietnam. Both events were Cold War phenomena;
both entered the daily lives of Americans through their television sets. We
cannot overemphasize the impact of audio-visual images transmitted into
the living spaces of virtually every home in the country, nor can we overlook the power of television as a propaganda tool that fueled Cold War tensions; Frank M. Folsom, president of RCA, claimed in 1951 that television
was a vital source of information "when swiftly changing events may otherwise cause confusion and alarm to the detriment of unity of purpose in
safeguarding the democratic institutions of our land and our determination
to assist other freedom-loving people against aggression."[3] Television, for
better or worse, provides Americans with a shared perspective on current
events. Its ever-increasing popularity over the last forty years explains why
anxiety over international affairs so thoroughly saturated the country during the Cold War. The nightly news repeatedly displayed Soviet troops
marching in lockstep in Moscow's snow-covered Red Square, or American
troops sweltering and paranoid in the jungle of Vietnam, or, perhaps most
disconcertingly, the repeated broadcasts of the mushroom clouds that followed the detonation of atomic bomb tests.

One cannot say that these disturbing images provide a coherent portrait
of a war. The many-faceted Cold War was a largely subjective experience
that changed as randomly and unpredictably as one Soviet leader replaced
another. Televised images are just one indication of how world events impacted American citizens during the Cold War and how a Cold War consensus was created and challenged. Due to an increased access to the far
reaches of the globe, Americans during the Cold War experienced a

3. Stephen J. Whitfield, *The Culture of the Cold War,* 154.

heightened awareness of world events, and of their own precarious position relative to them. Between the actual events of the Cold War and the American response to them, we can begin to see the post-1950s Cold War as a pattern of anxiety and confusion that threatened American stability.

Toward the beginning of his career, Updike's response to this anxiety and confusion was to avoid it as the overt subject of his fiction. About a decade into his career, though, there is a marked shift from closely bounded stories of rural and suburban domestic scenes to stories written with an eye toward the American identity crisis that contextualizes these scenes. There is an obvious development, in terms of both style and content, from his early Olinger stories, in which he repeatedly examines modern Americans in terms of Joycean epiphany and irony, to his later, broad-reaching novels such as *The Coup* (1978) and *In the Beauty of the Lilies* (1994), in which he reveals a deep concern for the national and global consequences of America's ongoing sense of crisis during the Cold War. While critics and reviewers have been baffled by these later works and have largely dismissed them in favor of the earlier works, it is noteworthy that his most famous and enduring body of work—the Rabbit tetralogy—is essentially a hybrid of the early and later types. As Updike's celebrated style becomes more complex, he increasingly makes use of actual events in history (often through television or radio broadcasts) and the middle-class response to global events. Defending himself against an interviewer's charge in 1968 that "American history is normally absent from [his] work," Updike asserts,

> Not so; quite the contrary. In each of my novels, a precise year is given and a President reigns . . . [a number of the characters] all talk about history, and the quotidian is littered with newspaper headlines, striking the consciousness of the characters obliquely and subliminally but firmly enough: Piet's first step at seducing Foxy [in *Couples*] is clearly in part motivated by the death of the Kennedy infant. And the atmosphere of fright permeating *The Centaur* is to an indicated extent early Cold-War nerves. My fiction about the daily doings of ordinary people has more history in it than history books, just as there is more breathing history in archaeology than in a list of declared wars and changes of government. (PP 482)

From the network of expressions and impressions of life during the Cold War that we have access to, we can articulate a notion of the type of cultural history Updike describes by placing his writings in the context of other cultural phenomena. Coming as it does at a crucial point in his career—just as he achieves monumental success with the publication of *Couples* and publishes the introspective, experimental poem sequence *Midpoint*—this quotation is also telling in terms of the shift I have spoken of: from the private writer he once was to the public writer he was rapidly becoming in the 1960s, when America's Cold War consensus reached its crisis point.

Even though Updike's writing career began and has continued through a period of tremendous global upheaval, and despite his defense of the historical significance of his fiction, the earliest Updike criticism attempts to remove his works from the atmosphere of current events that surrounds them. Unlike many of his contemporaries—Saul Bellow, Arthur Miller, Joseph Heller, Norman Mailer, and J. D. Salinger, to name a few—who have reduced their literary output or ceased writing completely, Updike has continued to be a major figure in American letters through the 1990s. Yet Updike's critical reputation was established in the early 1970s and remains heavily weighted toward his early works. During the 1970s a few major trends emerged that set the stage for much of the criticism that followed. Donald Greiner and Alice and Kenneth Hamilton approach Updike's works individually, as if there are no unifying themes connecting them. These critics lay down guidelines and provide admirable summaries of Updike's fiction, yet their appreciations underscore Updike's aesthetic achievement rather than his cultural significance. Similarly, Robert Detweiler is relieved that he, writing about Updike in 1972, can "expend less effort on the social-cultural implications of his writing and more on a comprehension and appreciation of his fiction as art." The works of criticism that do trace thematic development in Updike's work generally address religious searching, such as the book-length studies by Rachael Burchard and John Neary, or they address Updike's participation in archetypal traditions such as pastoral and anti-pastoral (Larry Taylor) and ritual and myth (Edward F. Vargo). Robert M. Luscher in 1993 begins to address the topic of "postwar development" in Updike's themes, and a special issue of *Modern Fiction Studies* devoted to Updike (spring 1991) contains a number of articles that engage with his uses of contemporary history, notably Stacey Olster's article on *Rabbit at Rest*. The only book-length study to take a cultural historical approach to Updike is Dilvo I. Ristoff's 1983 study *Updike's America: The Presence of Contemporary American History in John Updike's Rabbit Trilogy.* Ristoff's study is admirable for its ground-breaking treatment of Updike as historian and critic of contemporary culture; but the title of Ristoff's study alone indicates that more is to be done with the subject. Ristoff rounds out his study by discussing *Rabbit at Rest* in Lawrence Broer's *Rabbit Tales,* a recent collection of essays that also contains a number of historical and cultural studies; yet again, the focus is only on the Rabbit novels. The tide is unquestionably turning away from the early aesthetic and religion/myth schools of Updike criticism, but cultural/historical literary critics have not yet focused on Updike's entire career.[4]

It seems only fitting that a writer like Updike whose frequent popular culture allusions distinguish his work from less history-minded novelists would receive critical attention for his depiction of contemporary America. For all of his intellectual struggles—the theological, philosophical, literary, and scientific inquiries that give his work depth and solidity—Updike is first and foremost a social critic, and his legacy rests on his ability to depict contemporary America, which for most of his career was Cold War America. Updike's aesthetic involves incorporating the mass media into his fiction, as some recent critics such as Ristoff and Olster have demonstrated. The Updike reader can easily recall pivotal scenes from his fiction that suggest the connection between private crises and public events, such as Harry Angstrom's bored reaction as he watches the moon landing in *Rabbit Redux* or Foxy Whitman and Freddy Thorne deferring the substance of their conversation as they hear the news of Kennedy's assassination in *Couples.*

Yet the Cold War was more than just headlines and news broadcasts, and Updike frequently demonstrates the connection between his characters and the global conflict more subtly. It was a psychological war, a cultural war, a propaganda war, a war in outer space and in suburban back-

4. Robert Detweiler, *John Updike,* 7. Robert M. Luscher, *John Updike: A Study of the Short Fiction,* x. In the Broer collection see especially Jeff H. Campbell's "'Middling, Hidden, Troubled America': John Updike's Rabbit Tetralogy" (34–49), Dilvo I. Ristoff's "Appropriating the Scene: The World of *Rabbit at Rest*" (50–69), and Edward Vargo's "Corn Chips, Catheters, Toyotas: The Making of History in *Rabbit at Rest*" (70–88).

yards. It was so unrecognizable as a war that when American soldiers were shipped off to fight an actual war in Vietnam, ostensibly in the crusade against communism, Americans became confused, angry, and disillusioned. Lasting nearly half a century, the Cold War was never well-defined or stable, but it was unified by a few recurrent themes in American thought: the idea that communism represented a threat to American democracy, the sense that Americans were competing with a dangerous superpower for global supremacy, and the fear that the world could be destroyed at any time given the presence of nuclear weaponry.

In order to delimit the Cold War in this study I draw from official state relations between the United States and the Soviet Union and the consensus mood of Americans, both the public headlines and the semi-public and private reactions to them. By "littering" his fiction with newspaper headlines and allowing his characters to respond to these headlines, Updike records a distinct impression of the Cold War mind-set as it changes over the decades. Characters can either embrace or resist this mind-set, but their choices have consequences to their personal security and happiness. Patterns emerge over the course of Updike's career in such a way that the Cold War allows us to evaluate his characters' private lives against the backdrop of American identity. This national identity was in constant flux and in crisis throughout the Cold War, as the social turmoil of the 1960s makes clear. Recent historians have described "two major periods of cold war, the first of which petered out in the mid- to late 1960s, and the second of which began in earnest in the early 1980s."[5] This division is useful when applied to Updike; the years between the two periods described above—the Vietnam era, from the late 1960s to the late 1970s— contain some of Updike's most compelling, yet most conflicted, writing. The challenge to understanding this middle period in Updike's career depends upon understanding the difficulties many Americans of Updike's generation faced when it came to adapting to the changes in the Cold War. From Kennedy's assassination through the period known as détente, Americans were forced to come to terms with an enemy that was no longer absolute or well-defined. The fact that Updike's characters from the middle years of the Cold War face tremendous psychological and domes-

---

5. Ken Ruthven, *Nuclear Criticism,* 12.

tic difficulties reflects the upheaval of such changes, and underscores the overwhelming influence of early Cold War optimism on Americans who came of age in the 1950s.

It is crucial to try to understand the impact of the Cold War on the sweep of Updike's career. Some of his works, such as *Bech: A Book* (1970) and *The Coup* (1978) are particularly relevant in terms of the Cold War because of their overt treatment of it, and thus have a prominent place in my study; others, such as *Buchanan Dying* (1971) and *Roger's Version* (1985), are affected less obviously by the Cold War, and though they share many of the thematic characteristics of the literature I discuss in detail, they are not part of the study because they lack specific references to the actual Cold War. I have organized my material thematically, but also roughly chronologically, since the thematic development of Updike's career corresponds with global events.

The primary reason for the Cold War's grip on the American imagination was the threat of nuclear war. McCarthyism would not have had the impact it did were it not for the Rosenberg trials following the detonation of the first Soviet atomic bomb in 1949. Ronald Reagan would have had no cause to dub the Soviet Union an "evil empire" thirty years later if Americans were not imperiled by the continued threat of nuclear war. The Cold War begins with the fear of what nuclear weaponry is capable of, and it ends with that fear diminished, but far from totally erased. Though the Cold War is now officially over, American fears of nuclear war and perhaps a lingering distrust of former Eastern bloc countries remain with us. An investigation of Updike's status as a Cold War writer is relevant as a way not only to place his writings in a sociohistoric context but also to come to terms with the Cold War anxieties that remain a part of our culture.

The primary pressure of the Cold War—the threat of nuclear war—is the subject of my first chapter, "Knowledge of an Immense Catastrophe." The early period of Updike's writing—from his short stories in the 1950s through the publication of *Couples* in 1968—is characterized by widespread denial of nuclear fear and anxiety. Updike's characters during this period locate meaning in the past, treat the present as a game, and think about the future as little as possible. Faith in the future and in God diminish simultaneously, and characters tend to run around aimlessly, living their lives as though gratification in the present were all that mattered. When

placed in the context of the early Cold War, when the ever-increasing presence of nuclear weaponry threatened to destroy the world without warning, the fear and denial evident in Updike's early works becomes more
comprehensible. Updike's characters learn to live with the nuclear threat
in a typical way: they deny the danger that plagues their world, yet they
do so at a loss to their spiritual well-being. In *Couples,* Updike's characters
live through the Cuban Missile Crisis, the closest the world has come to
nuclear war. Surprised, in a way, that the world has survived nuclear peril,
these characters are forced to think beyond the inevitable end of the
world, a scenario that they had come to expect. The realization that the
world may not end in nuclear apocalypse forces them to come to terms
with the world they have created. After the initial fear of nuclear annihilation has subsided, Updike's characters begin to focus on other Cold War
concerns, such as the ideological conflict with the Soviet Union.

Though the fear of nuclear annihilation permeated the American consciousness during the Cold War, the fear of "losing" to the Soviets was often a more visible manifestation of this primary fear. While psychological
"flight" was a typical American response to the nuclear threat, the instinct
to "fight" was at least as common a response to the perceived existence of
a global enemy, and it was this latter impulse that preserved American optimism throughout the Cold War. The second chapter, "Zero-Sum Marriages, Global Games," discusses the presence of interpersonal competition in Updike's fiction, and reveals how that competition relates to the
global competition characteristic of the Cold War. America's anxiety over
the threat of nuclear catastrophe during the Cold War was balanced by the
potential for gain through competition with the Soviet Union. America in
the post–World War II era defined itself in relation to its global "other," and
Americans knew that they stood to benefit from this competition in terms
of economic gain as well as identity. Competition is generally seen as necessary in Updike's America, as it maintains postwar prosperity and ensures
the rights of the individual. But this type of competition does not translate
easily to interpersonal or romantic relationships. Beginning with his stories written in the early 1960s, Updike writes increasingly about the
breakdown of marriages. The cause for this disruption to the nuclear family is often linked directly to changes in the Cold War; the competitiveness
that enabled America to gain military and financial prosperity was devas-

tating to middle-class marriages. Marking the progression of the global game with such Cold War signposts as the launching of Sputnik, Nixon's "kitchen debate" with Khrushchev, and the landing of Apollo 11 on the moon, this chapter investigates how American competition with the Soviets threatened to unravel the social fabric of the domestic sphere in Updike's fiction even as the country prospered from such competition on a larger scale.

The third chapter, "Vietnam and the Politics of Undovishness," takes up the idea of the conflicted ideology covered in the second chapter. In this chapter I demonstrate how the Vietnam War, the testing ground for American anticommunist ideology, provided a source of prolonged tension in Updike's writing in the same way it divided America. Updike, who cut his teeth as a writer during the relatively unified 1950s, found it difficult to adapt to changes in the Cold War during the Vietnam era. Against his will, Updike became literary America's chief spokesperson for the pro-Vietnam War position in 1967 when he responded to a questionnaire that asked "Are you for, or against, the intervention of the United States in Vietnam?" The *New York Times* singled him out as the only American author "unequivocally for" such intervention. Though Updike disagrees with this assessment, he admits an "undovish" stance toward the war, and struggles for years to figure out why he was "out of step with [his] editorial and literary colleagues" (SC 117). His writings of the Vietnam era, particularly those that deal explicitly with the debate over the war, mark a turning point in his career. These works are characterized by extreme conflict, divorce, and a pervasive consciousness of current events of history. Because of the turbulence associated with the Vietnam years, Updike constructs the era before Vietnam as an Edenic time, setting up the nostalgia that is characteristic of his most recent works.

What makes Vietnam most interesting as a turning point in Updike's writing is his ongoing need to figure out why he was "so vehement and agitated an undove" (SC 116). He searches for the reasons behind his stance long after the war is over, especially in his 1989 memoir "On Not Being a Dove." There are a few possible explanations, mostly biographical: Updike's divorce seems inextricably linked to the Vietnam era, as is evident from his fiction as well as his memoir. There is also a rift between Updike and the younger generation, which can largely be explained by his feeling that the anti-war demonstrators on college campuses had not earned the right to protest since they did not have to work as hard as he did to attain the American Dream. All explanations point to the idea that Vietnam represented for Updike the breakdown of the Cold War consensus that had unified Americans throughout the postwar era, and to a successful author with his finger on the pulse of middle-class America, such a breakdown was unwelcome. Updike's characters from the middle years of the Cold War suffer crises of confidence, and repeatedly sabotage their domestic situations as a direct result of their inability to adapt to change. Updike's writings that reflect the debate over the Vietnam War are among the most tormented of his career; by viewing them as a part of the pattern that emerges within the Cold War context, we are in a better position to understand how they represent a development rather than an anomaly.

America's opponent during the Cold War was an unfamiliar empire whose citizens were stigmatized repeatedly in cultural images. The fourth chapter, "Seeing How the Other Half Lives," illustrates how Updike's idea of the necessity of competition is complicated by an investigation of one's competitor. Based on a state-funded trip Updike took to the Soviet Union in 1964, his fiction begins to treat the "Evil Empire" as a place of real character, essentially similar to the United States except in terms of Soviet governmental abuses, notably censorship. In contrast to his disastrous public statements about American involvement in Vietnam, Updike managed to ally himself with his literary colleagues on the issue of Soviet literary dissent; yet he stood apart from some of the more politically active writers of the late 1960s such as Robert Lowell, Arthur Miller, and Saul Bellow in his approach to this issue. He refuses to protest Soviet censorship by addressing the Soviet government directly as he becomes confident that his role as a writer is to write and to review, not to stage protests. He believes that all writers should have the freedom of expression that the Soviet government refused to allow, but he is wary of taking this point too far, especially at the risk of undervaluing American writing while praising Soviet dissidents. Authors should focus on writing before politics, he believed, and as a result he is careful to limit his connections to the plight of Soviet dissent to the strictly literary, confining them to his reviews of Soviet literature and to his fictional renditions of his 1964 trip, especially in *Bech: A Book*. His increasingly intricate prose style evolves as a direct result of his distaste for the deadening effect of communist oppression on Soviet literature. Confronting the Soviet Union in his fiction and taking on the topic of Soviet literary dissent in his reviews, Updike demonstrates a sympathy toward the people who live behind the Iron Curtain that leads to an intensification of his notion—born of 1950s optimism—that the communist system is antithetical to the basic right of individual freedom.

Having affirmed his position against communist governments in the post-Vietnam era, Updike casts a fond backward glance on the 1950s in his writings of the 1980s and 1990s. I study this development in "A Reason to Get Up in the Morning," the final chapter in the book. In his writings from the early 1970s until the present, Updike communicates a strong desire to return to the 1950s, "a waxy blue-white" decade before the "psychedelic red" 1960s arrived to "wreck our Fifties marriages, shatter our faith in the anti-communist crusade, and leave scarcely a hero standing" (MM 25, 29). Updike's characters long to return to a time when the world was more innocent and easier to understand because of America's unified opposition to the communist Other. Harry Angstrom dies at the same time the Cold War ends, declaring just before his death, "I miss [the Cold War]; it gave you a reason to get up in the morning" (RAR 293). Updike's worldview had become so steeped in early Cold War thinking that he found it easier to look back on the relatively stable past than to look forward into a radically uncertain future as the Soviet Union crumbled. This nostalgia is not entirely naive and idealistic, though; Updike realizes that "neither history (the determined study of past events) nor memory (in the form of nostalgia) can really bring back the past."[6]

It has become increasingly difficult for critics to make sense of the whole of Updike's career because he has experimented with a broad range of styles, subjects, themes, and voices and produced an astonishing body of work that defies easy categorization. Those critics who label him a regional writer of either eastern Pennsylvania or the north shore of Massachusetts can only account for a fraction of his work. Those who dub him the heir apparent to Cheever's title of the voice of suburban America cannot account for *The Coup* or *Brazil*. Those who think of him as the twentieth century's great white Protestant hope have a hard time classifying

6. James Plath, *Conversations with John Updike,* 233.

the three Bech books. The Cold War is a lasting and pervasive context for considering his work. Even as he continues to produce lively and experimental fiction in the post-Cold War period, he wrestles with problems that are rooted in the way the global conflict took hold of his imagination in the 1950s, when he began his career. Although the Cold War did not sustain the temperature it reached during that torrid week when Updike first stepped through the doors of the *New Yorker* office in 1955, it did burn itself into his consciousness enough to shape one of the richest writing careers in post-World War II America.

1

Knowledge of an Immense Catastrophe

"Apocalypse is in."

–John Updike, *Midpoint*, 1968

JOHN UPDIKE'S EARLIEST POEMS, stories, and novels reflect his desire to balance the characters and stories from his youth in rural Pennsylvania with the intellectual and literary tradition that had so intrigued him at Harvard. These writings do not indicate that he would within two decades become a writer interested in global issues whose primary subject was increasingly the Cold War American. On the surface, the stories contained in his first two collections, *The Same Door* (1959) and *Pigeon Feathers* (1962), are written by a young man more obsessed with Joycean epiphany and religious doubt than with his nation's identity lost in a precarious moment in history. In 1954 Updike graduated from Harvard and went to England on a Knox fellowship to study drawing. In the process of selecting writing as a profession he pointedly left his country to delve deeper into the artistic and intellectual issues that had been framed for him at college. The trip to England can be viewed as a fruitful period of artistic expatriation during which he sought to expand his breadth of experience and to deepen his worldview before embarking on his new career. But it can also be interpreted as a retreat from his country and its contemporary history. A notebook that he kept from his year in England contains a reading list in the form of quotations from mostly biblical, medieval, and philosophical texts. There are multiple titles by Hooker and by Karl Barth, and assorted titles such as *The Medieval Reader, Heretics,* and *The Monastic Idol.* Contemporary novels and current history were apparently not what Updike was seeking in England at the beginning of his career.

Yet he also saved a copy of the *Ocean Times,* a newspaper published aboard the Cunard Steamship Company, apparently from his return trip to America in July 1955, one month before he began his career as a writer for the *New Yorker.* The headline of this newspaper was about Khrushchev's defiant stance before an upcoming Big Four Conference in Geneva: "SOVIET LEADER MAKES PRE-TALKS STATEMENT. RIDICULES SUGGESTION OF AN AGRICULTURAL CRISIS IN RUSSIA." Updike probably saved the paper as a memento of his voyage, but it is significant because it demonstrates the anxiety of the America to which he returned in contrast to the deep philosophical and aesthetic retreat he had experienced in London. In short, as he was about to become a professional writer, he would have preferred the heady intellectual world of old texts, but he realized on some level that he could not deny the world around him.

Updike lived his adolescence in the wake of World War II, a momentous time in terms of global reconfiguration that centered around nuclear weaponry, the most destructive instruments of war the world had ever seen. In the late 1940s an entirely new geopolitical structure formed that was to dictate the fate of the entire world, directly or indirectly, for the next forty years. To be alive during the latter half of the twentieth century is to be conscious of the implicit threat of the Bomb. To be an American during this period is to be aware that this threat is part and parcel of our national identity. American writers during the Cold War, especially novelists of social realism such as Updike, reveal an awareness of nuclear weaponry that often manifests itself in discontent with the suburban veneer that made postwar America seem so perfect and prosperous, anxiety about the future, and a lack of direction. Any reader of Updike's novels can easily recognize these features; but the Bomb is often overlooked as instrumental in shaping his writings, particularly his works written up to and including *Couples* in 1968. The young writer worked hard to avoid the terrifying reality of the Nuclear Age, concentrating instead on the artistic and metaphysical questions that have intrigued him throughout his career; but, like his characters, Updike would gradually discover that the threats of nuclear war were undeniable, and that these threats must eventually be confronted.

The implications of the Bomb were enormous from its deployment at the end of World War II, but they became much more urgent when the Soviet Union detonated an atomic bomb in 1949 as Updike was preparing to go to college. This event made the Soviets a tangible nuclear threat and caused the superpowers to engage in an unprecedented escalation of their military arsenals to the point that the horrifying question, "can the world be destroyed in a nuclear war?" soon yielded to the absurd question, "how many times over can the world be destroyed with nuclear weapons?" After President Truman announced in 1949 that the Soviets had successfully exploded an atomic bomb, Americans tended to agree with their government's decision to view "the atomic bomb not as a terrible scourge to be eliminated as quickly as possible, but as a winning weapon to be stockpiled with utmost urgency,"[1] in the words of historian Paul Boyer.

Thus began a period of profound anxiety about the continued existence of the human race. Updike, like his contemporaries, had to live with the fact that nuclear war could happen at any time. He could deny that fact or evade its ramifications, but only to a point. Psychologist Robert J. Lifton, in a series of studies on the collective mental state created by the fact of nuclear technology, writes of "psychic numbing," a condition which includes "a new ephemeralism which tends to undermine interpersonal and family relationships" and "a sense of radical futurelessness due to an expectation of annihilation in our lifetimes."[2] The characters from Updike's early works try to deny their own fear and reflect this psychic numbing by sabotaging their own dream of a comfortable, monogamous, suburban life, partially because they have no faith in the future. The

1. Whitfield, *The Culture of the Cold War,* 5.
2. Jane Caputi, "Psychic Numbing, Radical Futurelessness, and Sexual Violence in the Nuclear Film," 58.

implications of this denial are evident throughout Updike's work; his characters consistently locate meaning in the past, treat the present as a game, and think about the future as little as possible. In addition to this behavior, the religious doubt that has been the subject of most Updike criticism can be explained by the fact that Updike's writings take place during a time when the fear of apocalypse made religion a prominent concern. Updike's preoccupation with describing the search for religious meaning in his writings and his depiction of Americans who seek to focus on the present rather than to confront the future are not surprising when we consider that his early writing grew out of an age of profound nuclear anxiety.

In her last published work, "Reflection on the Atomic Bomb" (1946), Gertrude Stein professes indifference to the fact of the Bomb's existence; referring to a nonspecific "they," a pronoun that can be taken to mean "everyone," she writes, "They think they are interested about the atomic bomb but they really are not not any more than I am. Really not. They may be a little scared, I am not so scared, there is so much to be scared of so what is the use of bothering to be scared, and if you are not scared the atomic bomb is not interesting." It could be said that Stein is protesting too much here, that she is trying to convince herself that the Bomb is of no interest, that rather than being scared of nuclear holocaust, one should be indifferent to it. This refusal to fear nuclear war is a typical way of coping with the fact that it is possible; in a 1946 poll, 65 percent of Americans "claimed that they were either not worried at all or not much worried" about the Bomb. Stein's insistence that she is "not so scared" triggers the realization that there is something to be scared of. Just before her death in 1946, she leaves the world with the flimsy exhortation to "just live along like always." Stein's final work is written three years before America learned that the Soviet Union had the Bomb, and two years before Walter Lippmann popularized the term "Cold War," which now describes the period of American history corresponding with Updike's career from the outset. Much would change over the next decade; Paul Boyer argues that Stein and her contemporaries were not ready to process "the central reality of a new era" and adds, "silence may have signaled not a failure of imagination, but intensity of imagination." Updike begins his writing career at a slight historical remove from Stein's pronouncement, but he and his contemporaries were not necessarily better equipped to process the new reality.[3]

In Updike's poem "Sonic Boom" (1959), the speaker takes the same stance as Stein does in her "Reflection on the Atomic Bomb," but the immediate danger of the nuclear condition and the speaker's fear are heightened far above what they would have been if written during Stein's time; the poem begins,

> I'm sitting in the living room,
> When, up above, the Thump of Doom
> Resounds. Relax. It's sonic boom.

The hesitancy in the final line of this stanza demonstrates the speaker's anxiety, as though his heart skips a beat and he stops breathing while waiting for the other scenario — nuclear war. He must warn himself to relax; he is still alive (in the "living room"), and his fear is offset by the familiarity of the supersonic jet overhead, which literally "resounds" — that is, repeats its noise. He then attempts to assuage his disconcerted child and concludes,

> Our world is far from frightening; I
> No longer strain to read the sky
> Where moving fingers (jet planes) fly.
> Our world seems much too tame to die.
>
> And if it does, with one more *pop,*
> I shan't look up to see it drop. (CP 29)

The sky, a text onto which the speaker can "read" his worst fears of the future, may *seem* too tame to die; but the speaker obviously knows that the world is in fact not too tame to die, given his acknowledgment of that possibility in the final stanza. By insisting that his world is "far from frightening," he admits the opposite; by explaining "fingers," his own metaphor for jet planes, he is further refusing to give in to his imagination, which is the source of his fear. His final defense mechanism, like Stein's, is to refuse to

3. Gertrude Stein, "Reflection on the Atomic Bomb," in *Reflection On the Atomic Bomb, Vol. 1 of the Previously Uncollected Works of Gertrude Stein,* 161. Paul S. Boyer, *By the Bomb's Early Light: American Thoughts and Culture at the Dawn of the Atomic Age,* 23, 250.

be interested. Here we see the speaker's attitude toward his life change over time as a result of his fear of nuclear war; in the past he read the sky in a search for meaning, in the present he shrugs off his fear and pronounces the world "tame," and the future doesn't interest him.[4]

This attitude is not uncommon in Updike's writings; his speakers or characters feel powerless when it comes to changing the larger world, so they test the limits of their power in their individual, private worlds. The all-too-real possibility of nuclear war lurks in the margins of their world as familiar as a plane's daily flight overhead, an event that causes fear, anxiety, and a widespread diminishment of faith. Characters who turn away from God are familiar figures in Updike's writing. Their presence can be at least partially explained by the anxiety produced by nuclear weaponry, compounded by American-Soviet rivalry. In his memoir "On Being a Self Forever" (1989) Updike writes, "an age of anxiety all too suitably takes God as a tranquillizer" (SC 233). Twice within the same memoir he links religion explicitly to nuclear anxiety; at one point he defines the very term "religion" broadly, "in the form of any private system," including "hatred of nuclear weapons" (SC 226). Later he speaks of "two kinds of people: those for whom [existential] nothingness is no problem, and those for whom it is an insuperable problem, an outrageous cancellation rendering every other concern, from mismatching socks to nuclear holocaust, negligible" (SC 228). Updike obviously belongs in the second camp; existential doubt haunts his characters throughout his writing, and faith is what makes life bearable for him, if not for his characters. Religion is quite obviously a more consistent subtext in Updike's writings than nuclear war is, but, as he demonstrates here and as I hope to prove elsewhere, the two are con-

4. The same scenario is described in Updike's memoir collected in Martin Levin's *Five Boyhoods* as a combination of the aurora borealis and a jet plane: "I was slapped by a sudden cold wave of fear that made my skin burn. 'Is it the end of the world?' one of the women asked. There was no answer. And then a plane went over, its red lights blinking, its motors no louder than the drone of a wasp. Japanese. The Japanese were going to bomb Shillington, the center of the nation. I waited for the bomb, and without words prayed, expecting a miracle, for the appearance of angels and Japanese in the sky was restrained by the same impossibility, an impossibility that the swollen waxy brilliant white of the flower by my knees had sucked from the night.

The plane of course passed; it was one of ours; my prayer was answered with the usual appearance of absence. We went home, and the world reconstituted its veneer of reason, but the moans of the women had rubbed something in me bare" (194).

nected. Updike may be earnest in his claim that the possibility of a God-less universe outweighs nuclear holocaust, but his comparing them in this profoundly introspective memoir makes it clear that the nuclear threat is a reality that has always weighed on him and influenced his fiction.

One of the most obvious manifestations of the fear of the nuclear threat in Updike's fiction is that characters seek immediate, transient pleasure rather than living their lives slowly and methodically, with an eye to the future and faith in an afterlife. In his own terms, his fiction contains more rabbits than centaurs. There is a sense of frantic energy in many of Up-dike's writings, an impatience with the world as it is coupled with the be-lief that there may be no tomorrow. Updike has made much of the fact that *Rabbit, Run* (1960), the novel that has gained him lasting recognition, was written in the present tense, and that its original title was to be *Rabbit, Run: A Movie,* underscoring the cinematic quality of the present tense. Harry Angstrom in this book demonstrates an obsessive need to escape, including a need to escape thinking about the future, which may be too horrifying to consider. The present tense continues to overshadow the narrative voice in the rest of the Rabbit tetralogy, and in countless of his short stories. In an essay on the status of the nuclear age, Jacques Derrida explains a similar emphasis on the present through the fact that "nuclear war has no precedent. It has never occurred, itself; it is a non-event. . . . The terrifying reality of the nuclear conflict can only be the signified ref-erent, never the real referent (present or past) of a discourse or a text. At least today apparently. And that sets us to thinking about today, our day, the presence of this present."[5]

Given Updike's preoccupation with the present tense in his Rabbit tetral-ogy, it is ironic that his first novel, *The Poorhouse Fair* (1958), takes place in the future. While much of Updike's later work is characterized by a strong yearning for the past, this novel projects a version of America in 1980.[6] The tone of his first book does not communicate a longing for the future, but instead subtly demonstrates how the world may change as a re-sult of a widespread disregard for the future. *The Poorhouse Fair* is not "fu-

---

5. Jacques Derrida, "No Apocalypse, Not Now: Full Speed Ahead, Seven Missiles, Sev-en Missives." *Diacritics* 14, no. 2 (summer 1994): 23.

6. Jeff H. Campbell, *Updike's Novels: Thorns Spell a Word,* 45.

turistic," in the science-fiction sense of the word; the world described within it is essentially the same for the characters who reside in and operate the poorhouse in 1980 as it would have been in 1958. Yet the novel contains hints that the world surrounding the poorhouse has changed, and is tending toward apocalypse. Any reader of future fiction knows that the projected fictional world is almost always meant to magnify some potentially frightening aspect of the present. In *The Poorhouse Fair* there is an undercurrent of anxiety about the nuclear condition, a fear that the world will become a more precarious place because of the fact of the Bomb. This fear was an intensified concern when the novel was published in 1958, the year after the Soviets launched Sputnik, the first man-made satellite, creating a crisis of confidence among Americans that sent them scrambling to build fallout shelters in their backyards. Following the launching of Sputnik, a top-secret report known as the Gaither Report fell victim to a press leak. The report, largely dismissed by Eisenhower, depicted America as vulnerable to Soviet nuclear attack, and in grave danger of slipping into second place in terms of military strength.[7] Such sensationalism in the press only confirmed what most Americans were sure of: the world was doomed.

The Poorhouse Fair sets forth what are to become familiar debates in Updike's fiction; there are apparent dualities between belief and busyness, spirituality and science, versions of history centering around Buchanan and Lincoln, all of which recur throughout Updike's career. These dualities are represented in the novel by Hook and Conner, respectively.[8] The conflict represented by various clashes between these two men—one the unofficial leader of the poorhouse residents, the other the director of the poorhouse—gives way to actual physical violence, as the poorhouse residents attack Conner by throwing small stones at him. Danger lies just below the surface of this group of seemingly benign, feeble residents. Updike indicates the same danger in the world at large. After a spirited debate between Hook and Conner, the two men fall into talk about mundane matters. Conner suggests that weather may be more variable now than it was in the past, and Hook replies, "Yes well: the bombs" (TPF 36). This

---

7. John Newhouse, *War and Peace in the Nuclear Age,* 119.
8. For a detailed discussion of this duality in *The Poorhouse Fair,* see chap. 1 of Susan Henning Uphaus, *John Updike.*

somber observation silences Conner; the alteration of the world by the existence of the atomic bomb puts their debate into perspective. Later, just
after the residents attack Conner with pebbles, Hook again sounds an apocalyptic note: "'This last decade,' Hook claimed, not clear what it meant but
feeling the words, momentous and rounded, yearning to be said, 'has witnessed the end of the world, if the people would but wake to it'" (TPF 105).
Hook's fear of the end of the world is unspoken most of the time, but it
haunts him, and undoubtedly his companions as well, as it threatens to
obliterate what little meaning they have held onto in the waning years of
their lives. He continues the prophecy, referring back to an earlier conversation in which he discussed a biblical passage: "I wonder, now, if the
lightning Matthew mentioned, as running from east to west, might have
referred to the a-tomic [*sic*] bombs" (TPF 106). The apocalyptic vision of
this aged man is as much a product of the nuclear age as it is of the Bible;
the only atomic bombs that have been detonated as an act of warfare were
in the East, and Hook's fear is that their destructive effects will inevitably
reach his own world, and the West more generally. The crowd listening to
Hook says nothing, except for Kegerise, who blatantly redirects the conversation. Hook, the oldest resident of the poorhouse, is confronting his
own mortality and sadly weighing it against the possible end of humanity
by way of nuclear war. The other characters refuse to acknowledge the
possibility. For them, in order to live with the possibility of war, one should
avoid discussing the subject directly, enact violence on a small scale as a
type of catharsis, and refuse to consider the ramifications of their actions.

Compounded with the undiminished threat of nuclear war in *The Poorhouse Fair* is the prediction that the Cold War will continue, essentially
unchanged, twenty years in the future. "The Russians" (TPF 105) are still a
global rival, and the peace between the superpowers is still precarious.
Updike's fictional prediction was accurate, and it underscores the fact that
during the Cold War, under the ever-looming dark cloud of nuclear apocalypse, there did not appear to be an end in sight. In the pre-détente Cold
War years the only possible end to the conflict was the unthinkable. As
long as our lives continued, we were to remain in a state of global hostility. In Updike's writing, this realization contributes to the emphasis on living entirely for the moment.

The relative meaninglessness of the present is as evident in Updike's early short fiction as it is in his early novels. The stories collected in *The Same Door* and *Pigeon Feathers* are characterized by instability and a sense that the world, though prosperous and full of potential, is plagued by the threat of global extinction. We see in these stories characters who try to fix upon a point of time or a palpable object in order to impose some stability on their lives. At key moments, this instability takes the form of nuclear anxiety. As in *The Poorhouse Fair,* the characters in these stories must find some psychological defense against the horror that their world may not last. The narrator of "The Blessed Man of Boston, My Grandmother's Thimble, and Fanning Island," describing his feelings of reminiscence created by the discovery of his grandmother's thimble, says,

> I felt at my back that night a steep wave about to break over the world and bury us and all our trinkets of survival fathoms down. For I feel that the world is ending, that the mounting mass of people will soon make a blackness in which the glint of this silver [of the thimble] will be obliterated; it is this imminent catastrophe that makes it imperative for me to cry now, in the last second when the cry will have meaning, that once there was a woman whom one of the continents in one of its square miles caused to exist. (PF 241)

This vision of impending apocalypse cannot be separated from anxieties of nuclear annihilation. This passage describes the transience of the present and explains the writer's need to record his impressions of the world, "to cry now, in the last second when the cry will have meaning." This fear that the world will end soon partially explains the conflicts that infiltrate the various stories in *Pigeon Feathers,* and accounts for the way actual Cold War events are treated in this collection. Cold War anxiety may be too great to confront directly, so the narrators and characters of these stories attempt to distance themselves from these events by retreating into language, myth, ritual, or any number of other subterfuges that make it possible to live in such an unstable present. These attempts at evasion are only partially successful, as the Cold War—both its actual events and its projected fears—is apparent throughout the story collection, even though Updike was trying to avoid the subject in favor of more universal themes.

In the final story in *Pigeon Feathers,* "Packed Dirt, Churchgoing, A Dying Cat, A Traded Car," Updike reaffirms the connection between personal

conflict and fear of nuclear annihilation. The narrator of this story meditates on human existence after having experienced lust for a woman who
is not his wife: "Each instant my horror was extended amplified God's non-
existence, so . . . as the magnetic motive-power in atom-smashers accel-
erates itself, I was caught in a gathering vortex whose unbearably shrill
pitch moved me at last to drop my weight on my wife's body and beg,
'Wake up. Elaine. I'm so frightened'" (PF 261). The narrator's analogy between his own anxieties and the motion of an atom-smasher give way to
his nihilistic fear, causing him to tell his wife "of the millennia when our
nation would be a myth and our continent an ocean" (PF 261). Despite his
wife's attempts to pacify him with stoicism, the narrator's anxieties remain
the next day; he says, "for the first time truly in my life I realized that each
face is suppressing knowledge of an immense catastrophe; our faces are
dams that wrinkle under the strain" (PF 262). Characters throughout *Pigeon Feathers* try to avoid this suppressed "knowledge of an immense catastrophe," but its presence under the narrative surface of the stories cannot be contained indefinitely.

By suppressing their knowledge of an immense catastrophe, the characters in Updike's early short stories respond in a typical manner to the nuclear condition. After all, these stories were written during the years when
schoolchildren were repeatedly taught how to "duck and cover" when they
saw the atomic bomb's flash. American suburbanites built bomb shelters
to accompany their backyard patios and stocked them with freeze-dried
foods that would outlast the danger of radioactive fallout. The Bomb was
responsible for creating a culture of isolation, also fueled by the suspicion
of communist infiltration that pervaded the McCarthy years. Nearly all of
Updike's early stories are thematically concerned with isolation. Characters
in these stories are not able to communicate effectively or connect with
one another. This isolation can partially be explained in terms of the "psychic numbing"[9] that Lifton characterizes as endemic to the nuclear age. Updike's characters frequently embody the frustration of such isolation, and
they unconsciously associate this isolation with the fact of the Bomb.

More often than not, these characters are lovers or would-be lovers who

9. Nancy Anisfield, ed., *The Nightmare Considered: Critical Essays on Nuclear War
Literature,* 58.

painfully fail to communicate. For instance, Leonard Hartz in the story "Still Life" (1960) discovers himself to be one of a handful of representative Americans in an art school in London. While courting Robin, a British student, he confronts the differences between their cultures. He comes to terms with Robin's assessment that "Americans are never serious" (PF 35) by asserting, "All Americans are bores" (PF 48) in the final line of the story. He can never see things as she does, coming to Europe as an outsider: "She was eighteen, and described looking up as a child and seeing bombs floatingly fall from the belly of a German bomber, yet there was something flat and smooth behind her large eyes that deflected his words oddly; she seemed to be empty of the ragged absorbent wisdom of girls at home whose war experiences stopped short at scrap drives" (PF 35 - 36). The differences between them become apparent to him as the story progresses, as he realizes they are "two creatures thrown together in the same language exchanging, across a distance wider than it seemed, miscalculated signals" (PF 35). In the middle of the story, Robin reveals her anxiety about the current instability of the world by announcing to Leonard, "I have a friend who's an atheist and hopes World War Three blows everything to bits. He doesn't care. He's an atheist" (PF 35). This comment, without an apparent context, dictates how the distance between them—as man and woman as well as American and Brit—is exacerbated by the global situation. Robin's friend is a nihilist more apparently than an atheist and he symbolizes an unspoken lack of hope in her life. The hopelessness of the potential for romance between Robin and Leonard is fueled by this tragic position made possible by the threat of nuclear annihilation. Their future becomes impossible to consider as Robin's knowledge of an immense catastrophe is revealed. At the story's conclusion, Leonard resigns himself to the fact that they have no future, and the narrator observes, "she had exploded as he watched" (PF 40). The end of their relationship is not a calm slipping away; a character metaphorically explodes, forcing us to recall her apocalyptic vision of the future. Leonard remains isolated at the conclusion of the story, caught, like the protagonists of many of Updike's early writings, in an endless present without a clear indication of the future.

Some of these early stories initiate Updike's tendency to situate his fiction in the past. This tendency suggests that, in the nuclear age, meaning can be found in the past given the instability of the present and the uncertainty of the future. Knowledge of an immense catastrophe is less of an issue in his third novel, *The Centaur* (1963), than in some of the stories in *Pigeon Feathers,* partially because *The Centaur* takes place in 1946 before the Soviet Union had nuclear capability. America in 1946 was not in the complex "fix" of 1963 America, the year the novel was published. "What fix?" Peter Caldwell asks Minor Kretz. "This country is sitting on top of the world. We got the big bomb and we got the big bombers" (Centaur 202). The novel reflects a certain nostalgic yearning for a time when nuclear war was not a threat in the same way it was in 1963, when the Soviets had set up the big bombers as close as Cuba. Life was simpler in 1946 in Olinger, Pennsylvania, from Peter's perspective, without the threats and responsibilities Harry Angstrom faces in *Rabbit, Run,* in the same locale during the late 1950s. Yet the world of *The Centaur,* preoccupied though it is with rendering mythically the father-son experiences of George and Peter Caldwell, is still haunted by Cold War anxiety, fear, and paranoia. Peter's notion that America is safe with its possession of the "big bomb" touches off an ice cream parlor debate about the future. The most horrifying effect of the debate comes from Johnny Dedman, who sits apart from Minor and Peter, commenting irrelevantly on the points they make.

Dedman represents the "knowledge of an immense catastrophe" shared by the reader of *The Centaur* if not by the characters in it. As the debate over the merits and realities of communism between Minor and Peter begins, Dedman chain smokes Camel cigarettes and blows smoke rings. Suddenly he joins the debate: "Now he cries, without warning, the word 'War!' and with his finger rat-tat-tats the big brown button knotted onto the end of the light chord above his head" (Centaur 203). The volatility of this outburst seems to be characteristic of Dedman, as he continues to add to the debate: "'I love Hitler,' Johnny Dedman announces. 'He's alive in Argentina'" (Centaur 203). Like a character in *Dr. Strangelove* or the speaker in Gregory Corso's poem "Bomb," Dedman enthusiastically continues his rant: "'Bam. *Bam,*' Johnny Dedman cries. 'We should've dropped an atom bomb on Moscow, Berlin, Paris, France, Italy, Mexico City, and Africa. Ka-*Pow.* I love that mushroom-shaped cloud'" (Centaur 204). The other debaters ignore Dedman's reckless outbursts, but the reader in 1963 could not have been immune to the danger of this type of character, or to his symbolic function as the repressed fears within us all. The instability of the global situation in 1963, due to the superpowers' buildup of nuclear stockpiles, assigns a value to a character like Dedman that his contemporaries do not grant him in 1946. Like some characters in *Pigeon Feathers,* Dedman shows a lack of regard for the unstable present; when George suggests a possible career to the shiftless Dedman, the boy replies, "I'm waiting for the war." George responds with the most chilling prophecy of the debate, "You'll wait until Doomsday, kid" (Centaur 206).

At the end of the novel, which takes place over the course of three days, not much has changed, either globally or in the life of George Caldwell. He forgets to buy a newspaper for his father-in-law, but defends himself by saying, "I'll get you one tomorrow. Nothing'll happen until then, I promise you. The Russians are still in Moscow and Truman's still king" (Centaur 289). At the same time, George discovers that he does not have cancer. Yet there is an undeniable weariness, as though the ability of the world to hold up against such pressure—the face-off between the superpowers and George's resistance to his own death—is slipping. During the mid-1960s this weariness was compounded by turbulence on the domestic front— the assassination of Kennedy, the violence that precipitated the Civil Rights movement, and the sexual revolution. In his short novel *Of the Farm* (1965), as in most of the stories collected in *The Music School* (1966), Updike attempts to isolate his fictional world from the turbulence of the larger world. His fiction of the mid-1960s is characterized, like *Rabbit, Run,* by the will to escape. "The Hermit," the final story in *The Music School,* epitomizes this impulse, as the protagonist exiles himself in the woods near his home. *Of the Farm* depicts a similar (though not so drastic) escape; Joey Robinson returns with his second wife Peggy and her son Richard to his mother's farm, where the rustic world of his youth represents an escape from his fast-paced adult life in New York. Severe conflicts arise between the three adult characters; though they are seemingly isolated from geopolitical conflict in this rural setting, the possibility of nuclear disaster infiltrates their world through the vehicle of a science fiction book Richard is reading; he describes the story: "There's been an atomic war or something," Richard said, "it never exactly says, and there's this single man, the last man left on the planet Earth, crawling over that radioactive desert to get somewhere, and then you realize he's trying to reach the sea" (OF 52). The three adults listening to the story interrupt the tale to describe the things that upset them in the night. Their common fears are precipitated by the larger unspoken fear of "an atomic war," and perhaps these fears only exist to mask their greatest fear, the same scenario Richard has read about in his sci-fi story. Richard continues his tale by relating how the character in the story believes, "if he could die in the sea the cells of his body would keep on living and form the basis for new life, so evolution could begin all over again" (OF 52).[10] There is a clear parallel between the protagonist of the story Richard is reading and the protagonist of *Of the Farm;* both are trying to achieve renewal. Joey's idea of renewal manifests itself by returning to the farm, but his mother's emotional manipulation is so painful to him that he can relate to the prospect of a man who has survived nuclear war. The atomic age becomes a metaphor for all the anxieties Joey is trying to resolve.

Richard's appetite for such science fiction is limitless, as too is its availability. Later in the novel he says to Joey,

> "This morning I was reading in that anthology about a mutie, that's short for mutant. There's been an atomic war — "
> "Again?"
> "It's a different story. This time, lots of people survive, but the radiation mixes up the genetics and most of the babies are born freaks, that's why they're called mutants. Most are mistakes, but some are improvements, people with four hands, and so on. It sounds silly — "
> "No." (OF 64)

The story emphatically does not sound silly to Joey because it is the type of fantasy he shares with Richard and with the culture at large. Atomic war represents to Joey and Richard the fear for the future of the human race — its possibility for survival, and its dependence on the whims of nature. The specter of nuclear war haunts the simplicity of a rural existence in the book just as the struggles between Joey's youth and adulthood — his wife and mother — are in sharp contrast to the peaceful existence he is seeking at the farm.

10. Louise Erdrich and Michael Dorris point out in their 1988 essay "The Days after Tomorrow: Novelists at Armageddon" that "a majority of postnuclear war novels of the last 25 years are irrationally optimistic, if only in their lack of true realism. Often degraded, mutated and dazed, human beings — or some facsimile of them — *do* survive to tell the tale" (Anisfield, *Nightmare Considered,* 54).

Of Updike's four novels published in the 1960s, the final one, *Couples,*
expresses most fully an engagement with the apocalyptic possibilities of
the Cold War and with current events in general. *Couples* represents a
crossroads in Updike's oeuvre, where his tendency to chronicle his fictional world in terms of contemporary news, prevalent in the mature years
of his career, becomes evident. Contemporary news events are sometimes
evident in Updike's work prior to *Couples,* notably in *Rabbit, Run,*[11] but
from this work on, especially in his novels, global events are a force infiltrating the domestic spheres of the characters through television, radio,
and the newspaper. The narrator of *Couples* tells us, "Television brought
them the outer world. The little screen's icy brilliance implied a universe
of profound cold beyond the warm encirclement of Tarbox, friends, and
family" (C 214). It is not likely that Updike's choice of adjectives in this
quotation (icy, cold, warm) is accidental; the world that attempts to invade
the suburban community is cold, the very word applied to the ongoing
war that pervades this world.

Couples, published in 1968 when the Vietnam War was unquestionably
the basis for the unrest that characterized America during the latter half
of the 1960s, takes place during the turbulent Kennedy years, and demonstrates how Cold War produces anxiety even in insulated communities like
Tarbox, Massachusetts. While the novel's primary concern is the morality
of this "post-pill paradise" (C 52), Updike also indicates how this new
morality arises out of the anxiety fueled by, even created by, America's
ideological face-off with the Eastern bloc and its potentially apocalyptic
nuclear weaponry. "Our fundamental anxiety is that we . . . will cease to
exist," Updike writes in a 1963 review of *Love Declared* by Denis de Rougement (AP 283), and his use of the plural subject indicates that he is referring to anxiety about the human race, not just individual death. The nuclear threat has made this anxiety immediate, and it is one of the factors
that explains the behavior of the characters in *Couples.*

Amid the cocktail parties, the swapping of sexual partners, and the rampant infidelity that characterize *Couples,* there is also a narrator who is
aware that the world is not at peace. This narrator selects and arranges di-

11. See Dilvo I. Ristoff, *Updike's America: The Presence of Contemporary American History in John Updike's Rabbit Trilogy.*

alogue that communicates the troubles of the world, but he generally re-
frains from commenting. Early on in the book the characters discuss the
sinking of the *Thresher;* Harold little-Smith states, "I think it's shocking . . .
that in so-called peacetime we send a hundred young men to be crushed
at the bottom of the sea" (C 30). When Janet Appleby asks him, "Why 'so-
called'?" he snaps, "We'll be at war with China in five years. We're at war
with her now. Kennedy'll up the stakes in Laos just enough to keep the
economy humming" (C 31). Given America's engagement in Vietnam in
1968, little-Smith's 1963 prediction is accurate, as is his realization that
America is involved in an ongoing war. This war, lying just below the consciousness of the characters, is potentially dangerous and constantly in
flux, not unlike their extramarital relationships.

Ironically, John Ong, the only member of the Tarbox couples who clearly has never had an extramarital affair, is the one who is most directly related to the actual Cold War. "If they ever dropped an H-bomb on Tarbox
it would be because of him," Angela Hanema tells Foxy Whitman. "He's a
nuclear physicist who works in MIT. *At* MIT? Actually, I think he works *under* MIT, in a huge underground workshop you need a password to get into"
(C 59). This connection serves to isolate Ong from the rest of Tarbox;
Angela says, "Neither he nor Ben [Saltz] can ever talk about their work because it's all for the government. It makes everybody else feel terribly ex-
cluded" (C 59). More likely, it makes everyone else feel terribly frightened,
as they blame Ong for endangering the town's future safety. Given Ong's
status as first-strike target, Piet jokes about Ben's relative unimportance
when Georgene suspects FBI agents are after Ben: "Do you think he'll be
electrocuted like the Rosenbergs or traded to Russia for Gary Powers?" (C
253). No one communicates well with Ong; his presence is a reminder of
the volatility of the world. We later learn that "one of their unspoken rules
was that professions were not criticized; one's job was a pact with the
meaningless world beyond the ring of couples" (C 233). Ong's job is different, though, as it connects him with a world beyond the couples that
has meaning and a definite impact upon their world.

Kennedy is at the center of this world; his death becomes a pivotal point
in the couples' relationships with each other. The first connection between Kennedy and the couples' extramarital affairs comes in the form of
a joke, in which Kennedy attempts to explain a rumpled collar and lipstick

on his chin to Jacqueline Kennedy by saying first, "I've been having a conference with Madam Nhu" and then, "saying that he was sitting up late arguing ideology with Nina Khrushchev" (C 96 – 97). The couples clearly see their own world, notably their infidelity, in terms of global conflicts. Frank Appleby and Harold little-Smith, before overtly sleeping with each other's wives, discuss "Kennedy's fumblings with Cuba and steel, the similarity of JFK's background to their own" (C 138). When things begin to turn sour between these two couples, the connection to Kennedy, and to the potential crisis he represents, is reiterated: "Meanwhile, our advisory capacity in Vietnam was beginning to stink and the market was frightened, frightened yet excited by the chance of expanding war. Basically business was uneasy with Kennedy; there was something unconvincing about him" (C 158). This uneasiness serves as a definite parallel to the uneasiness the Applebys and little-Smiths feel about their own situation. In this way, global unrest — as represented by allusions to Kennedy — provides a context for instability among the Tarbox couples.

Kennedy is assassinated on the same night the Thornes had planned a black-tie dinner party. Upon the first announcement of the assassination, Freddy Thorne's receptionist, "wide-eyed from having overheard the radio," communicates fear before sorrow: "'Do you think it was Communists?' the girl asked" (C 293). What had been uneasiness about Kennedy while he was alive becomes full-blown paranoia now that he has been killed. The Thornes' party forces many of the novel's conflicts to become crises — Freddy Thorne threatens to harm Piet physically, and Piet renews his affair with Foxy, causing him to jump out of a second-story window to avoid being caught. In short, the false confidence of the couples is undermined as the world suddenly lurches into even greater instability with Kennedy's death. Foxy, writing to Piet of new friends she has made in St. Thomas, makes the connection between JFK and the Tarbox couples more concrete:

> They think LBJ a boor but feel better under him than Kennedy because K. was too much like the rest of us semi-educated lovables of the post-Cold War and might have blown the whole game through some mistaken sense of flair. Like Lincoln, he lived to become a martyr, a memory. A martyr to what? To Marina Oswald's sexual rejection of her husband. Forgive me, I am using my letter to you to argue with Larry in. But it made me sad, that he thought that somebody like us (if K. was) wasn't fit to

rule us, which is to say, we aren't fit to rule ourselves, so bring on em-
perors, demigods, giant robots, what have you. (C 449)

The residents of Tarbox see something of Kennedy in themselves, and they
retrospectively recognize the precarious positions they were in—similar
to Kennedy's precarious position as president during the most dangerous
year of the Cold War. To downplay the precariousness of the situation,
Foxy calls the Cold War a "game" that Kennedy might have blown, as opposed to a planet that he might have blown up; the word "game" also applies to the sexual foibles of the couples, as the chapter title "Applesmiths
and Other Games" makes clear. Foxy's sense that they "aren't fit to rule"
themselves acknowledges the volatility of their sexual behavior, which is
analogous to the volatility of the world during the Kennedy years. America is, of course, just as turbulent during Johnson's reign; Foxy's assessment
of this period as the "post-Cold War" may be attributable to her oblivious-
ness to the global situation, or to her inability to think of the world in terms
other than the ones she has lived with.

The most volatile incident in the Kennedy era, and in the Cold War in
general, came on October 25, 1962, when the world waited anxiously to
see its knowledge of an immense catastrophe come to fruition. The Cuban
Missile Crisis is chronicled in *Couples* alongside the characters' typical ir-
responsibility. Freddy Thorne foreshadows the connection between the
sexual behavior of the couples and the international crisis when he proposes to Janet Appleby that she have an affair with him; he says, "Let it simmer. As Khrushchev said when he put the missiles on Cuba, nothing ventured, nothing gainski. I'm there if you think you can use me" (C 165). The
glibness of Freddy's proposing an extramarital affair is undercut by his
Cold War simile: sexual misconduct threatens to explode the suburban
bliss of Tarbox just as the presence of missiles in Cuba is potentially catastrophic for the entire world.

The connection between the Cuban Missile Crisis and the sexual games
of the Tarbox couples is reinforced later in the novel; Piet meditates in detail on his affair with Foxy one month after the affair has begun:

Only one other time had been so ominous: the Wednesday in October of
1962 when Kennedy had faced Khrushchev over Cuba. Piet had had a
golf date with Roger Guerin. They agreed not to cancel. "As good a way

to go as any," Roger had said over the phone. Stern occasions suited him. As Piet drove north to the course, the Bay View, he heard on the radio that the first Russian ship was approaching the blockade. They teed off into an utterly clear afternoon and between shots glanced at the sky for the Russian bombers. Chicago and Detroit would go first and probably there would be shouts from the clubhouse when the bulletins began coming in. There was almost nobody else on the course. It felt like the great rolling green deck of a ship, sunshine glinting on the turning foliage. As Americans they had enjoyed their nation's luxurious ride and now they shared the privilege of going down with her. (C 224)

Like the speaker of "Sonic Boom," Piet and Roger accept the inevitability of nuclear holocaust almost stoically, merely glancing toward impending disaster from a golf course instead of cowering in a fallout shelter. Having enjoyed prosperity and global hegemony for so long, they feel as though they deserve to die in the ensuing war, that it is indeed a "privilege." The narrator characterizes the state of the country as "a climate still *furtively* hedonist, of a country still too overtly threatened from without to be ruthlessly self-abusive, a climate of time between, of standoff and day-by-day" (C 106). This sense of hedonism followed by punishment clearly serves as another analogy for the sexual experimentation of the couples, as we learn that the Cuban Missile Crisis takes place one month after Piet has begun his first extramarital affair with Georgene Thorne, just as he remembers this day on a similarly "ominous" day, one month after he has begun his affair with Foxy:

Piet had played less well [than Roger]. He had been too happy. He played best, swung easiest, with a hangover or a cold. He had been distracted by the heavensent glisten of things—of fairway grass and fallen leaves and leaning flags—seen against the onyx immanence of death, against the vivid transparence of the sky in which planes might materialize. Swinging, he gave thanks that, a month earlier, he had ceased to be faithful to Angela and had slept with Georgene. It had been a going from indoors to outdoors; they met at beaches, on porches, beneath translucent trees. Happy remembering her, picturing her straight limbs, Piet sprayed shots, three-putted, played each hole on the edge of an imaginary cliff. Driving home, he heard on the car radio that the Russians had submitted to inspection and been allowed to pass. He had felt dismay, knowing that they must go on, all of them, Georgene and Angela and Freddy and himself, toward an untangling less involuntary and fateful. (C 224)

Piet feels disappointed that the conflict between the superpowers will be extended indefinitely because he feels that his affair with Georgene will also have to continue. In both cases he invites retribution for his guilt. His whole life has been motivated by guilt and a desire for punishment, for the enforcement of rules. To be bombed by Russia, in Piet's mind, is an appropriate punishment for a nation that has failed to give thanks to the God that made it, and that made it so wonderful. Piet gives thanks that he has been unfaithful just as he remembers his happy ride on the crest of America's prosperity, but he only feels this elation because he is certain that both are about to end in the apocalypse of atomic warfare.

A metaphoric apocalypse does eventually occur in the book—the revelation of all of Piet's affairs to Angela coupled with the destruction of the Congregational church in a lightning storm. Yet the Cold War continues at the end of the book, and there is evidence that the cycle of infidelity will continue along with it, as Piet and Foxy, in Lexington, "have been accepted, as another couple" (C 458). The cycle of renewal in *Couples,* which ends with a section entitled, "It's Spring Again," can be variously interpreted; perhaps there is forgiveness and the chance to begin again, or perhaps the cycle is leading toward destruction. There is, at least, the *hope* for renewal, though, which parallels the hope that Americans held out for in the 1960s that the immense catastrophe would never come, or at least be deferred indefinitely.

There is a comic way of dealing with nuclear apocalypse that runs alongside the knowledge of an immense catastrophe in Updike, an absurdist strain that enables the golfers in *Couples* to finish their round despite the threat of nuclear war. In two pieces written for the *New Yorker* in the early 1960s, Updike demonstrates how humor, like avoidance, can effectively deflect our anxieties about the Bomb. The first piece, entitled "Doomsday, Mass.," reports on the construction of a motel north of Boston that will accommodate "a community capable of creating the world anew in the event of a holocaust" (AP 98). Updike envisions this community, whose members include various professionals from the local community as well as "sixty motorists lucky enough to be stopping at the motel on Doomsday" (AP 98), as a sort of post-apocalyptic circus, grotesque and cartoonish in nature. The essay ends on a grim note, as Updike suggests that a writer be included in the list of survivors so that someone "could while away the long cave nights with fabulous tales of the world when men walked upright, in sunshine, only intermittently afraid" (AP 100). Yet this bleak vision is tempered by humor; Updike notes that it is "a sobering thought" that "the brave new world . . . will speak with a Danvers accent" (AP 98). He runs through the list of potential members, wryly noting the contrast between a "social director organizing square dances and pinochle tournaments in the shelter" and a "machine-gunner busily mowing down the interested crowds that have come up from Lynn" (AP 99). The humor here is dark indeed, but Updike is not creating his own vision of the post-apocalyptic future so much as he is commenting on someone else's vision. Laughing at this vision is a way of refusing to accept it.

Another *New Yorker* piece from the same period, an untitled "Talk of the Town" essay from August 1962, analyzes six various responses to the question "What would you do if notified that the world was going to end in four days?" The responses were comic, in Updike's eyes: "All in all, it was a reassuring picture these six conjured up, of a hundred and eighty million doomed souls reaching for their car keys, giving the airport a ring, rather shyly veering between the saloon and the cathedral, quietly keeping natural, and—though no one said this—presumably maintaining that indispensable American virtue, a sense of humor" (AP 101). Responses to absurd questions about the future are, of necessity, humorous. Updike sees the humor in someone booking a flight to Bermuda for the last four days of the world's existence.

To avoid such humor is to risk sinking into despair. The first ten years of Updike's writing career were especially plagued by the anxiety that can cause such despair. Characters in his early writings respond to the nuclear condition with a mixture of fear ("what makes us bastards run," according to Harry Angstrom), a search for religious meaning, and humor. All of these responses allow Updike's early characters to move on with their lives despite the Bomb. An author cannot hope to continue to write if he or she gives in to the despair over the nuclear condition. Like Samuel Beckett, who expresses repeatedly during his writings of the 1950s and 1960s the futility of continuing to speak, coupled with the necessity to do so, Updike expresses a similar sentiment in a 1966 interview: "It's true that we live on the verge of a catastrophe—not worldwide annihilation, perhaps, but surely something drastic. Still, since 1945 our little dramas have generally

been played out somewhat short of catastrophe. We do survive every moment, after all, except the last one."[12] There is a hint of optimism in this
observation; Updike indicates that, since World War III has not happened
yet, it *may* not happen. As the Cold War continued past the Cuban Missile
Crisis a general feeling began to unfold that nuclear war became less likely with each passing day. Updike's anxiety over the end of the world subsides in the late 1960s, but does not fully disappear. Once this anxiety is
overcome, other Cold War concerns rise to the surface of the American
consciousness, as evidenced in Updike's writings. The fear that nuclear
war is inevitable gives way to the related fear that our global rivals will begin to surpass us culturally and technologically, threatening the American
ideal of freedom.

12. Jane Howard, "Can a Nice Novelist Finish First?" 78.

2

Zero-Sum Marriages, Global Games

"Who needs Afghanistan? Fuck the Russkis . . .
We'll go it alone, from sea to shining sea."

–John Updike, *Rabbit Is Rich*, 436

HARRY ANGSTROM'S defiant isolationist attitude in this quotation from the end of *Rabbit Is Rich* (1981) is consistent with the worldview he espouses all his life. For Harry, competition is a necessary element of survival; yet when competition becomes stale or dangerous, he tends to retreat into his private world—to "duck and cover" in the way that school children during the early years of the Cold War were instructed to behave when they saw the atomic bomb's flash—or he runs frantically in no particular direction. Much of Harry's life is dictated by the fleeting sense of accomplishment he experienced as the star of his high school basketball team. The events of his adult life, spanning four novels published over the final thirty years of the Cold War, hearken back to the days of his youth when excellence on the court was all that mattered. It is not merely coincidental that Harry's adult life, based as it is upon competition, corresponds exactly with the Cold War (he turned thirteen in 1946 and died at fifty-seven in 1990). Updike acknowledges the connection between his most persistent protagonist and the Cold War in a 1990 *New York Times Book Review* article, "Why Rabbit Had to Go": "Like me, [Harry] has lived his adult life in the context of the cold war. He was in the Army, ready to

38

go to Korea, hawkish on Vietnam, proud of the moon shot, and in some sense always justified, at the back of his mind, by a concept of freedom, of America, that took sharpness from contrast with Communism. If that contrast is gone, then that's another reason to put him, regretfully, to rest in 1990."[1] By killing off Harry just as the Cold War ends, Updike suggests not only that Harry's life "took sharpness" from American competition with the Soviet Union but also that it depended directly upon this competition. Harry's undiminishing need to compete—to approach both his friends and his family as he would approach a rival on the basketball court—is one of the qualities that makes him unlikable; but Harry and many of his fellow Americans might insist that life during the Cold War wasn't about being liked: it was about *winning*.

Harry's competitive views do not automatically lead to happiness. Competition, though necessary for maintaining American power during the Cold War, does not translate easily to the domestic sphere in Updike's writings. From the early 1960s onward, Updike increasingly places domestic problems alongside their global analogue: Cold War tensions. This heightened engagement with the Cold War in Updike's books profoundly affects personal relationships, notably marriages and, to a lesser degree, relationships with other family members. The strain of global tension alters the way people communicate and indicates a weakness in the notion that domestic bliss can be based on the same philosophy of competition that serves as the foundation for Cold War success. To appreciate (if not identify with) Harry Angstrom and many of Updike's other protagonists, we must recognize the importance of this need to compete. Harry's behavior, his attitude, and his sometimes misguided reason for being can largely be explained by his sense of the need for competition, which is consistent with his government's behavior toward the Soviet Union. Problems arise in Updike's fictional world when characters misappropriate the importance of global competition by attempting to translate it into marriage. It is a paradoxical Cold War truth that what strengthened the country as a whole weakened its most basic, stable middle-class institution: the family.

Nonetheless, in order to identify oneself as an American in Harry's lifetime, it was necessary to respond in some way to the global competition

---

1. Updike, "Why Rabbit Had to Go," 24.

that defined the times. Like Updike, Harry came of age in the 1950s, when Americans sought fervently to define themselves in relation to the Soviet Union; as Stephen Whitfield points out,

> the need to express and celebrate the meaning of "Americanism," was the flip side of stigmatizing Communism; to decipher the culture of the 1950s requires tracing the formulation of this national ideology. It was not invented but inherited, and some of its components were intensified under the political pressures of the era. The belief system that most middle-class Americans considered their birthright—the traditional commitment to competitive individualism in social life, to the liberal stress on rights in political life, and to private enterprise in economic life—was adapted to the crisis of the Cold War.[2]

This commitment to competitive individualism is particularly relevant to Updike's fiction; without it, America as Updike depicts it would not be America, and Americans would have less to be certain of in an already uncertain world plagued by the ongoing threat of nuclear war.

Competition was fundamental to America's place in the Cold War world for three fundamental reasons: the desire for supremacy in the arms race, the fear that Soviet aggression threatened the American ideal of liberty, and the hope for continued economic prosperity. The Cold War world was a kind of global game between the superpowers; the winner was determined by military and economic might, and the stakes were two belief systems symbolically bifurcated by the Berlin Wall. As the Cold War reached crisis levels in the late 1950s and early 1960s, the rivalry between the superpowers overshadowed all other facets of international politics; the field was reduced to two belligerent players. In a 1987 article historian David Calleo explains the American-Soviet relationship during the Cold War as follows:

> Attempts to develop Soviet-American economic relations have foundered on recurring American efforts to bargain trade for political concessions or fears that trade would strengthen Soviet war-making capabilities. The Russians themselves have a natural tendency to emphasize the military relationship. It is the only sphere where they are, in any sense, equal to the Americans. In commercial weight or cultural prestige,

---

2. Whitfield, *The Culture of the Cold War,* 53.

they are notably inferior to the United States as well as to the major European states and Japan.

This bilateral Soviet-American preoccupation with security questions
reinforces a tendency in both to see world politics in military terms and,
as a result, to exaggerate each other's role in shaping world events. In
Washington as well as in Moscow, international politics can still be seen
as a global duel—a zero-sum game where all events are significant only
insofar as they represent a gain for one or a loss for the other. Since bipo-
lar competition is thought to be the underlying reality, conflict in one ge-
ographical region is seen as tied to conflict in another.[3]

This view in American foreign policy mirrored mainstream America's
views of the Soviet Union throughout much of the Cold War. All geopolitical incidents were potential steps toward either triumph or defeat, yet
equally important is the ongoing sense that cultural prestige mattered as
much as military fortitude, at least from the point of view of the average
American who had no real say in military matters. Civilians of previous
generations contributed to the war effort by joining the workforce or col-
lecting scrap metal to build ships and weapons. Cold War Americans contributed to their country's cause in a more abstract way: by adhering to
the competitive principle that affirmed the integrity of the middle-class
American dream.

Cold War competition has a negative effect on Updike's characters, who
are frequently out of step with their contemporaries and are almost always
unable to sustain a peaceful monogamous relationship. The will to compete in Updike's fiction is accompanied by a need to withdraw—an os-
cillation between fight and flight that mirrors American foreign policy during the Cold War. Historian Stanley Hoffman interprets some early Soviet
Cold War maneuvers not as aggressive, but as an effort "to drive a frustrated and exasperated United States back into isolationism,"[4] and he notes a
similar trend toward American isolationism in the early years of détente.
Historians still debate whether the United States acted offensively or de-
fensively in its relations with the Soviet Union during the Cold War,
whether our policy was one of containment or aggression. The answer

3. David P. Calleo, *Beyond American Hegemony: The Future of the Western Alliance*,
269–70.
4. Stanley Hoffman, "Revisionism Revisited," 20.

seems to fall somewhere in between these two possibilities; American foreign policy makers at times sought to provoke competition and at other
times to retreat from it. The action of running, the defining characteristic
of Harry Angstrom's life, can serve as a metaphor for a similar duality in
Updike's fiction: Harry runs to keep himself physically fit in order to maintain the competitive edge he enjoyed in high school, but he also runs to
escape his problems, retreating to shelter when the pressure is on. The
metaphor of running is prevalent in Cold War rhetoric as well; the United
States and the Soviet Union were said to be competing in an "arms race"
and a "space race," terms that suggest a winner will eventually emerge,
even though the possibilities for stockpiling arms or exploring space are
seemingly infinite.

America's fear that Russia would surge ahead in the races for military
and galactic supremacy reached a high-water mark on October 4, 1957,
the day the Soviet government caught the world—especially the American government—off guard by launching Sputnik I, a radio satellite that
placed the Soviets far ahead of America in terms of technology and the
capacity for espionage. In addition, the Soviets announced that they had
launched an intercontinental ballistic missile less than two months prior
to Sputnik. These announcements devastated Americans who had become
complacent in their belief that America was and always would be the most
formidable military and technological power on the planet. The Eisenhower administration downplayed the Soviet achievement immediately;
Sherman Adams, Eisenhower's closest personal assistant in the White
House, said that America was not interested in getting caught up "in an out-
erspace basketball game" with the Soviet Union, a metaphor that certainly would not be lost on Updike. Cultural historian David Halberstam points
out that "*Sputnik* was only the first of several psychological setbacks for
America. . . . Soon after, in November 1957, the Gaither report leaked out
. . . [which] implied that we were slipping in our nuclear capacity while
the Soviets were becoming stronger all the time."[5] Eisenhower was aware
that the Gaither report was exaggerated at points and downright inaccu-
rate at others. Having seen classified photos of Soviet nuclear stockpiles
taken from U-2 spy planes, Eisenhower knew that the perceived threat

5. David Halberstam, *The Fifties,* 625, 699.

should not be taken too seriously. Yet this information was top secret; Americans did not share their president's sense of calm, and the final years of the 1950s were tense times. Fearing that they were losing the race, Americans reacted by building bomb shelters, and concentrated on defense: the Gaither report recommended that the government spend $25 billion on bomb shelters and an additional $19 billion on weaponry. The sense of global competition had never been greater, and America alternated between the urge to fight back and the urge to take shelter.

Americans felt they could fight the "war" by building bomb shelters that acted as a symbolic defense of the American Dream of a stable, secure middle-class home. The creation of the modern American suburb in the 1950s—a massive human migration from the perceived threats of the urban world as well as a removal from population centers that could be potential targets for nuclear strikes—can be seen as an outgrowth of the need to maintain security through withdrawal. The so-called "kitchen debate" between Khrushchev and then–Vice President Nixon in 1959 captured the spirit of the American suburbanite who felt that his comfortable, applianced household marked a victory over the Soviets who, though they had launched Sputnik, were woefully behind us in terms of kitchen appliances and automobiles (the two commodities Harry Angstrom sells in the Rabbit novels).

The "kitchen debate" was occasioned by an international exposition held in Moscow on technology and how it affected modern lifestyles. Nixon scored a Cold War victory, in the eyes of most Americans, simply by touting the conveniences of the modern American suburb and contrasting them with the relatively Spartan Soviet domestic sphere. Responding to Khrushchev's angry rejection of the American propensity for materialism and free market choice, Nixon gallantly replied, "Isn't it better to talk about the relative merits of washing machines than the relative strength of rockets? Isn't this the kind of competition you want?" The burgeoning American suburb and its attendant lifestyle was a kind of Cold War weapon, as the unintentional pun "nuclear family" makes clear. Beginning with Levittown, the Long Island community of mass-produced homes created by Bill Levitt in the late 1940s, American suburbs grew at an astonishing pace, accounting for an urban population loss from 1950–1980, while the suburban population grew by 60 million. Understanding the geopolitical significance of his business endeavor, Levitt declared, "No man who owns his own house and lot can be a communist. He has too much to do." It is a happy accident for readers of Updike's fiction that Levittown became known as "the Rabbit Hutch."[6] Rabbit Angstrom, like many of Updike's protagonists, epitomizes the attitude of the Cold War suburbanite; when the Soviets launched satellites, Americans responded by trying to match their achievements. When we failed, Americans like Harry withdrew from a sense of global connectedness, vowing to "go it alone, from sea to shining sea" (Rich 436).

Updike's most overt proclamations about America's competition with the Soviet Union come in the form of "Notes and Comment" pieces written for the *New Yorker* in the late 1950s and early 1960s. This anonymous forum, characterized by its use of the third-person plural subject, allowed Updike to exercise his voice as a social commentator without allowing that voice to interfere with his fiction, which was, during that time, relatively disengaged from the Cold War. As a "Notes and Comment" writer, Updike was free to speak out as a kind of well-heeled everyman about topical issues without being controversial. Yet these pieces are never straightforward editorials. The best of them aspire to the condition of poetry, and at the very least they are well-crafted belletristic essays, topical and lyrical at once. Two such pieces, both published in the fall of 1959, indicate Updike's feeling toward his nation's global game. In both cases he tries to mask his nation's anxiety over its status as cultural victor, first with bravado, then with humor. Both essays also advance the notion that although cultural victory is a weak replacement for military supremacy, culture is the only sphere over which the average Cold War American could exert any influence. Khrushchev and Nixon arguing over washing machines became more relevant to the average American than atomic bombs and satellites: suddenly it was possible for all Americans to get into the game.

Updike's "Notes and Comment" piece published on September 26, 1959, takes on the subject of the Soviets' unmanned moon landing. It is a three-paragraph essay that begins with a general assessment of the event, follows with an observation of an old woman tending a grave in a ceme-

6. Ibid., 142. Whitfield, *The Culture of the Cold War,* 74, 73. Elaine Tyler May, *Homeward Bound: American Families in the Cold War Era,* 171.

tery, and concludes with a vignette about waiting in a railway station late at night until the evening paper arrives with news of the moon landing. Updike feigns nonchalance throughout the essay and tries to communicate a sense of reassurance at the end. He begins the essay with an admission of fear: "Twenty-two months ago, we wrote in this space of our deep, primeval fear that Soviet Russia would celebrate the revolution's fortieth anniversary by splashing red paint on the face of the moon. This threat of heavenly vandalism was in the wind, you may remember, shortly after the first sputnik violated the azure serene of our national vanity."[7] The violence in this description— "splashing red paint," "vandalism," "violated" —describes an assault directed toward America, but more specifically toward American innocence and smugness, our "national vanity" that amounts to complacency. The tone quickly changes after this sentence, though: the missiles surrounding the moon are compared to "a panel of Krazy Kat," space race lingo has "entered our advertising slang," "the fizzles at Cape Canaveral have blended with the friendly sizzling of breakfast bacon," and "the backs of Kix boxes have made this whole awesome business too familiar to all of us." In short, mainstream American culture, especially the mundane routine of the breakfast table (comics, bacon, cereal) has triumphantly remained at the forefront of American consciousness, and the Soviet's moon victory is not a big deal. This paragraph is a condensed, symbolic version of the recent "kitchen debate"; riding this optimism, Updike manages to conclude the first paragraph with, "At any rate, the Soviet flag is on the moon, and we feel surprisingly little pain."

Americans in general and Updike in particular may not have felt pain at this event, but it is suspicious how quickly he moves from "deep primal fear" to the blasé final sentence of the first paragraph. There is a sense of bewilderment underlying this transformation that becomes much more apparent when one observes the early corrected drafts of the manuscript. In one such draft Updike deletes the words "forboding" [sic], "ominous," "queer" (twice), "odd," and "strange" from the first paragraph of the essay.[8] Moreover, Updike's original terms for our national "vanity" —not neces-

---

7. John Updike, "Notes and Comment," September 26, 1959.
8. By permission of John Updike and the Houghton Library, Harvard University, bMS Am 1793.1.

sarily a negative term, as Ben Franklin's *Autobiography* makes clear—
were "pride," then "conceit," words that connote a nation in much greater
danger of falling, or falling behind. It is clear from these changes that the
speaker's easy dismissal of the event may not be entirely honest: his gaze
does move morosely to a cemetery in the second paragraph, after all. Yet
the final paragraph, like the first, attempts to put things in perspective, to
cover up deep, primal fears and lonely observations about death by returning to the cheerful mundane routine of American middle-class life.

The final paragraph begins with a consideration of the event in terms
removed from the personal fears of the first paragraph: "That evening, we
found ourself in a railroad station. In the interval, a hermetically sealed
sphere weighing 858.4 pounds had crashed into the moon, at a speed of
about seventy-five hundred miles an hour, at two minutes and twenty-four
seconds after twelve o'clock Monday morning Moscow time, presumably
creating a huge cloud of dust. Three hours later, it was still Sunday evening
in an American railroad station." Updike presumably emphasizes numbers
here to make the whole affair seem boring and impersonal, hardly the
"heavenly vandalism" it was presumed to be in the first paragraph. Yet the
extreme attention to detail indicates how closely the speaker has been paying attention, like someone pretending not to care about the outcome of
a baseball game who proceeds to rattle off its most obscure statistics. The
porter who brings the papers declares, "Sorry they're late. We had to wait
for the Russians to hit the moon," and the speaker reacts: "There it was:
democracy, indifference, persistence." The porter, like the newspapers he
carries, is meant to represent the essence of America that will eventually
triumph despite setbacks like the Soviets landing on the moon: the American gumption and work ethic that leads us back, through the production
and delivery of newspapers, to the sanctity of the breakfast table.

If the reader finds this solution a bit disingenuous, he can again find evidence in the manuscript version of the essay in which Updike is unsure
about both the reason why the porter's remark is comforting and about
his own identity, the paradoxical "ourself" who observes the porter. A passage that Updike deleted after the porter's remark, with corrections, reads:

> The remark, with the ~~superb~~ fair easy democracy ~~that welded him~~ of the
> "we" that welded him to the ~~elegant~~ giants of the editorial room (quite

unlike the "we" of this piece, which ~~claims~~ enlarges and makes ~~formida-~~
~~ble~~ presentable the fitful timorous "I" that is trying to press upon you, so
obliquely, a crumb of comfort) made a light cast a light as simple ~~as calm~~
~~as the heavenly globe pale heavenly globe that for tens of thousands of~~
~~years, after all, has been hit by the flights of men's imaginations.~~[9]

Another version begins, "We can hardly isolate the element in [the
porter's] short speech that gave us so much comfort." It is clear that the
speaker is desperately seeking and wanting to provide comfort, but the situation is, from the point of view of an early Cold War American steeped in
the pride, conceit, or vanity of having always been in the lead, uncomfortable.

At the time this piece was published the country was engrossed in a trial over the so-called "quiz show scandals," the most egregious of which occurred on a game show called "Twenty-one." Under investigation, the pro-
ducers of the television show ultimately admitted to having fixed the
game by feeding correct answers to some contestants while bribing others to answer incorrectly. The case became a setback to Cold War Americans who had regarded the shows as evidence that their countrymen and
women were still brilliant in the face of Soviet advances in technology.
Charles Van Doren, the show's most charming and eloquent winner, was
discovered to be a cheat, and his status as the embodiment of American
intelligence and wisdom turned out to be a sham. Confidence in the American way and optimism about America's cultural superiority dimmed with
this scandal. In sum, these shows were at once an embodiment of the
American will to compete and an indication that this competition was a
potentially dangerous threat to the foundations of national integrity. Updike published a satiric "Notes and Comment" piece in the October 24,
1959, issue of the *New Yorker* written partially as a dialogue between a
cynical game show host and an initially naive contestant. The skit ends
with the two characters fixing on a sum, and according to the final stage
directions, "They embrace, and, as the Curtain Falls, the West Declines noticeably."[10] The original version of this piece was not written as a dialogue,
but rather as a straight essay; it ends with a note in Updike's hand: "Rewrite

9. By permission of John Updike and the Houghton Library, Harvard University, bMS
Am 1793.1.
10. John Updike, "Notes and Comment," October 24, 1959, 34.

completely." There are a few elements of the original draft that make it into the published draft, notably the peevish observation that "the contestants . . . were meant to be us—you and me and the bright boy next door. This was America answering."[11] In one manuscript version that line is followed by an explicit link to the Cold War: "The ~~appeal rose~~ the appeal of the programs, with the ~~threat~~ rising challenge of Soviet ~~brainpower~~ brainpower ~~making~~ as ~~the ominous~~ a backdrop, was ultimately patriotic; the contestants were a cross section of our nation ~~just~~ as deliberately as the GIs in a war ~~were~~ are a cross-section." In the original manuscript version, in place of the fictional dialogue are actual quotations from the contestants who benefited from the scandals:

> Mr. [David] Enright, however, shows a degree of repentance that is morbidly Calvinist compared to some of the contestants. Mrs. Antoinette Hillman, who won $1,460 on Dotto, a ~~show that~~ battle of wits that had a daily meeting to decide what was going to happen the next day, ~~said, when~~ was asked what she thought of the "moral situation"—a quaint phrase that the newspaper account ~~perhaps~~ judiciously puts in quotes. "I was perfectly happy about it," this bonny wife ~~responded~~ answered, "they were having a happy time, I was, everybody was." Well, we for one are not having a happy time as we write this, and Mrs. Hillman's blitheness seems scarier than twenty Sputniks.[12]

Updike's decision to transform this strongly worded indictment into a satirical play may have been inspired by his fear that his voice had become too strident, his opinion too visible, or his tone not humorous enough for a "Notes and Comment" piece. In any case, the original version makes explicit something that is oblique in the published version: that Updike felt the quiz show scandals represented a national failure, one that was not only comparable to the military and technological battle for superiority in the solar system, but one that overshadowed that battle twenty-fold. As in the September 24 piece, the quotidian American lifestyle is of primary importance, but it suffers as a result of America's ongoing global competition with the Soviet Union. Since Updike believed strongly that the American

11. Ibid., 34, 33.
12. By permission of John Updike and the Houghton Library, Harvard University, bMS Am 1793.1.

way was "the distinctly better mousetrap" (SC 139) when compared to Soviet communism, he may have been reluctant to admit that competition
between the two could negatively affect American culture.

In theory, competition between the Cold War superpowers was supposed to strengthen and unify American society so that day-to-day life in
middle-class America would be harmonious and peaceful. Yet these two essays demonstrate that, in practice, Updike was aware of how competition
could be a potentially destructive force. This force is more apparent as Updike trains his gaze on smaller and smaller spheres of social interaction. In
the "Notes and Comment" pieces he writes of the relationship between individual and nation, but in his fiction he is more preoccupied with the relationship between individual and community, and even more preoccupied
with family relationships. As global competition trickles down to private
lives in Updike's writings its destructive potential becomes more evident.

During the period following the launch of Sputnik, Updike wrote a number of stories that were eventually collected in *Pigeon Feathers* (1962).
These stories reveal Cold War jitters more than any other collection of Updike's short fiction, and they mark a turning point in his career, as they are
the first of his stories to take on the subject of familial dysfunction, the
most prevalent topic of his writing. Writing about the appeal of a stable
home life during the Cold War, Elaine Tyler May observes, "As the chill of
the cold war settled across the nation, Americans looked toward the uncertain future with visions of carefully planned and secure homes, complete with skilled homemakers and successful breadwinners. The fruits of
postwar America could make the family strong; the family, in turn, could
protect the nation by containing the frightening potentials of postwar
life." May also observes that the pressure to maintain a peaceful domestic
life placed a great strain on husbands and wives in the 1950s; she writes,
"As these couples sealed the psychological boundaries around the family,
they also sealed their fates within it."[13] In Updike's writing married couples are frequently condemned to a fate of mutual resentment between
husband and wife, which generally leads to infidelity, which in turn leads
to divorce. The American divorce rate began rising steadily in the mid-
1960s both in Updike's writing and in fact. Contrary to the dream that the

13. May, *Homeward Bound,* 90, 36.

American family could provide stability against an uncertain future and the perils of communism, Updike's characters discover that their individual freedom is inhibited by family life. This circumstance is due in part to the principles of global competition that were ultimately irreconcilable with domestic bliss.

Not unlike the leaders of the superpower nations, Updike's fictional husbands and wives tend to withdraw from one another rather than to negotiate for mutual peace and understanding. "Walter Briggs," the first story collected in *Pigeon Feathers,* demonstrates how the connection between the Cold War and domestic life coincides with a thematic pattern of competition and isolation. The story seems little more than a car ride in which Jack and Clare play a memory game, "one of their few devices for whiling away enforced time together. A poor game, it lacked the minimal element of competition needed to excite Jack" (PF 4). Jack's boredom with the game shifts to anxiety as he realizes he is failing to match his wife's abilities. He recalls the profession of a past acquaintance "with triumph," and reveals his insecurities: "'I can remember their professions but not their names,' he said, anxious to put in something for himself, for he felt his wife was getting ahead of him at this game" (PF 7–8). He admits, "It made him jealous, her store of explicit memories" (PF 9). This minor detail indicates an undercurrent of competition and jealousy between a husband and wife that is given more substance by the only connection in the story between Jack and Clare and the larger world that surrounds them. Once they return from the car ride, they perform a ritual that connects them briefly to this world: "Downstairs, the two adults got the ginger ale out of the refrigerator and watched the midnight news on provincial television, Governor Furcolo and Archbishop Cushing looming above Khrushchev and Nasser, and went to bed hastily, against the children's morning rising" (PF 10). The ritual aspect of this act—Jack's and Clare's evening routine—serves to highlight specific Cold War events, the Hungarian and Suez Canal crises of 1956. The competition between world powers symbolized by this detail enhances the competition between Jack and Clare, which continues after Clare falls asleep as Jack struggles to recall an old acquaintance's name. Jack's need to win his trivial competition with Clare makes sense only as an exercise in one-upmanship, symbolized by the presence of Khrushchev and Nasser in the story.

"Walter Briggs" serves as an early paradigm for much of Updike's work that follows it. By demonstrating how Cold War competition infiltrates the domestic sphere, Updike begins to, in his words, "elicit the violence and tension that does exist beneath the surface of even the most peaceful-seeming life."[14] His earlier stories, collected in *The Same Door* (1959), are not as fraught with domestic tension as the stories in *Pigeon Feathers* are, nor are they as concerned with geopolitical affairs. The presence of domestic dissolution in his stories corresponds with a heightened awareness of Cold War events; the breakdown of happy marriages illuminates the global tension that looms behind them. The anxiety created by the global situation in "Dear Alexandros," another story in *Pigeon Feathers,* is linked to the dissolution of a marriage. In this story, Kenneth Bentley writes a letter to Alexandros, a needy child who Kenneth supports through an organization called "Hope, Incorporated." In the letter Kenneth tries to explain why he and Mrs. Bentley "no longer live together" (PF 104). Kenneth attempts to blame the breakup on "so much plumbing and fast automobiles and rapid highways" (PF 106), as well as alcohol and friends who are "tedious people" (PF 107). For Alexandros's sake, he tries to explain the breakup in terms of a poem from Alexandros's language—the *Iliad*—but his analogy becomes muddled. One paragraph in the letter stands out prominently; it obliquely connects the Cold War to the Bentleys' breakup, and explains the breakup more clearly than Kenneth's other attempts do:

> There has been much excitement in the United States over the visit of the head of Soviet Russia, Mr. Khrushchev. He is a very talkative and self-confident man and in meeting some of our own talkative and self-confident politicians there has been some friction, much of it right on television where everybody could see. My main worry was that he would be shot but I don't think he will be shot any more. His being in the country has been a funny feeling, as if you have swallowed a penny, but the American people are so anxious for peace that they will put up with small discomforts if there is any chance it will do any good. The United States, as perhaps you will learn in school, was for many years an isolated country and there still is a perhaps childish wish that other nations, even though we are a great power, just let us alone, and then the sun will shine. (PF 105)

14. J. M. McNally and Dean Stover, "An Interview with John Updike," 102.

In this paragraph Kenneth describes the growing anxiety in his country, but he also creates a metaphor for the failure of his marriage. He says that Americans are "anxious for peace" as though they are involved in an actual war; he eventually admits that they are merely anxious to be left alone, to be taken out of situations fraught with "friction." He claims that Americans "will put up with small discomforts" in order to achieve peace, yet admits two paragraphs later that "we have forgotten how to live with inconveniences" (PF 106).

The Cold War during this period (Kenneth's letter is dated September 25, 1959) was perpetuated by the failure of both the United States and the Soviet Union to negotiate. Nixon had scored what seemed like a victory over Khrushchev in the kitchen debate the summer before the Soviet leader's visit to the United States, touting the merits of increasingly automated American middle-class life. Khrushchev's rhetoric during this period was characterized by suggestions that America with all of its modern conveniences was losing its competitive edge. The leaders of the two nations seemed unable to get together on even mundane issues. We realize, through Kenneth's unintended analogy, that the failure of his marriage may be due in part to his own unwillingness to negotiate; immediately after writing about Khrushchev he writes, "That was not a very good paragraph and perhaps the man or woman who kindly translates these letters for us will kindly omit it" (PF 105). In a letter to me written after the Cold War's conclusion Updike acknowledges this desire of the average American to avoid the Cold War whenever possible: "The thing about the Cold War was you ignored it if you could."[15] The need to avoid the subject may have something to do with a fear of too much self-analysis; Kenneth wants to distance himself from the discomfort of the Cold War situation because it is so close to his domestic situation, characterized by anxiety, discomfort, and failure to negotiate. The fact that Khrushchev's visit is available via television, "where everybody could see," exacerbates Kenneth's anxiety by connecting him inextricably to his fellow Americans. Kenneth projects onto America his own desire to isolate himself when he claims that his country wants to be left alone. He has apparently taken this course of action; he has moved away from

15. Updike, letter to the author, September 19, 1995.

his wife and children in an unsuccessful attempt to escape the "friction" of his world.

The domestic situation in "Wife-Wooing" is not as painful as in "Dear Alexandros," but there is a similar link to the Cold War that reveals marital tension. Once again characters are both sexually isolated from one another and incapable of effective communication, and once again this situation is placed alongside allusions to the larger global situation. The narrator's attempts to seduce his wife are thwarted by her interest in contemporary history; his interior monologue goes, "In bed you read. About Richard Nixon. He fascinates you; you hate him. You know how he defeated Jerry Voorhis, martyred Mrs. Douglas, how he played poker in the Navy despite being a Quaker, every fiendish trick, every low adaptation. Oh my Lord. Let's let the poor man go to bed. We're none of us perfect" (PF 113). As the narrator attempts to speed up the seduction, his wife pleads, "Wait. [Nixon]'s about to get Hiss convicted. It's very strange. It says he acted honorably" (PF 113). The narrator becomes impatient: "'Honey, Hiss was guilty. We're all guilty. Conceived in concupiscence, we die unrepentant.' Once my ornate words wooed you" (PF 113). The narrator is pained to notice that his wife's interest in Nixon and Hiss outweighs her desire for sex: "Suddenly it slips. The book has slipped from your hand. You are asleep. Oh cunning trick, cunning" (PF 114). In the narrator's mind, seduction becomes a type of game in which he and his wife are trying to trick one another. Unlike Nixon's dogged pursuit of Hiss, the narrator's sexual pursuit of his wife does not pay off. He blames his failure indirectly on the Red-baiting that was characteristic of the early years of the Cold War, which holds more interest, in modern times, than the ancient rituals of wooing that he describes. Husband and wife, competing with each other through subtle "cunning tricks," are left isolated from one another in the end. The protagonists of these three stories from *Pigeon Feathers* experience the marital competition that they need to maintain forward motion, but, as in the Cold War, alienation, not victory, is the ultimate effect.

There are two possible outcomes for the type of marriage described in these stories: couples can either negotiate or separate. The perception that the world was divided into two mutually exclusive spheres that were unable to communicate with or clearly see one another was bound to have some impact on American marriages. In Updike's fiction of the 1960s and

1970s, the competitive model had its logical corollary in separation, the subject most often associated with his writing. Beginning with the so-called "Maples stories" (collected partially in *Museums and Women* [1972] and more extensively in *Too Far to Go* [1979]), Updike's fiction is increasingly characterized by marital strife, infidelity, and the specter of divorce. Just as Harry Angstrom's life "took sharpness from contrast with communism,"[16] Updike's fictional marriages take sharpness from their nation's ongoing rivalry with the Soviet Union. Updike uses the Cold War to illustrate the difficulty of marital peace in a world characterized by deceit, suspicion, and unwillingness to negotiate.

The story "The Day of the Dying Rabbit" (1969) subtly chronicles a day in the life of a family that is struggling to preserve its frail sense of harmony. The story is initiated when a stray cat brings the narrator and his family a dying rabbit and the narrator, a photographer, feels the inexplicable need "to get the day on some kind of film . . . however underexposed" (MW 29). The story seems harmonious enough—a family on vacation going about their pleasant routine—but there is clearly a disturbance between the narrator and his wife occasioned by his attraction to his tennis partner, Jenny Pingree. After a lengthy description of this woman he declares, "I could look at her forever" (MW 30), yet he has not granted his wife Margaret the same type of descriptive attention. He indulges in another lavish description of Jenny on the tennis court, and his attention to her must also be evident to Margaret, who says, "Say. I don't mind your being partners with Jenny, but you don't have to toss the balls to her in that cute confiding way" (MW 34). The underlying conflict between the narrator and Margaret is suggested by a Cold War metaphor, as they "make love for the first time in, oh, days beyond counting. She's always tired, and says the Pill depresses her, and a kind of arms race of avoidance has grown up around her complaints" (MW 31). The narrator does not devote much time to his marital conflict, but his comparison of their marital difficulties to the arms race and to the idea of "avoidance" suggests that he and his wife are competing rather than negotiating, that the problems are growing, and that alienation is the ultimate result. They play tennis against one another with other partners, after all, and the only nice thing he says to

16. Updike, "Why Rabbit Had to Go," 24.

her throughout the story is, "That second set . . . your backhand was terrific" (MW 35). He describes her brilliant play as "a moral triumph" (MW 33), suggesting that there is something deeper than just physical achievement at stake here. Like the "memory game" that Jack and Clare play in "Walter Briggs," this physical competition between them seems to keep the marriage alive; yet given his clear interest in another woman, and his wife's lack of sexual interest in him, there is a profound problem at the heart of this marriage that threatens to drive them apart.

In the final pages of the story the narrator retreats into his own world, contemplating how he would photograph the world around him if he were behind a camera rather than socializing with family and friends. He is only half paying attention to the voices around him, and records them ("underexposed") in snippets, leading in or trailing off with ellipses. His son Jimmy complains that his sisters are ignoring him: "Showing off for their boyfriends . . . whacked me for no reason . . . just because I said 'sex bomb'" (MW 37). Another snippet comes from the mouth of Jenny, the object of his affection: " . . . *must* destroy the system! We've forgotten how to *love*!" (MW 38). These seemingly meaningless fragments of conversation emphasize his description of his sexual relationship with his wife as an "arms race of avoidance." Competition has seeped into the marriage and weakened it, but the "system" of Jenny's comment—the competitive global structure—is formidable, so there isn't much hope that he will remember how to love. The narrator retreats into his own world rather than working toward a level of mutual understanding with his wife. The only opportunity for a lesson in negotiation comes from an older friend of the Pingrees who became rich by trading wheat with Stalin before the war; he tries to instruct the narrator, claiming, "The thing we must realize about your Communist is that he's just another kind of businessman" (MW 38). Success is achieved only when you come to terms with the person you had regarded as your adversary, in other words, and when you find a mutually beneficial arrangement. This advice could apply to his marriage, but the narrator refuses to listen, and he instead drifts deeper into his obsession with the photographic possibilities of the world immediately surrounding him.

If we follow this story's trajectory, it is clear that the rift between this couple will isolate them further until they are divorced: it is possible to substitute the word "marriage" for "rabbit" in the title. Rabbits can never be taken at face value in Updike, after all, and Rabbit Angstrom is not too far removed from the narrator of "The Day of the Dying Rabbit." Harry's life, as I have said, is characterized by competition, and his life changes with the rhythm of the times. The Cold War during the 1960s began with near apocalypse in the form of the Cuban Missile Crisis, reaffirming the notion of the Soviet Union as a clear and absolute enemy, but it eventually became fragmented into many smaller fronts during the final years of that decade, notably Vietnam and the space race. These two Cold War phenomena respectively tore America apart in terms of public opinion and brought it together in terms of national achievement. In this way, the space race represents the last remaining vestiges of the old Cold War; America was competing directly with the Soviet Union in the quest for galactic supremacy, and both sides had a common goal. Vietnam, on the other hand, signifies the advent of the new Cold War: America was, in theory, still battling the spread of Soviet-style communism in Vietnam, yet the Soviets were not fighting the war, and the enemy seemed to be the Viet Cong, Red China, or even America itself, given the dissent the war caused on the home front. Both scenarios offer the competition or resistance that seem necessary in Updike's world; but in the new Cold War of the late 1960s, the object of competition is less clearly defined, and the tentative optimism associated with competition is hard to find, if it exists at all.

The space race and Vietnam are also recurrent touchstones in *Rabbit Redux* (1971); as is the case in many of Updike's works of the 1960s, Cold War competition in this book is analogous to the conflicts between men and women, but it is also a metaphor for the way Harry's life is given to rapid and disorienting change during these years. Reflecting the confusion and complexity of international politics during the late 1960s, *Rabbit Redux* is the darkest book in the tetralogy. Vietnam complicates the subject of the Cold War to signify more than the simple "we-they" of the Eisenhower years, but Harry obstinately believes that nothing has changed, and his stubbornness threatens to destroy his home completely. Simple competition with the Soviet Union in *Rabbit Redux* manifests itself in the form of the moon landing, which, given American paranoia over Sputnik in the 1950s, was as much a demonstration of military and technological might as it was a scientific "giant leap for mankind." The moon landing, which

Updike calls "our space invasion,"[17] exists in defiance of the social upheaval of the late 1960s, and Harry uses it as an excuse to continue his life
as if the Cold War had not changed since the 1950s. Essentially, he is still
keen on the principle of competition, but the object of that competition
and the identity of the opponent are so confusing that they lead directly
to his alienation and to the potential dissolution of his marriage. His excitement over the Cold War and his marriage falter at the same time, and
the novel poses difficult questions about the way he should respond to
these changes in his life. While the debate over the Vietnam War—the subject of chapter 3 of this study—is the more contentious of the Cold War
battlefields in *Rabbit Redux,* the space race dictates Harry's behavior
more directly because it appeals to the reassuring competitive instinct
that characterized his young adulthood.

Each of the four sections of *Rabbit Redux* begins with an epigraph from
the Soviet Soyuz 5 space mission or the United States' Apollo 11 mission,
its first successful attempt to put astronauts on the moon.[18] The moon
landing, a peaceful Cold War triumph for the United States, comes just before Janice leaves Harry in Updike's novel. Harry had anticipated both
events a few days earlier, as we can see in a quotation that reflects both
his knowledge that the Cold War is not over and his suspicion that Janice
is cheating on him: "Harry is beginning . . . To feel the world turn. A hopeful coldness inside him grows, grips his wrists inside his cuffs. The news
isn't all in, a new combination might break it open, this stale peace" (Redux 16). Having accepted his role as a husband, father, and provider following the tragic death of his daughter in *Rabbit, Run,* Harry feels his life
has become dull; the competition upon which he thrives has been flat, just
as the Cold War has suffered no direct confrontation (such as the U-2 incident or the Cuban Missile Crisis) in the latter half of the 1960s. Because
of his need for competition, Harry labels this period "stale peace" as opposed to "thaw," the more common term and a word Updike uses else-

17. Plath, *Conversations with John Updike,* 88.
18. In a 1976 interview with Jeff Campbell, Updike affirms a connection between
"intimate and domestic and personal" problems and "issues that affect international relations and world affairs"; he says, "Sure, there's some attempt in these epigraphs to remind the reader that these domestic events are occurring simultaneously with this unparalleled venture into space" (Plath, *Conversations with John Updike,* 87).

where to describe the same period (Bech 4). "Coldness," a metaphor taken directly from the Cold War, is "hopeful" for Harry because it might rekindle his competitive spirit. The word "inside" is repeated within a single sentence, emphasizing Harry's isolation and his innate desire for competition. After he realizes that this desire might be fulfilled, Harry watches the moon shot blast-off on television along with his coworkers at a bar, and the narrator contrasts this event with their lives: "The men dark along the bar murmur among themselves. They have not been lifted, they are left here" (Redux 16). Harry feels differently after a drink with his father over conversation that intimates Janice's infidelity: "Rabbit has ceased to feel cold, his heart is beginning to lift off" (Redux 18). Frightened of mediocrity, Harry rises to the call for competition, illustrated by advances in the space race in the world at large and by Janice's infidelity in his smaller world. In terms of the Cold War it is significant that this competition begins as something "cold," and that this coldness is what inspires action.

Harry notices mediocrity all around him, a condition made more apparent by the grand achievement of the space race. As William D. Atwill points out, Updike's project in the first section of *Rabbit Redux* "is to take the event the media has heralded as 'the greatest week in history' and reveal the paucity of response it creates in the lives of people constrained by their own problems."[19] This is certainly true of Harry's coworkers, but it is only initially true of the protagonist himself. The book is partially about the way this event gradually becomes meaningful to Harry. In the above passages he is directly contrasted to them: they "have not been lifted," but "his heart is beginning to lift off." Self-involved as usual, Harry has failed in the beginning of the novel to connect himself to his nation's achievement. He reflects on his father's life from what seems like miles away, and what he sees scares him: "Pop stands whittled by the great American glare, squinting in the manna of blessings that come down from the government, shuffling from side to side in nervous happiness that his day's work is done, that a beer is inside him, that Armstrong is above him, that the U.S. is the crown and stupefaction of human history. Like a piece of grit in the launching pad, he has done his part" (Redux 20). Despite the

19. William D. Atwill, *Fire and Power: The American Space Program as Postmodern Narrative*, 50.

patriotic appeal of his father's life, Harry is wary of replicating it, especially since they work together. He feels no more connection to the astronauts and their accomplishment than if he were just a piece of grit in the launching pad; when he returns home from the bar and his son Nelson exclaims, "They've left earth's orbit!" he responds nonchalantly, "Good for them. . . . Your mother here?" (Redux 23). There is a definite but unclear link at this moment between Harry's concern over Janice's infidelity and his perception of the moon mission. That night, watching the evening news, the connection becomes more explicit as Harry can see only emptiness in the astronauts' objective, the same emptiness he feels in his marriage. After a suspicious conversation with Janice followed by another evening apart from her, he reflects: "The six o'clock news is all about space, all about emptiness. . . . They keep mentioning Columbus but as far as Rabbit can see it's the exact opposite: Columbus flew blind and hit something, these guys see exactly where they're aiming and it's a big round nothing" (Redux 28). America is still "something" to Harry, but he cannot feel passionate about the moon because, like his marriage, there is nothing there worth the effort. America's colonization of a cold, lifeless satellite does not personally offer him the competition he requires. There is no visible opponent, so the achievement is hollow, the equivalent for Harry of sinking a miraculous jump shot while playing basketball alone in the driveway.

Harry can only become passionate about life in general and the space race in particular after Janice has left him and his foundling teenage lover Jill has replaced her, threatening his sense of security as she does so. By infiltrating his secure home she represents a new force of resistance (or competition) to replace Janice. He initially yields to her, but not for what would appear to be the obvious reason of sexual attraction. He is in fact not physically aroused by her (Redux 130–34), probably because he regards her as a child, closer in age and sensibility to Nelson than to him. Emphasizing the book's central symbolism, their sexual relationship is briefly described as "moonchild and earthman" (Redux 179).[20] His initial accep-

20. For a discussion of Harry's ongoing search for a daughter in the Rabbit novels see Mary O'Connell, *Updike and the Patriarchal Dilemma: Masculinity in the Rabbit Novels*, 164–85 and Campbell, "'Middling, Hidden, Troubled America,'" 34–49. Janice, like Jill, is described as "moonchild" when Harry makes love to her on the pile of gold coins in *Rabbit Is Rich* (Rich, 202).

tance of Jill is related to his passivity at the beginning of the novel before his characteristic resistance has resurfaced. He finally takes issue with Jill and her generation when she brings Nelson to the streets to beg for money. Harry tries to convince her that her life is too easy, that she is essentially dead because she has not had to work for anything, that she doesn't "have a fucking clue what makes people run. Fear. That's what makes us poor bastards run." When she suggests love as an alternative to fear, he responds, "Then you better find yourself another universe. The moon is cold, baby. Cold and ugly. If you don't want it, the Commies do. They're not so fucking proud" (Redux 152). Harry has not exhibited any emotion about the space race until this point; but once his personal security is threatened and his worldview is challenged he allows his heart to "lift off" for the purpose of competition rather than transcendence. Using hard-nosed rhetoric from the previous decade, Harry employs his competitive pro-American voice here in order to put Jill in her place and to maintain his position as leader of his house.

His different responses to the space race during his separate times with Janice and Jill reflect how much it means to him, how much he relies on global competition—preferably competition he can win, but not without effort—since his personal life has never equaled the competition he once experienced on the basketball court. Harry identifies his enemy variously through the novel as his wife, the younger generation, African Americans (in the person of Skeeter), the privileged classes (including Jill), his intolerant neighbors, and Janice's lover Charlie. The fact that he redefines his enemies so frequently and with such violent force during this novel is testimony to the rapid changes in the Cold War at this time. The enemy is no longer clear or visible, as it was a decade earlier under the satellite-launching, bombastic Khrushchev. The Soviet Union, like Janice, has temporarily receded from view, leaving Harry to scramble in search of an opponent. He instinctively needs to struggle or fight with these enemies, but the challenge presented to him is to learn to adapt to a changing world. Though he seems to make progress and to soften his outmoded conservative rhetoric, he ultimately returns to his safe core values and fails to adapt to new ones. Jill, Skeeter, Nelson, and his lover Peggy are all damaged or destroyed by his behavior. In the absence of clear competition, his destructive potential is randomly unleashed.

The problem for Harry and for his nation as they wander through what Updike described as the "most dissentious American decade since the Civil War" (HS 858) may be that the goal is no clearer than the enemy. He believes that the moon is "a big round nothing" and "cold and ugly." If America was still fighting the same Cold War in the 1960s as it fought in the 1950s, the spoils of this war were no longer desirable: in Harry's eyes, a lifeless satellite could not take the place of a well-furnished suburban home. The moon landing was only an abstract, distant victory like Sputnik was an abstract, distant loss. Conversely, the kitchen debate was a more tangible victory while the quiz show scandals were a more tangible loss for Americans like Harry (and Updike) who identified with these battles, or at least knew their terrain. For Harry to become excited about the moon landing as Nelson is, he must learn to see things through the eyes of someone younger than he is. If Harry does not adapt to such changes in the Cold War he will remain out of touch with his peers: his coworkers, his neighbors, and his wife. At stake in Harry's reaction to the moon landing, then, is the status of the early Cold War consensus that was rapidly breaking down in the late 1960s. Consciously or not, he chooses to reconcile with his peers at the expense of the younger generation. Jill, Skeeter, and Nelson are all sacrificed—symbolically or literally—so that Harry can regain stability in his life. Jill dies, Skeeter is sent into permanent exile, and Nelson suffers irreversible psychological damage as a result of Harry's choice to reunite with his own generation, first in the person of Peggy Fosnacht and eventually with Janice. The new, more complicated, more abstract Cold War is too difficult for Harry to comprehend. Life without Janice is similarly difficult and ultimately undesirable.

His separation from Janice ends at the book's conclusion; yet the reconciliation between them is tempered by the novel's ambiguous final lines: "He. She. Sleeps. O.K.?" (Redux 352). The "O.K.?" echoes the recurrent "O.K."s in the epigraph to the book's final section, a dialogue between astronaut Neil Armstrong and Mission Control. The connection between Harry's life and the space race is complete, but complicated. The question mark at the book's conclusion effectively questions the achievement of the U.S. Manned Space Program as well as the reconciliation of Harry and Janice. Updike has claimed that all of his novels pose a moral dilemma to the reader, and in *Rabbit Redux* this dilemma is encapsulated in the final sentence: is it simply "okay" that such a tragic novel ends with the comic trope of lovers reunited, or that Harry has not paid the price for his actions? A broader question ensues in light of this discussion: is it "okay" that Harry has essentially retreated into the relative safety of marriage given the fact that the bulk of the novel is devoted to his education into the ways of the younger generation? Updike poses these questions for the individual reader to answer, but the Cold War clarifies the context for them. In reuniting with his wife, Harry has chosen an early Cold War solution, for better or worse, which favors simplicity and clarity. The new Cold War will demand increasingly that Americans of Harry's generation adapt to complexities of this kind. The Cold War is not over when Armstrong sets foot on the moon, nor are Harry's domestic problems solved by his temporary separation from and reunion with Janice. In short, Harry continues to regard his marriage as he regards his Cold War life: there won't be any clear resolution to either of them, but Janice's resistance to him is necessary to keep him going, just as the presence of the Soviet Union is what keeps America on its toes. For Harry, the semblance of simplicity—life with Janice—is preferable to the educative chaos of life with Jill and Skeeter. With the final "O.K.?" Harry has made the moon landing meaningful to his life, and in doing so has accepted the competitive early Cold War mentality that the younger generation encourages him to reject, or at least to question.

In this sense, *Rabbit Redux* encourages us to wonder if separation is inherently bad. In Updike's frequently anthologized story "Separating," the Maples' separation is tainted by the fact that Richard cannot remember the answer to the fundamental question, why are they separating? (TF 211). In the case of Harry and Janice, though, the reason is clear—because they do not love each other—as is the reason they reunite: to regain stability. Yet if Harry had assimilated Jill's and Skeeter's values more thoroughly, the tragedy of the book's apocalyptic final evening might have been avoided. Stability for Harry and Janice is devastation for their son. Harry's unconscious attempt to regain the mood of the early Cold War is logically flawed because he has failed to account for Nelson's expressed needs and desires. Early Cold War logic held that the American family, if strong and united, could act as a bulwark against the threat of communism. Sensing a renewal of American fear for its favored position on the global stage, Harry in *Rabbit Is Rich* attempts to do his part toward winning the Cold War game by working hard, investing courageously, and trying to keep his family together. In some senses he succeeds, but his success seems impermanent and lacks something essential. *Rabbit Is Rich* is characterized by a strong sense of entropy, of a life, a country, and a global standoff that are "Running out of gas," to quote the first words of the novel. Coupled with the awareness of this world weariness is a sense of defiance and rebellion; Harry Angstrom and his fellow Brewerites are, in 1979, "getting frantic," for "they know the great American ride is ending" (Rich 1). The Cold War seemed to be coming to a close as the 1970s ended, but it was not over. The decade was marked by renewals of Cold War tensions on surprising fronts, from Iran to Afghanistan, and the rhetoric of the early Cold War returned in the early 1980s, notably with President Reagan's flourish of Eisenhower-era bravado in christening the Soviet Union "the Evil Empire." Since Harry is now accepted by his peers and is in tune with the mood of mainstream middle-class America, he should be happy and well adjusted. He is, except where Nelson is concerned.

Harry and Janice declare a sort of truce with one another at the end of *Rabbit Redux,* but his competitive instinct must find an outlet. In *Rabbit Is Rich* he transfers this instinct away from Janice and throws himself into the business of making money. His competition is more individualized now, pitting him against his golfing friends as opposed to his wife. He has unconsciously replicated the "kitchen debate" of his youth, amassing the comforts and appliances that herald American prosperity. He takes this pursuit to its grotesque extreme when he spreads gold Krugerrands across his bed and makes love to Janice on top of them (Rich 200–203). An overabundance of money itself in its most garish form—gold coins—appears to have made the struggles of Harry's life worthwhile. British journalist and social commentator Godfrey Hodgson writes of a "consensus mood" in American culture, which becomes the "dominant American ideology" by 1960, the year *Rabbit, Run* was published; the two notable qualities of this consensus mood, he writes, are that Americans became "Confident to the verge of complacency about the perfectibility of American society, anxious to the point of paranoia about the threat of communism." Hodgson sees this ideology emerge from the discovery of the simple fact that

"Capitalism, after all, seemed to work,"[21] while communism led to economic woes. He points to the way American economists put a new spin on the ideas of John Maynard Keynes—that capitalism worked best when combined with aggressive governmental spending and competition—after postwar economic success in the 1940s.

Updike affirms the neo-Keynesian viewpoint as late in the Cold War as 1989, writing that the economic conditions of the superpowers during the Cold War did not render them "six of one and a half-dozen of the other. It was more like eleven of one and one of the other. It was Athens and Sparta, light and shadow. Ours was the distinctly better mousetrap" (SC 139). To see Updike's view of the necessity of global competition strictly in economic terms would be reductive; yet there is something resonant about the way many of Updike's characters approach their lives in general, but more specifically the idea that American capitalism is competing with Soviet communism for more than just global stability in the nuclear age. Updike's generation believed to varying degrees that America was superior to its global counterpart in terms of the lifestyle of its citizens as well as the strength of its military. Hodgson sums up the essential elements of the predominant ideology of Updike's generation as follows: "the optimism, the confidence that more means better, the faith in the harmony of interests between capitalism and social progress, the cankerous sense that all this must be related to the competition with communism."[22] Harry Angstrom's behavior throughout the Rabbit tetralogy reflects this philosophy exactly; his struggle to gain and maintain power—whether on the basketball court, in the bedroom, or as a functioning member of his local community—is motivated by a strong belief in competition as the means to success and well-being, and his conservative views on communism bear out and largely explain this competitive instinct.

Harry certainly seems more content, less flappable, and less in danger in *Rabbit Is Rich* than in the previous two novels in the tetralogy. His relative wealth and level of social comfort allows him to transfer the global pressure exerted by the Cold War from his relationship to Janice to his place in the community. Gradually, though, this competition is transferred

21. Godfrey Hodgson, *America during the Cold War,* 74, 75.
22. Ibid., 81.

back to his family, but this time it is directed toward Nelson. Just as America has retreated in order to focus on its own problems in the late 1970s, Harry tries to exist as though he can "go it alone," eliminating from his mind any troubling thoughts from outside his insulated little world. Just before the scene in which he makes love to Janice on top of the gold coins, he meditates on Nelson, concluding, "To hell with this scruffy kid. Rabbit has decided to live for himself" (Rich 199). This isolation from his son can only be temporary despite Harry's efforts to run from Nelson or to set up blockades against him. Similarly, awareness that America's ongoing conflict with the Soviet Union is still very much alive creeps into Harry's consciousness at various times. To a young couple wanting to buy a car early in the novel, he backs off temporarily from his determined sales pitch, claiming, "It's still a free country, the Commies haven't gotten any further than Cambodia" (Rich 14). Underlying this seemingly meaningless banter is the fear that it is still possible for America to fall to communism; Harry's use of the word "Commies" intensifies this sense of fear, as it is a word associated with the paranoia of McCarthy-era rhetoric, and the very word he used to intimidate Jill in *Rabbit Redux*. His use of the word "still" also indicates a lingering fear that America must keep up its guard against communist infiltration. The link between Harry's perception of the Carter years and of the 1950s is later made explicit: "Carter is smart as a whip and prays a great deal but his gift seems to be the old Eisenhower one of keeping much from happening, just a little daily seepage" (Rich 117). This idea is both a comfort and a bane to Harry; coupled with the absence of a direct threat to global stability, which characterized the Kennedy years, is the notion that a threat is seeping into the American landscape, definitely and steadily, toward some inevitable end.

Harry's friends in *Rabbit Is Rich* cling to the notion that the world behind the Iron Curtain must continue to be stigmatized; Buddy Inglefinger believes that "in countries like East Germany or China they're pumping these athletes full of steroids, like beef cattle, they're hardly human" (Rich 53). Inglefinger expresses a typical American perception of Soviet athletes during the early 1980s, rendered heavy-handedly in media images and films like the propagandistic *Rocky IV* in which the American boxing hero, literally wrapped in the American flag, defeats his Soviet opponent who has been made inhuman through countless steroid injections. Athletic competition with the Soviet Union was prevented the year before *Rabbit Is Rich* was published when President Carter canceled U.S. participation in the 1980 Moscow Olympics due to Soviet military involvement in Afghanistan. The atmosphere during the late Carter years was tense due to the renewal of such showdowns between the superpowers; one unnamed Carter administration official declared in 1980, "this is the Cold War in the most classic, extreme form."[23] After making his pronouncement about Russian athletes, Inglefinger has no problem transferring old Cold War rhetoric to the new Cold War situation: "Jesus, those Arabs," he says, "Wouldn't it be bliss just to nuke 'em all?" (Rich 159). Buddy later treats Harry and his friends to a banal pun about a Russian ballet dancer who defected to the United States "because Communism wasn't Goodunov"(Rich 168). The presence of Buddy and his old-fashioned xenophobic attitudes in the novel signals a lingering paranoia in Harry's world, as well as a tinge of fear about America's economic slide, which Harry uses as a metaphor for his fear that he will fall from the position of power that he has attained; he muses, "Get out of it in this society and you're as good as dead, an embarrassment. Not Goodunov"(Rich 168). Competition is still the core of Harry's philosophy of success, and even when the Soviet Union and its global allies do not provide an immediate threat to American hegemony, they seem to lurk in the margins of Harry's consciousness, ready to take over if America falters. To Americans at this time the nation's primary weakness was its fragile economy, so Harry fights this battle by getting rich.

As is the case with many of the protagonists of Updike's 1970s novels, Harry in *Rabbit Is Rich* is trapped by nostalgia, and resents this quality in himself when Janice points it out to him: "It stung him, that she thinks he lives in the past" (Rich 229). Immediately after this realization, he "switches on the radio to shut off their conversation," and he hears about "Soviet tanks patrolling the streets of Kabul in the wake of last Sunday's mysterious change of leadership in Afghanistan" (Rich 229). Harry's resistance to being caught in the past is coupled with the sense that the past, at least in terms of the Cold War, has parallels in the present. His ideas about competition and about the Cold War have essentially not changed since the

23. Bernard A. Weisberger, *Cold War, Cold Peace*, 292.

late 1950s; "he pulls for the Rams [to win the Super Bowl] the way he does for the Afghan rebels against the Soviet military machine" (Rich 435). He proclaims, in his support of the long-shot football team and the Afghan rebels, that "he doesn't like overdogs," but in the case of Afghanistan, he would also be uncomfortable if the Russians were to exert power successfully.

It is obvious to the reader, if not to Harry, that the Cold War in 1979 resembles the old Cold War only on the surface. The new enemy of middle-class America, according to Harry's coworker (and Janice's former lover) Charlie Stavros, is Big Oil, an extension of OPEC, which represents the new area of countries with divided loyalties between the United States and the Soviet Union. The narrator notes that a riot over gasoline on television "looks like old films of Vietnam or Budapest but it is Levittown right down the road" (Rich 44). The connection between the suburban gasoline riots and former Cold War battlefields is subtle, yet terrifying for Harry, who still retains his crucial need for space around him—a concept he developed in relation to Vietnam in *Rabbit Redux*—and his need to feel as if he can still compete. Like other Americans, Harry in 1979 feels strongly about America's inability to do anything about the hostages in Iran or about the angry Iranians who could be seen on the nightly news desecrating the American flag. It is evident from Updike's "Notes and Comment" pieces from the late 1950s that mainstream Americans believed the way to counter Soviet achievements was to revel in the triumphs of American culture. Having been raised on that paradigm, Harry fights back by making money. But like the 1950s quiz shows, there is something false about the way Harry achieves his wealth. He is no more satisfied with his job as a car salesman than he was with his job as a Magipeel salesman in *Rabbit, Run* or as a linotype setter in *Rabbit Redux*. Moreover, he has essentially inherited this job and the money that accompanies it from Janice's father. Finally, he amasses his wealth on gold speculation, the purest gamble and the most fleeting and illusory form of wealth.

Despite the relative bliss of Harry's world in this novel, then, things may not be what they seem. Updike believed that America would pay a price for its blithe dismissal of the quiz show scandals, and he also believed that Harry would have to pay a price for becoming rich on the inflationary fears of others. That price comes not in the form of a devastated marriage but rather in the form of a ruined son.[24] The fourth section of the book begins bluntly with a reaction to the crisis in Iran: "The hostages have been taken," and is followed immediately by, "Nelson has been working at Springer Motors for five weeks" (Rich 292), as though these two events are directly related to one another. There is, of course, no causal relationship between the two, but in Harry's mind, hiring Nelson has been catastrophic, as much of a crisis as the taking of political hostages in the new battleground of the Cold War. Harry has spent the majority of the novel avoiding both the global crisis and the deep problems that exist in his family, and the two crises resurface at the same moment. The old Cold War solution of making money works for Harry, but since he has dismissed the perspective of the younger generation in *Rabbit Redux* he has yet to account for the complexities of the new Cold War.

Harry makes a weak, narcissistic effort to care about his son, declaring, "You're too much me" (Rich 194). There are many ways in which they are alike, of course, in that Nelson impregnates a woman and tries to run from his responsibilities, but these comparisons are to the young Harry of *Rabbit, Run*. Nelson and Harry may be the same type of man, but they are from different generations. As a young man Harry had a completely different context for the way he thought about the world. His relatively simple version of the way the world works cannot be compared to Nelson, who grew up during the turbulent 1960s and was exposed to profound turmoil when Janice moved out and Jill and Skeeter moved in. Nelson has no idea of the larger ramifications of the hostage crisis, and no insight into its effect on his life or his new career at Springer Motors; he muses, "This Iranian thing is going to scare gas prices even higher but it'll blow over, they won't dare keep them long, the hostages" (Rich 297). Yet something bothers Nelson about the hostage situation, as though he senses the threat of another empire to his existence despite the fact that he was not indoctrinated in the Cold War the way Harry was. Nelson recognizes his own fear, using an image similar to Kenneth's perception of Khrushchev's visit in "Dear Alexandros" ("like swallowing a penny"): "[Nelson] thinks of those hostages in Tehran and it's like a pill caught in his throat" (Rich 298). His

24. See D. Quentin Miller, "Updike's Rabbit Novels and the Tragedy of Parenthood," 195–216.

earlier thought that the hostage crisis will not last long is undermined by this fear, and he reacts accordingly: "Drop a little tactical A-bomb on a minaret as a calling card" (Rich 298). We see evidence here that the Cold War affects Nelson's generation in much the same way that it affected Harry's generation, as represented by Buddy Inglefinger. There is an illusion of national solidarity shared by the two generations demonstrated by Nelson's and Buddy's desire to flex America's nuclear muscle against Iran, a Soviet ally. However, the differences in perspective between the younger and older generations (made evident in the late 1960s) simmer dangerously under the nation's surface. The hostage crisis bogs down into the same type of standoff that occurred with failed negotiations in earlier decades; the news in *Rabbit Is Rich* becomes in Harry's mind "the latest version of nothing happening. Khomeini and Carter both trapped by a pack of kids who need a shave and don't know shit" (Rich 331). Harry tries to blame the standoff (like everything else) on the new generation, and it is clear that he regards this generation as his new enemy, with Nelson as its point man.

Despite some superficial similarities between Nelson and Harry, their differences underscore how dramatically the early Cold War consensus has broken down. Their opposite interpretations of the new Cold War build into a crisis at a rare scene in which the two actually talk to one another. The generational differences between the father and the son have always been a point of contention between them, but in this scene their differences are contextualized specifically in terms of the Cold War. Harry is on the verge of firing his son as a car salesman; he begins the conversation by talking about basketball, the game from his youth that he still holds dear, even though he admits, "it's changed a lot since my day." Nelson's reaction to the conversation is, "Basketball is all goons, if you ask me" (Rich 353). Harry senses that the discussion is off to a poor start and switches to politics; he begins,

> "What do you think about those Russkis in Afghanistan? They sure gave themselves a Christmas present."
> "It's stupid," Nelson says. "I mean, Carter's getting all upset. It's no worse than what we did in Vietnam, it's not even as bad because at least it's right next door and they've had a puppet government there for years."
> "Puppet governments are O.K., huh?"

"Well *every*body has 'em. All of South America is our puppet governments."

"I bet that'd be news to the spics."

"At least the Russians, Dad, *do* it when they're going to do it. We *try* to
do it and then everything gets all bogged down in politics. We can't do
*any*thing anymore."

"Well not with people talking like you we can't," Harry says to his son.
"How would you feel about going over and fighting in Afghanistan?"
(Rich 353–54)

Nelson, who came of age during Vietnam when the new Cold War began,
laughs off Harry's question and says, "Dad, I'm a married man. And way
past draft age besides" (Rich 354). Harry is startled by this response, first
because he himself "doesn't feel too old to fight" and second because he
was prepared to go to Korea when he was in the army during the early
Cold War. He reminisces about the "straight-on way of looking at the
world" (Rich 353) that characterized his time in the army. The distance between them is evident; Harry belligerently addresses his son as "people like
you" as if he is back discussing Vietnam with Charlie Stavros in *Rabbit Redux*. He accuses Nelson of getting married to avoid going to war and Nelson replies, "There won't be any next war, Carter will make a lot of noise
but wind up letting them have it, just like he's letting Iran have the
hostages. Actually, Billy Fosnacht was saying the only way we'll get the
hostages back is if Russia invades Iran. Then they'd give us the hostages
and sell us the oil because they need our wheat" (Rich 354). Harry uses
this opportunity to voice his negative opinion of Billy Fosnacht, and a confrontation ensues about the fateful night when Jill died in the house fire.
As he becomes heated Harry feels "his heart rising to what has become a
confrontation" (Rich 354) with his son just as he hopefully felt his heart
"lift off" in *Rabbit Redux* as he prepared to fight against Janice. Even
though Harry has recently demonstrated his nostalgia for the past, his advice to Nelson is, "You got to let it go, kid. Your mother and me have let it
go. . . . The past is the past" (Rich 355). Since Harry returns to the past
when it is more appealing than the present, his advice to Nelson is in-
consistent and perhaps insincere, just one of many instances when he effectively dismisses his son. Nelson's troubled presence in Harry's life is testimony to the fact that the world is more complex than Harry allows, and

the "straight-on way of looking at the world" that characterized his youth is only a temporary defense against the difficulties of the present. As in the previous novel of the tetralogy, Nelson disappears at the end of this one and Harry seems happy enough to be isolated, crowing, "Fuck the Russkis. . . . We'll go it alone, from sea to shining sea" (Rich 436). His will to withdraw despite his competitive instinct emphasizes how poorly he has adapted to changes in the Cold War world. Nelson's disappearance is only temporary; neither personal nor global conflicts have been truly resolved.

Even so, Harry's competitive instinct is perfectly understandable in terms of his Cold War upbringing, which fostered a deeply ingrained belief that America is a better place, in terms of military power and economic health, because of its rivalry with the Soviet Union. Yet since marriages and family relationships deteriorate in Updike's fiction as a direct result of the competitive instincts exhibited by his patriarchal protagonists like Harry, we can conclude that competition for its own sake does not lead to happiness. At some level, the object of the competition becomes less clear. If Americans were trying to demonstrate the superiority of their lifestyle through the promulgation of happy, well-apportioned homes, then why are these homes the sites of so much despair in Updike's fiction? It is clear from these stories and novels that the competitive global structure was not meant to infiltrate the domestic sphere, but there was no way to stop it. The tension between the global power structure and the mistranslation of this structure into the private worlds of characters is often at the heart of Updike's fiction, especially during the middle period of his writings— the period spanned by the two middle novels in the Rabbit tetralogy. The threat is heightened by the division of public opinion during Vietnam, the subject of my next chapter. Though theoretical competition with the global "other" put pressure on the fragile domestic sphere in Updike's writing, America's divisive response to actual competition in the mysterious jungles of Vietnam threatened to shatter it altogether.

3

Vietnam and the Politics of Undovishness

Power is a dirty business, but who ever said it wasn't?

–John Updike, "On Not Being a Dove," 1989

THE COLD WAR during the 1960s began with a single, coherent struggle between two military superpowers, but it gradually became fragmented into many smaller, unfamiliar fronts, notably the Vietnam War and
the space race. The space race represents the last remaining vestiges of
the old Cold War in which America's goal and its competitor were recognizable. While NASA did what it could to bring America together in terms
of popular opinion, the debate over American military involvement in Vietnam threatened to tear the country apart. Vietnam signified the advent of
the new Cold War. America during the Vietnam era was still battling the
spread of Soviet-style communism, in theory; yet the Soviets were not fighting this particular war, and the enemy seemed to be the elusive Viet Cong,
Red China, or even some faction of America itself, given the dissent caused
by the war on the home front. In the new Cold War of the 1970s and 1980s,
the object of competition, like the enemy, is less clearly defined. The debate over the Vietnam War becomes especially pertinent to Updike's writing career because of his public declaration in 1967 that he was not fundamentally opposed to U.S. intervention. In the slow process of working
through the implications of this declaration, he permanently alters the trajectory of his fiction by simultaneously intensifying within it the presence

of world politics and illustrating an increasingly disharmonious domestic world.

Vietnam becomes a contentious issue in Updike's thinking and in his writing because it represents the passing of a world order that had become deeply embedded in his consciousness. The advent of this new phase in the Cold War has a profound and lasting effect on Updike's fictional writings, which become noticeably more conflicted beginning with *Rabbit Redux* (1971). Familiar motifs in Updike's fiction change drastically; conversations give way to highly charged debates, characters who previously existed in society's margins surrender to their impulse to withdraw completely, and a world previously wounded by adultery becomes a world scarred by divorce. The debate over the Vietnam War is a source of extraordinary tension in Updike's writing, and its lasting effect is to cause Updike's protagonists to associate the pre-Vietnam era with a sort of Edenic innocence. The debate represents a schism between the suburban complacency of the early Cold War and the nationwide chaos of the late 1960s and 1970s.

In the preceding chapters I have demonstrated how Updike's characters respond to Cold War anxiety through fight or flight instincts. In his earlier writings the threat of nuclear war causes characters to take shelter in their private worlds; but as the Cold War heated up and the threat of global annihilation receded in the wake of the Cuban Missile Crisis, Updike's characters rise to the challenge of global competition, unconsciously sabotaging their domestic safety as they allow their belligerence to surface. The Vietnam era marks the high point of this latter tendency in Updike's works, and the presence of contemporary history takes a position of prominence in his fiction. In his works written during the most intense years of the Vietnam War—notably *Couples* and *Rabbit Redux*—reports of contemporary events originating from television, radio, and newspaper sources become increasingly prevalent and eventually develop into a hallmark of his work. Updike's fiction of the Vietnam era suggests that it is useless for Americans to attempt to isolate themselves from global events.

History in general also takes on greater importance in Updike's writings of this period, substantiating his claim that his novels "contain more history than history books"; his play *Buchanan Dying* (1971) finds him digging back into America's collective history and combining it with

Buchanan's personal history. Even this play, far removed from current events, may illuminate Updike's view of the 1970s scene; as Arthur Schlesinger, Jr., writes in a review of the play, Updike sees in Buchanan "the emblem of the house divided against itself, the recapitulation of half a century of the American descent into chaos."[1] This description could apply just as easily to the Vietnam era as to the Civil War; the divided house that was Vietnam-era America sparked an identity crisis that continues to haunt Americans just as the aftermath of Buchanan's war does. The Vietnam debate held special importance for Updike because he was shocked that no one in his circles shared his position on it. His unpopular stance, which was as surprising to himself as it was to his fellow writers, makes perfect sense in the context of the larger Cold War. The complexity of the Vietnam debate and the fact that he eventually seems to change (or at least examine) his stance help to explain why Updike holds interest as a writer of complex and conflicting impulses. Although they are tormented, his Vietnam-era works genuinely mirror the confusion of the times.

Updike's emphasis on global and individual competition carries over into the Vietnam era, but he begins to question the usefulness of this ideal when he senses that his opinion is no longer aligned with the status quo. When Vietnam became a public issue in the mid-1960s, Updike was convinced that American involvement in Vietnam was really another Cold War attempt to battle communism and that the American ideal of personal liberty was a cause worth fighting for. Many Americans of Updike's generation in his social class had long accepted that capitalism preserved American ideals, that the Soviet Union posed a threat to these ideals, and that America needed to maintain military superiority to ensure protection against its global enemy. Divided opinion over the Vietnam War, made possible by the changing ideals of a young and visible American counterculture, suddenly rendered this consensus obsolete. This counterculture questioned the value of fighting not only a war against communism but also of fighting any war, and they even went so far as to suggest the possibility that communism was not America's enemy in the first place. What ensued was a moral crisis that fragmented America like no other issue since the Civil War. The Vietnam debate was especially thorny because of

1. Arthur Schlesinger, Jr., "The Historical Mind and the Literary Imagination," 57.

the difficulty of articulating the moral terms of America's objectives, as Updike's pronouncements on the subject demonstrate.

It is helpful to see Updike's career as bifurcated by the Vietnam War; before the war, "we-they" competition provided the backdrop for his writings. After the war, his writing takes a nostalgic turn; his characters long for earlier times when their lives were simpler, a time when Americans were largely united against the Soviet Union and marriages lasted, even though they had problems. In his middle years, Vietnam is a burden, representative of the rough transition between the high years of the Cold War in the 1950s and early 1960s and the renewal of earlier Cold War rhetoric in the late 1970s and 1980s. If we think of American involvement in Vietnam in terms of National Security Advisor McGeorge Bundy's slippery slope metaphor, we should regard Updike as a Sisyphus figure, repeatedly charging the hill pushing a stone of ideals that had become, at least for liberal intellectuals and writers, too weighty to bear.

Updike's stance on Vietnam was first made public in what for him became a controversial book entitled *Authors Take Sides on Vietnam* (1967), comprised of various authors' responses to two simple questions on the war in Vietnam: "Are you for, or against, the intervention of the United States in Vietnam?" and "How, in your opinion, should the conflict in Vietnam be resolved?" Updike was listed as the only American author "unequivocally for" U.S. involvement in the war, and the *New York Times* drew attention to this circumstance. This unpopular public declaration had a lasting impact on Updike's writing; echoes of it plague his protagonists, who confidently support the war only to find themselves isolated from their friends, families, and lovers. As one of the only major American authors to refrain from attacking American intervention in Vietnam, Updike was not quite prepared to accept the idea that the clear-cut global issues of the 1950s had become complicated and difficult to think through in the 1970s. Twenty-three years after his stance on Vietnam was made public, he writes, "It pained and embarrassed me to be out of step with my editorial and literary colleagues" (SC 117). These emotions of pain and embarrassment help to explain the heightened presence of the Vietnam debate in Updike's writings of the 1970s, and they also mark the development of the trend within his writings toward nostalgia for the happier (if more precarious) days of the old Cold War.

It is no news that the debate over Vietnam dealt American identity one of its most devastating blows. Even setting aside for the purpose of the debate the many young men who fought in and were traumatized by the war, all Americans who lived through the era can still conjure up scenes of profound violence on the home front—the National Guard firing on college students rallying for peace at Kent State University, or pro-war blue-collar workers in New York tearing into a crowd of peaceful demonstrators and students at Pace University. In his clear-eyed retrospective study of the debate, David W. Levy hardly overstates the significance of the era when he concludes "that the debate over American participation in the Vietnam war was one of those times when the most basic faiths, the most dreadful fears, the most profound hopes of the nation were spoken, considered, and judged."[2] America, in other words, was questioning its role as a superpower during Vietnam for the first time since the Cold War began. Updike, who had hardly been a controversial public figure or a political novelist before this point, was placed at the center of the debate against his will. The writer of what many readers considered to be isolated suburban fictions found himself becoming more involved with the way global dramas affected his suburban scenes.

Before analyzing Updike's position, it is important to frame the issues of the debate. In very broad terms, Americans in the mid-1960s who opposed the war argued that their country had no place intervening in what could be considered a civil war in a far-removed country; they saw American involvement as just another example of capitalist imperialism with little to be gained and many lives to be lost. On the other side of this argument, Americans in favor of the war saw the North Vietnamese as purveyors of communist expansionism, with the fall of South Vietnam representing the beginning of a "domino effect" that would allow communism to spread until it became a direct threat to U.S. security. "Communism" was a term that had swelled in importance in the minds of Americans who had been raised to believe in the ideas of the Cold War consensus; as Levy points out,

> two large, general defenses of American involvement—that national security was endangered and that the enemy was immoral—were tightly linked, in the minds of most Americans by a single, fearful, demonic

2. David W. Levy, *The Debate over Vietnam,* xii–xiv.

specter: communism. After almost two decades of Cold War the word had
come to symbolize for millions of Americans both everything that was
endangering and everything that was immoral in world affairs. . . . Thus
the fact that Americans were resisting *communism* in Vietnam went a
long way, by itself, toward justifying the effort.[3]

Morality is the central focus for this aspect of the debate; considerations
over legality, cost, the dissolution of a nation, the dehumanization of its soldiers, the brutality of the nature of this particular war, and so on, entered
into the debate as the war sank deeper and deeper into a hopeless quag-
mire. Before television brought the war into the living rooms of most
Americans, the debate was shaped by the old Cold War idea that America
needed to fight communism regardless of individual circumstances posit-
ed against the new Cold War idea that communism should not be thought
of in the same terms as it always had been. Americans began to question
that communism was in fact the enemy in Indochina, or whether it truly
posed any threat to our national security or our ideology.

Morality can be strongly influenced by social institutions, such as
churches and colleges, but in modern times morality is often swayed by
contemporary popular opinion. Updike's colleagues in the literary world
also construed their response to the Vietnam question in moral terms, but
their collective concept of morality caused them to draw conclusions opposite to those of Updike, as can be seen in the many responses recorded
in *Authors Take Sides on Vietnam* by writers who voiced unequivocal opposition to the war, such as James Baldwin ("I am against United States intervention in Vietnam on moral grounds because it is wrong"), Arthur
Miller ("I was and am opposed to intervening in Vietnam, for political, military and moral reasons"), and the irrepressible Joseph Heller ("By fighting
and attempting to justify this war of ours in Vietnam, we are reducing ourselves to the low moral level of Nazis"). Updike's moral perspective caused
him to focus on his distrust of the ability of communist leaders to ensure
the rights of the individual, as the quotation by Updike from *Authors Take
Sides* published in the *Times* makes evident: "I do not believe that the
Vietcong and Ho Chi Minh have a moral edge over us. I am for our intervention if it does some good, specifically if it enables the people of south

3. Ibid., 38.

Vietnam to seek their own political future." Updike was for U.S. intervention insofar as he was for political self-determination, pure and simple. The type of communism practiced by the North Vietnamese did not offer this option, based on the record of totalitarian communist nations in the twentieth century. Updike stuck to these beliefs, even while others began to believe that, in the words of Arthur Schlesinger, Jr., "Communism is no longer a unified, coordinated, centralized conspiracy."[4]

"On Not Being a Dove" is enlightening as an analysis of Updike's reliance on competition and as a realization of how his idea of global competition is complicated by Vietnam. He writes the memoir as a corrective to what he felt was an injustice on the part of the *Times,* claiming that he wrote out his stance on Vietnam quickly, "with some irritation" (SC 112) at being interrupted from an island vacation. He also points out that the *Times* cut a page from a letter to the editor that Updike wrote to clarify his position, including his plea to be "released from the responsibility of having an opinion on the Vietnam involvement" (SC 114-15), a wish that was certainly shared by countless other Americans. Updike also protests that, despite the *Times'* assessment that he is the only author "unequivocally for" American involvement in Vietnam, he in fact "was not the only non-dove" (SC 115) included in the book, citing responses written by W. H. Auden and James Michener as evidence. Once Updike has made his case for being misunderstood on the subject of Vietnam, he makes some telling observations about his actual stance, looking back from a 1989 perspective.

What Updike tells us in "On Not Being a Dove" about his stance on Vietnam is evident in his fiction: Vietnam represented for him a great challenge to the way he thought about the world and about America's place in it. Consequently, the world he has created in his fiction (and the world in which he lives) becomes complicated, a game in which the rules have suddenly been reinvented, a lost paradise marred by divorce. Pre-Vietnam

4. There is also the consideration of what non-authors thought of the war; just a year before Updike's statement in *Authors Take Sides on Vietnam,* polls showed that 70 percent of Americans supported a bombing strategy as the "only way" to "save" Vietnam, and 80 percent felt that American withdrawal would open Southeast Asia to communist domination. See Steven M. Gillon and Diane B. Kunz, *America during the Cold War,* 157-58. Quotes from Cecil Woolf, ed., *Authors Take Sides on Vietnam,* 14, 37, 29; "The War Assayed by 259 Writers"; and Allen Matusow, *The Unraveling of America: A History of Liberalism in the 1960s,* 219.

takes on the weight of an era of innocence, "domestic bliss" (SC 122) within which a ski trip can become "a holiday back into adolescence" (SC 123). He argues how difficult it is for him to complain about a nation that had provided him with so much to be thankful for. Updike's answer to the Vietnam question is for him an easy one: "What was Vietnam but Korea again, Korea without an overt invasion, without a UN resolution, and without a Syngman Rhee, but all the more honorable a cause for its added difficulties? Were the people in the State Department utterly stupid to think we shouldn't let Southeast Asia go down the drain? Were we really secure enough—high and mighty and smug enough—to become a pacifist nation? You don't get something for nothing" (SC 125). By this logic, Vietnam is simply a manifestation of the larger war America had been fighting for all of Updike's adult life. This was also the view of President Kennedy during the early years of his administration, when Updike was securing his identity as a writer; according to historians Steven Gillon and Diane Kunz, "Kennedy shared the bi-partisan consensus which saw the Communist world as monolithic. Virtually all American policy makers maintained that a victory for Communist forces in Indochina was equally a victory for the Soviet Union. Furthermore, Communism seemed on the move during the early sixties."[5] Of course, American policy makers and many American citizens began to question these assumptions as the war dragged on. Given the impact that Updike's position on the war has on the direction of his writing, it is obvious that Vietnam was more complicated than Korea, and especially more complicated than the Cold War as a whole.

Updike struggles in his memoir to figure out just what changed during Vietnam, and just why he was "so vehement and agitated an undove" (SC 127). The issue is so perplexing that one manuscript version of *Self-Consciousness* mistakenly lists the title of the memoir in the table of contents as "On Not Being a *Hawk*." Updike searches for autobiographical reasons, attributing his stance to everything from the predictable (his father's politics) to the absurd (his own recurrent dental pain). But the most involved statements come from his unwillingness to alter his views on competition. He adheres to his original beliefs, even when writing his memoir in 1989: "'You *must* fight,' none other than a Russian had told me,

5. Gillon and Kunz, *America during the Cold War,* 152.

in late 1964, in the Soviet Union, concerning Vietnam" (SC 131). His willingness to fight extends to his willingness to agree to war, based on what
he feels is human nature: "The Vietnam war—or *any* war—is 'wrong,' but in
the sense that existence itself is wrong. To be alive is to be a killer" (SC 131).
This view casts Vietnam-era pacifism as a luxury available only through
American military might; Updike writes, "It was all very well for civilized
little countries like Sweden and Canada to tut-tut in the shade of our nuclear umbrella and welcome our deserters and draft evaders, but the United States had nobody to hide behind" (SC 131). Updike's rhetoric is not
unusual for one brought up with the notion that his country is superior
to its rival in terms of military might, economic power, and the individual
rights of its citizens. Yet this rhetoric is bold; by equating the human condition with the capacity for murder—"to be alive is to be a killer"—Updike accounts for our warlike tendencies, and by comparing the United
States to smaller pacifist nations, he underscores the historical importance
of Cold War America. By the very fact of writing the memoir he acknowledges that these realizations are problematic; he never achieves his goal
of understanding why his position wasn't universally accepted. Updike's
essay is full of conflict, and he searches for explanations as to why he was
out of step with his contemporaries on this issue.

The answer to this question remains unclear by the end of the essay, but
Updike does offer two explanations that correspond with two of the recurrent topics of his fiction: religion and marital difficulties. "My religious
and Vietnamese opinions were clearly allied" (SC 141), he writes, "both
made me feel vulnerable, excited, apologetic, and angry, and both were, in
my adopted social milieu, rather original" (SC 141). Updike's tough Barthi-
an theology can be seen in terms of his stance on Vietnam; he asks, "Where
was the ingenuity, the ambiguity, the humanity (in the Harvard sense) of
saying that the universe just happened to happen and that when we're
dead we're dead? Where, indeed, was the intellectual interest of saying that
Johnson and Nixon were simply dreadful Presidents? Truth had to have
more nooks and crannies, more ins and outs than that" (SC 142). In the
same way Updike searches for religious truth through his writing, he
searches for historical truth, or at least clarity of vision. He regards the debate over Vietnam as a worthwhile subject because it throws a wrinkle
into our national pattern of thinking, which becomes troubled in a way it

did not seem to be before. Though Updike claims that the sixties were a prosperous time for his career, he also recalls, "The Vietnam era was no sunny picnic for me; I remember it as a sticky, strident, conflicting time, a time with a bloody televised background of shame" (SC 146). Updike's ongoing investigation of Vietnam stems from the fact that he sees the debate over the war, like religion, as a source of productive tension.

In addition to providing grounds for intellectual inquiry, the conflict over the war also gives Updike a context for marital conflict, a subject that pervades his fiction. He writes, "my wife's reflexive liberalism helped form my unfortunate undovish views . . . I assumed these views out of a certain hostility to her, and was protesting against our marriage much as campus radicals were blowing up ROTC buildings" (SC 134). As we have seen in chapter 2, Cold War conflicts find their way into the domestic sphere in Updike's fiction. Vietnam becomes a battleground for other conflicts to be fought; Updike remembers his "children wincing and leaving the room when the subject came up at the dinner table" (SC 134), which demonstrates how heated the discussions could be. Vietnam created conflict within the home, the dissolution of the nuclear family that had seemed so unified in the 1950s.

Two of Updike's most prominent fictional topics—religious doubt and divorce—begin to explain his stance, and the generation gap between himself and the baby boomers might also help to paint the picture. Updike sees within the artistic endeavors of the Flower Children a "consciously retrieved Edenic innocence" (SC 148). The inherent loss of innocence in this assessment also applies to the characters in his fictional world for whom Vietnam becomes the era of disruption. Updike's most vocal pro-Vietnam characters—Harry Angstrom in *Rabbit Redux* and Tom Marshfield in *A Month of Sundays* (1975)—express outright contempt toward members of the younger generation who protest the war without giving thanks for their blessings as young Americans. Yet other writers who were Updike's age or older do not express the same type of distance from the younger generation. The reason behind Updike's stance may have something to do with his humble beginnings. The debate over Vietnam highlights the two sides of Updike; on the one hand we have the Harvard-educated, wildly successful author of upper-middle-class suburbia, and on the other we have the son of a rural Pennsylvania junior high school teacher who brought his family through the 1940s on less than two thousand dollars a year, according to a 1968 *Time* article. "The Updikes were so poor and isolated, [Updike] recalls, that 'in a way I've always felt estranged from the middle class—locked out of it.'"[6] For someone who has written so extensively and almost exclusively about the middle class, this observation is bound to cause some problems. He regards his success as a writer as hard-earned, and he unconsciously resents the new generation's anti-war protests, because he feels that they are of a privileged class that has not earned the right to criticize their country; he writes,

> A dark Augustinian idea lurked within my tangled position: a plea that Vietnam—this wretched unfashionable war led by clumsy Presidents from the West and fought by the nineteen-year-old *sons of the poor*— could not be disowned by a favored enlightened few hiding behind college deferments, fleeing to chaste cool countries, snootily pouring pig blood into draft files, writing deeply offended Notes and Comments, and otherwise pretending that our great nation hadn't had bloody hands from the start, that every generation didn't have its war, that bloody hands didn't go with having hands at all. (SC 135–36, emphasis added)

Class must be added to the list of possible explanations for Updike's stance, and regionalism added as a footnote to it. Apparently overlooking Kennedy, Updike highlights the "clumsy Presidents from the West" who were responsible for the war and the "sons of the poor" who fought it. Conversely, he must have regarded the protesters as the wealthy offspring of East Coast socialites, his adopted neighbors in Massachusetts who were also the subjects of much of his fiction.

All of these possible explanations for Updike's stance on Vietnam, in fact, represent the breakdown of a consensus that together signal an American identity crisis. Such a crisis was not welcome to a writer like Updike for whom America had offered an approximation of its elusive dream— fame, fortune, and critical acclaim, all of which came together for him at the height of the Vietnam War when his picture appeared on the cover of *Time* magazine in 1968. This high visibility was undoubtedly uncomfortable for Updike given his unpopular stance on the war. Gone forever were his days as an anonymous "Notes and Comment" writer for the *New Yorker;* public scrutiny was now the order of the day. Yet prior to his procla-

6. "View from the Catacombs," 73.

mation in *Authors Take Sides* he had voiced his opinions on the war in the *New Yorker*'s "Notes and Comment" pages, sharing space with the "deeply offended" pieces written by the "favored enlightened few" he speaks of in his memoir. In one early draft of the memoir, "deeply offended" was "unctuous peacenik." This moderated tone was something that Updike would have to develop with regard to the Vietnam debate. His "Notes and Comment" pieces from the mid-1960s found him arguing with a polite but indignant voice that often expressed his opinion that the United States should not shrink from its global responsibility, but that always admitted the difficulty of the debate.

His dissenting opinion with regard to the literary world becomes apparent in one "Notes and Comment" piece published on June 5, 1965, in which he fears that the debate over the war may weaken "the ties of respect and exchange between the intellectual community and the federal administration." The essay indicates Updike's undovish position on the war, stating, "a nation utterly unwilling to use its power has abdicated reality," but it also demonstrates his early realization that a new Cold War is dawning: "Communism no longer appears a monolithic menace, so our own position feels deprived of grandeur." Perhaps the most resonant statement of his position is contained in the simple sentence, "There are no simple alternatives."[7] In another piece published on November 6 of that same year he uses the paintings of Robert Motherwell to contemplate the question, "Why is it . . . that only black-and-white really satisfies us?" Updike admits in this essay that the Cold War has changed and that Vietnam represents the terrifying complexity that results from this change: "The edge between the free and the Communist worlds, never as distinct as some people thought, has blurred. The edge between Russia and China seems hard but jiggly. Vietnam is gray within gray within gray, an unfathomable impasto of blood and money and good intentions and jungle rot. Student protests double back on each other in a self-cancelling gumbo." The essay concludes that what we seek in art is something clarifying, something that can "redeem from the enveloping muddle the black-and-white fact of our own existence."[8] In order for art to do that, it must "mag-

7. John Updike, "Notes and Comment," June 5, 1965, 31.
8. John Updike, "Notes and Comment," November 6, 1965, 43.

nify" the difficulties of our lives. The debate over Vietnam, in this sense, directly affects the way Updike regards his craft as a fiction writer. It is up to the reader to figure out how art clarifies our lives, but the writer must at least concentrate on those gray areas of our lives that need magnification, and Vietnam is, after all, "gray within gray within gray." Updike's early writings had taken on difficult religious questions, but from this point on his writings were also destined to take on difficult social problems based on world politics.

In a 1971 "interview" with his alter-ego Henry Bech in the *New York Times Book Review,* Updike tries to sort out his position regarding American ideology, and regarding America's position on the world stage. Updike's praise of America and of its commitment to the individual is clear, but not absolute, at the beginning of the 1970s. He offers the following ambiguous assessments: "[Updike] said he was pro-American in the sense that he was married to America and did not wish a divorce. That the American style and landscape and impetus were, by predetermination, his meat; though he had also keenly felt love of fatherland in England, in Russia, in Egypt. . . . That, given the need for a [social] contract, he preferred the American Constitution, with its 18th-century bow to the pursuit of individual happiness, to any of the totalisms presently running around rabid" (PP 29). Updike asserts in this quotation that America offers the best available option in terms of individual liberty, but his statement isn't mere flag-waving; it is cautious patriotism at best. His metaphor for patriotism—a married man who does not wish a divorce—is not surprising, given the prominence of divorce in his writings from *Couples* on. The Vietnam era, if not the war itself, was about the break-up of a nation, and it is no accident that divorce becomes Updike's leitmotif during Vietnam and after, biographical considerations aside. The fact that the divorce rate in America grew from 11.2 percent in 1967 to 20.3 percent in 1975—nearly doubling during the Vietnam years—is not merely coincidental with the meteoric divorce rate in Updike's writings of the 1970s.[9] While Vietnam cannot be said to *cause* divorce in Updike's writings, it can be seen as a recurrent metaphor for the breakdown of the same type of consensus that determines the success of marriage. Marital contentment (if not bliss) corre-

9. Thomas Edsall, *Chain Reaction,* 260.

sponds with a unified national attitude toward the mission of Cold War America in the pre-Vietnam era.

Evidence of Updike's own discomfort about his Vietnam stance becomes a commonplace in his fiction during the 1970s. His protagonists live with the burden of being isolated in their pro-war stances, which are tremendously unpopular among their social sets. Henry Bech is haunted by paranoia as he tours South America in "Bech Third-Worlds It" (1979). Bech's growing sense of persecution becomes tangible in Venezuela, where students in an audience draw a caricature of him with the caption, roughly translated, "Intellectual reactionary. Imperialist. Enemy of the people." The English words "Rolling Stone" leap up at him from the page; the narrator glosses, "Some years ago in New York City he had irritably given an interviewer for *Rolling Stone* a statement, on Vietnam, to the effect that, challenged to fight, a country big enough has to fight. Also he had said that, having visited the Communist world, he could not share radical illusions about it and could not wish upon Vietnamese peasants a system he would not wish upon himself" (Back 40). Like his experiences with representatives from Vietnam and Korea, Bech's feelings about Vietnam have become confusing to the point that "he was sorry that he had said anything, on anything, ever" (Back 40). The fragmentation of the monolithic ideologies associated with the early Cold War complicates Bech's worldview and alters his impulse to write. It is clear that Bech, Updike's only fiction-writing character, in many ways embodies some of his own feelings, especially given the thinly veiled allusion to *Authors Take Sides On Vietnam* in the passage above. The reception of Bech's stance on Vietnam causes him to doubt his own identity as a writer. It is clear that the debate represents a crisis in Updike's world.

The crisis caused by the Vietnam debate affects not only identity in Updike's fiction, but also marital and extramarital relationships. Richard Maple, another of Updike's recurrent short-story protagonists, is also haunted by his stance on the war. As the title indicates, "Eros Rampant" (1968) is about a world suffering from the condition of love gone mad. In describing who loves who, the narrator mentions that Richard "as well seems to love, perhaps alone in the nation, President Johnson, who is unaware of his existence" (TF 134). Richard clearly experiences isolation, from not only his countrymen but also his wife, who asks him regarding his affair with an office mate named Penelope, "What went wrong, darley? Did you offend her with your horrible pro-Vietnam stand?" (TF 134). After finding out that he himself has been cuckolded, he begins to alter this stand: "When the usual argument about Vietnam commences, he hears himself sounding like a dove. He concedes that Johnson is unlovable. He allows that Asia is infinitely complex, devious, ungrateful, feminine" (TF 139). It is clear that Richard Maple's position on Vietnam gets in the way of his happiness, and that the crisis-filled Vietnam era represents a turning point in his ill-fated marriage. This scenario becomes increasingly familiar in Updike's writings beginning at this time and notably affects his two novels of the early 1970s. The shift from the relatively playful world of *Couples* to the dark, brooding world of *Rabbit Redux* and *A Month of Sundays* is a direct result of the contentious debate over Vietnam.

Vietnam acts as a sort of fulcrum in *Rabbit Redux* on which Harry Angstrom balances his own ideals against the ideals of his family, friends, neighbors, and enemies. Vietnam is the ideological issue that separates Harry from nearly everyone around him. In this separation, Harry is not unlike Updike, who states in a 1971 interview, "Intellectually, I'm not essentially advanced over Harry Angstrom . . . I quite understand both his anger and passivity, and feeling of the whole Vietnam involvement as a puzzle, that something strange has gone wrong" (PP 489). What has gone wrong is that the global power struggle that has structured Updike's and Harry's adult lives has manifested itself as a real war in a remote country, as opposed to a psychological war fought largely in America's collective imagination. Harry has become predictably paranoid as the Vietnam era begins; his anxiety about communist aggression amounts to a primal fear about his territory, an idea that gains new meaning from the space race, which is a contemporary version of the frontier, the ongoing battle for territory.

Harry uses a basketball metaphor to describe his position on the war to his sister Mim: "It's a, it's a kind of head fake. To keep the other guy off balance. The world the way it is, you got to do something like that once in a while, to keep your options, to keep a little space around you" (Redux 310–11). Harry's perception of Vietnam is boyish and naive from the perspective of the early 1970s when the world is not divided along the relatively clear lines of the 1950s. Mim questions his we-they theory; she asks,

"You're sure there is this other guy? . . .You don't think there might be a lot of little guys trying to get a little more space than the system they're under lets them have?" (Redux 311). Mim's questions reveal the fragmentation that the Cold War has undergone in the last half of the 1960s, but Harry clings to the idea, more typical in the late 1950s, that there is a single fundamental difference between Soviet communism and American-style capitalism: "'Sure there are these little guys, billions of 'em'—billions, millions, too much of everything—'but then also there's this big guy trying to put them all into a big black bag'" (Redux 311). "This big guy" with his "big black bag" is a personification of America's once-monolithic enemy, the oppressive Soviet Union; but while the metaphor is recognizable, it is unusual, owing more to Harry's own childlike insecurities than to accurate perceptions of communism. Harry has evidently voiced this theory before, as Janice later reflects on Harry's fear that "the Communists wanted to put everybody in a big black bag so he couldn't breathe" (Redux 332). Harry's feelings about Vietnam and the Cold War in general are revealed in this theory; he is frightened that the threat of communism jeopardizes his freedom as an individual, that it will suffocate him, and that like the kids on the basketball court in the initial sequence in *Rabbit, Run,* communists are trying to "crowd him up." Vietnam is important as territory; it acts as space between himself and what he feels is an oppressive system designed to make him powerless and anonymous.

Harry expresses his theory about Vietnam more succinctly to Mim than he does to Janice and her lover Charlie Stavros in a lengthy, heated debate in a Greek restaurant. Stavros tries to convince him that Vietnam is more complex than his simple "we-they" theory allows; Stavros says, "my theory is it's a mistaken power play. It isn't that we want the rice, we don't want *them* to have it. Or the magnesium. Or the coastline. We've been playing chess with the Russians so long we didn't know we were off the board" (Redux 48). Stavros's theory—much more thoughtful and expressed more eloquently than Harry's—reflects the new complications of the Cold War, and also echoes the very situation between the two men and Janice. Harry senses instant competition with this salesman and rises to the occasion. He is fighting territorially for his right to Janice, as he senses that she is on Stavros's side in the conversation and rightly suspects that she is sleeping with him. In Stavros's terms, it isn't that Harry wants Janice, only that he doesn't want *him* to have her. Stavros makes this observation to Janice later:"I get it. You're his overseas commitment" (Redux 54). The truth of his statement stings Janice. She is for Harry a territory, like the moon or Vietnam, that allows him to put space between himself and his competitors, real or imagined.

Harry reaffirms his need for competition during this argument, just as he does when arguing with Jill about the threat of the Soviet Union in terms of the moon. He accuses Stavros of biting the hand that feeds him in his attitude toward America, and he accuses the country at large of apathy:"This country is so zonked out on its own acid, sunk so deep in its own fat and babble and filth, it would take H-bombs on every city from Detroit to Atlanta to wake us up and even then, we'd probably think we'd just been kissed" (Redux 50). His own actions throughout the novel follow his theory that "you have to fight a war now and then to show you're willing" (Redux 50). The problem with this theory is that Harry ends up fighting for the sake of fighting, without any clear goals in mind; the issues, as with Vietnam, are more complex than Harry's theory allows for. Stavros asks Janice, "How can [Harry] think that crap? We-them, America first. It's dead" (Redux 54). She responds with a telling pronouncement that illuminates Harry's character in general: "He put his life into rules he feels melting away now" (Redux 54). In a review of the novel, Charles Thomas Samuels points out that Harry, like Bellow's Artur Sammler, has "survived an age that puts [him] out of step with its successor."[10] Harry's attachment to Vietnam is partially a longing for the old days of the Cold War, when the conflict was clearer. This type of dangerous nostalgia affects his career, his child-rearing, and his sexual relationships; his unwillingness to update his beliefs eventually causes catastrophe.

Harry's father notices Cold War pressures in Harry's life and deems himself unfit to cope with them:"If I'd of had the atomic bomb and these rich kid revolutionaries to worry about, I'd no doubt just have put a shotgun to my head and let the world roll on without me" (Redux 149). Harry, however, is determined to be less complacent than his father, and will fight an occasional war to show his willingness to stand up for his rights. This is why he takes on Charlie Stavros in a debate. Yet he is uncharacteristically

10. Charles Thomas Samuels, "Updike on the Present," 29.

passive when he allows Skeeter, Jill, and Nelson—representatives of the younger generation—to attempt to change his outdated ideas about Vietnam and race by instructing him in history. Jill points to Harry's lack of foresight in terms of his false sense of goals: "Because of the competitive American context, you've had to convert everything into action too rapidly. . . . But now, you see, we must [think], because action is no longer enough, action without thought is violence. As we see in Vietnam" (Redux 202-3). The history lessons Harry receives from his son, his teenage lover, and a radical Vietnam veteran constitute some of the most belabored and implausible scenes in the Rabbit novels. It is clear that Updike was working through a difficult point; these are long lectures, and they are pared down considerably from an earlier manuscript version from which Updike deleted long passages and interior monologues about Skeeter's experience in Vietnam. Skeeter's association with Jesus is more obvious in these earlier versions and he and Harry both repeatedly assert that God is on America's side. The war is somehow holy, in this sense; when Harry asks Skeeter point blank, "Do you think our being in Vietnam is wrong?" Skeeter answers, "Wrong? Man, how can it be wrong when it's just the way it is? We just bein' ourselves. . . .We are *the* place. Like France in the eighteenth century, that was the place then. If he'd come down then, Jesus would have come down there."[11] Skeeter was confusingly pro-Vietnam in these early versions, affirming Harry's position that American involvement in the war is moral insofar as it is economic. The published version leads the debate away from Vietnam itself and back into Harry's community; he eventually identifies his real enemy not as the communist world, but rather as the wealthy residents of his own hometown. "I hate those Penn Park motherfuckers," he finally admits, "'If I could push the red button to blow them all to Kingdom Come'—he pushes a button in mid-air—'I would'" (Redux 220). This realization is a major turning point in Harry's education, and he reconfigures the nuclear condition to conform to his new attitude, directing the "red button" at the upper class rather than at Vietnam or the Soviet Union. Harry's development is crucial insofar as he needs to experience renewal, as indicated by the title of the novel, and his old-fashioned

11. By permission of John Updike and the Houghton Library, Harvard University, 75M-53 (1018).

view of the Cold War (which parallels his outmoded view of the world in general) must change before he can do so.

Harry's problem with Vietnam in *Rabbit Redux* emphasizes his differences with society in general. During the course of this novel Harry finds himself isolated from his coworkers, friends, neighbors, and family. In *Rabbit, Run,* he also experiences isolation from the world around him, but he manages to maintain in the earlier novel a viable connection to at least one other character at any given time. In *Rabbit Redux* he is on his own. Harry's alienation contributes to the sense that he essentially takes a step backward at the end of the novel because he can think of no other way to cope with the catastrophe of Jill's death and the loss of his house. There is the suggestion that the depravity of Skeeter's and Jill's lifestyle is irreconcilable with Harry's respectable middle-class home. By extension, Harry's early unpopular stance on the war is irreconcilable with the point of view Skeeter and Jill try to foist upon him. The friction caused by the encounter between them is enough to burn Harry's house down: what else could happen to a house divided against itself? In the book's final pages Updike does what he says art should do in his *New Yorker* piece on Robert Motherwell, magnifying the gray area of our nation's collective life that was the debate over Vietnam. In his review of the novel, Charles Thomas Samuels is dissatisfied with this method of addressing the problem, concluding that the reader, upon completion, is "still waiting for the perhaps impossible novel that will not only show us how we live now but also why we live in this awful way."[12] There can be no question that this novel is representative of "a poisonous time" (SC 116), as Updike describes the era in which he took his unpopular stance on Vietnam, but there is also the sense that Harry is going through a necessary period of growth and experiencing some of the pain that goes with it. The conclusion of *Rabbit Redux* is ostensibly comic—Harry and Janice reunite after their separation—but the novel is so dark, with so many painful and turbulent events, that most readers put it down with the sense that Harry's life is becoming more deeply immersed in an impossible conundrum, just as American troops were becoming more deeply entangled in the jungles of Vietnam.

Jill, Nelson, and Skeeter spend a good deal of time and effort in *Rabbit*

---

12. Samuels, "Updike on the Present," 30.

Redux trying to educate Harry to be more tolerant of women, the younger generation, and black Americans in addition to their attempt to alter his stance on Vietnam. Exhibiting a similar need both for reflection and for the willingness to change his beliefs, Reverend Tom Marshfield, narrator of *A Month of Sundays,* is forced into exile from his community after a scandalous series of extramarital affairs. He is sent to a retreat for wayward clerics to regain his faith and to work through the problems that have plagued his personal and professional life by narrating his story in a journal. The novel is fairly localized and does not engage itself with Vietnam as overtly as *Rabbit Redux* does; yet Marshfield reveals some glimpses into his position on American involvement in Southeast Asia that help to explain his crisis. Like many of Updike's other characters he has built his life around competition, and he finds it necessary to work obsessively on his golf game, to wrestle with the ideas of other theologians, and to seduce women, especially women who initially resist him. After a come-from-behind victory on the golf links at his retreat, he declares jubilantly, "[I] felt myself irradiated by the Lordly joy of having defeated — nay, crushed, obliterated — a foe" (MS 222). Marshfield's will to convert all aspects of his life into competition forces him into isolation from his community. Yet even in isolation he finds worthy golf opponents and a woman worthy of a seductive conquest. Having been raised during the early Cold War, Marshfield's competitive instincts are not surprising. His flaw stems from the fact that global rivalry has changed by 1973, yet he has failed to adapt to this change. The reasons for this failure again include the breakdown of Marshfield's marriage, his fear of the younger generation, and especially his tough theology.

Marshfield, more so than Harry in *Rabbit Redux,* acknowledges the idea that the Cold War has become more complex in the 1970s than it was in the 1950s. He describes his sister-in-law as "crazy" in the 1950s because "in those years, she opposed Truman's intervention in Korea, and spoke of his dropping the atomic bomb as an atrocity" (MS 68). Any foray into dovish thinking was apparently grounds for insanity in the 1950s, due in part to the Red scare. Marshfield finds a certain comfort in this idea; he disparages his wife's "infuriating politics" in the 1970s, which he describes as "a warmed-over McGovernism of smug lamenting" (MS 73). He resents his wife's liberal thinking, which she shares with Ned Bork, Marshfield's deacon;"never did they think to see themselves," he writes,"as two luxurious blooms on a stalk fibrous with capital and cops"(MS 73)—that is,they take for granted the security and prosperity that American capitalism offers its citizens. Underlying this sentiment is Marshfield's belief that Americans take for granted in the 1970s what they were thankful for in the 1950s; he describes the fifties as a time "when the global plum pudding,full of dimes and brandy, seemed served up all for Uncle Sam, because he had been so good" (MS 142). It was of course easier for Americans to be unified behind such beliefs when the enemy seemed so clear, and when economic prosperity was so evident. Marshfield's anger, like Harry's anger in *Rabbit Redux,* grows out of the disintegration of the idea of an absolute enemy, and out of the sense that Americans have become complacent and vulnerable. He describes his world in terms of the summer of the Watergate disclosures:"everything sure was coming loose, tumbling" (MS 158). He later muses,"when does an empire begin to die? When its privileged citizens begin to disdain war" (MS 228). The allusion to Vietnam in this quotation is unmistakable, and Marshfield's anger is without question a product of the confusion of the times.

Ned Bork becomes for Marshfield the representative of the "infuriating politics" that so disturb him, a politics associated with youth, femininity, and softness toward communism. In Marshfield's mind, Bork and his generation will be responsible for the inevitable collapse of Cold War America:"Ned is in charge; the androgynous homogenizing liberals of the world are in charge, and our American empire obligingly subsides to demonstrate how right they are. The East, the dust between the stars, will prevail" (MS 240 – 41). Bork also becomes a source of competition, since Marshfield catches him sleeping with Alicia, his first extramarital mistress. Marshfield attempts to associate Bork with all that is soft about the next generation of Americans, who are unfit and unwilling to defend their country. In a typical diatribe, he proclaims, "Perfidy, thy name might as well be Bork. The present writer, his nose and eyeballs still stinging from his first afternoon of desert brightness, can scarcely locate what is most signally odious about this far-away young man. His unctuous, melodious, prep-school drawl? His rosy cheeks? His hint of acne? The chestnut curls of his preening beard? His frog colored eyes? Or was it his limp-wristed theology" (MS 18). All of the adjectives Marshfield uses here and elsewhere to describe Bork indicate weakness, privilege, youth, and a propensity toward comfort rather than a willingness to fight. These are the same complaints Harry holds against Jill in *Rabbit Redux;* America's enemy, according to Harry and Marshfield, is as much the privileged, thankless younger generation as it is the communist world. Marshfield uses the differences between himself and his deacon to initiate a debate with him. The situation here is similar to a debate between Harry and Charlie Stavros in *Rabbit Redux;* in both cases cuckolded men argue over ideology with the men who cuckold them. The topic, again, is Vietnam. Bork believes, "We went into Vietnam to keep things open, to keep the world open for trade" (MS 106). Marshfield agrees, but sees the war as necessary: "'Better open than closed,' I offered. 'Better Mammon than Stalin'" (MS 106). He describes the situation in easy, either-or terms in order to bring the issue back into the "absolute enemy" realm of the 1950s Cold War. Marshfield feels that the new situation, after "Kissinger's Houdini-truce had been effected," allows for weakness and a lack of the competition necessary for progress: "we were de-vietnamized and could attempt dispassion where the flames of rage and counter-rage had danced" (MS 106). Marshfield feels America has gone soft, and is worried that he, too, is losing his edge. Just after he laments the loss of "rage and counter-rage" in the global theater, he remarks, "Ned's furniture, I might say, was beanbag and paper ball tattily mixed with Good Will" (MS 106). He sees softness creeping in all around him, and it causes him to inveigh against the complacency of his community, which manifests itself in behavior that is increasingly characterized by irreverence and infidelity. His competition with Bork fulfills for him the necessary tension that has been obscured or fragmented by the new Cold War.

In other words, much of Marshfield's most outrageous behavior—his rampant adultery and his irreverent statements—can be explained by his desire to maintain the competition of the old Cold War. He has great contempt for "all the fat cats and parasites of the system poor Johnson was sweating to save" (MS 107), a group which includes clergymen, he admits. Like Harry in *Rabbit Redux,* Marshfield resents those privileged anti-war protesters who have failed to earn the right to protest. He defends himself against a charge of indifference by describing himself as "vigorously pro-Caesar" and saying, "I tend to trust the Caesar that is against the Caesar that might be. The Caesar that is, at least has let us live, which the next might

not" (MS 108). Bork points out the contradictions in Marshfield's thinking
by asking him, "Do you think . . . in Stalin's Russia, say, you would have trust-
ed and served *that* Caesar?" Marshfield yields at this point, and acknowledges that his ideology is becoming confused: "I was grateful to him, for
seeing this, and stopping me. My head and tongue were whirling with an
angry excitement I didn't understand and didn't like" (MS 108). This angry excitement again springs from Marshfield's stubborn notion that the
Cold War has not changed since his youth. Yet Updike's objective in *A
Month of Sundays* is to educate Marshfield, similar to his objective in *Rabbit Redux* to educate Harry. Bork aids Marshfield's education through his
patience and persistence in debating with Marshfield, who eventually admits, "[Bork's] views, which I had earlier dismissed as hopelessly compromised by topical fads . . . now had some interest for me" (MS 104-5).
These debates center around Marshfield's conservative positions on theology and Vietnam. In Marshfield we see a magnified manifestation of Updike's own confusion about the falling away of old ideals.

Even so, Updike is much more self-aware than Marshfield is; though
Marshfield softens to Bork's position and seems as though he might mend
his promiscuous ways, he refuses to change at the end of the novel, which
corresponds to the end of his month-long retreat. His return to the familiar territory of sexual promiscuity is akin to Harry's return to the familiar
territory of marriage to Janice in *Rabbit Redux*. Toward the end of Marshfield's narrative he reacts to a pamphlet handed to him by a religious youth
that depicts "Nixon collapsed beneath a 'Shield of Incredibility' " and which
predicts apocalypse within the next eighty days: "we recoil from this gib-
berish," he writes, "but . . . is not the content of this miserable throwaway
. . . the content of our life's call and our heart's deepest pledge?" (MS 245).
The pamphlet describes an apocalyptic war resulting from "America's
wickedness." Marshfield values the idea of the prospect of such a war to
the extent that it is his "heart's deepest pledge." In other words, life in
America is worth living only insofar as we maintain our readiness to defend our beliefs against a global enemy. He asks Bork, "is war always the
worst possible alternative? The Bible says not. I say not" (MS 106-7). Indeed, it seems, the idea of war—and the Cold War is largely an idea—is
actually essential to Marshfield's life. But it is this attachment to early Cold
War-style competition that causes Marshfield to relinquish his parish and

his marriage. Like many of Updike's other protagonists who take their cue
from their country's rivalry with the Soviet Union, Marshfield's need to
compete might benefit him on the golf course, but is destructive to his
personal relationships. His life follows a pattern of confrontation and withdrawal, and he reveals in his writing a profound dissatisfaction with the
way his life has turned out. Like all characters in Updike's novels, Marshfield needs to grow, and his rigid stance on Vietnam indicates that he has
not learned to do so by the book's conclusion.

Growth and mutability become a central focus for Updike's attitude toward the Vietnam issue from this point on. *A Month of Sundays* was published during the year that the last American troops withdrew from Vietnam; after 1975 the debate takes on entirely new meanings both for
Updike's characters and for Americans in general. Even Secretary of Defense Robert McNamara, the man who spearheaded American involvement in Vietnam, altered his views on the war in a 1995 memoir, *In Retrospect:*

> I want to put Vietnam in context.
> We of the Kennedy and Johnson administrations who participated in
> the decisions on Vietnam acted according to what we thought were the
> principles and traditions of this nation. We made our decisions in light of
> those values.
> Yet we were wrong, terribly wrong.[13]

Updike's retrospective analysis of the debate in "On Not Being a Dove" is
similarly characterized by the desire to explain his stance but also by a desire to put the debate in perspective. There is a sense in many current revisions of the meaning of the war in Vietnam that, although the debate may
be easier to analyze now, its significance to American identity has not been
resolved; as historian Norman Podhoretz points out, "one can, if one wish-
es, make the consoling point that everyone on all sides of the argument
turned out to be wrong about the political character and implications of
the Vietnam War."[14] Beyond self-consolation, Updike's intent in looking
back from a postwar perspective is to derive a lesson from the Vietnam

13. Robert McNamara, *In Retrospect: The Tragedy and Lessons of Vietnam*, xvi.
14. Norman Podhoretz, *Why We Were in Vietnam*, 174.

experience. All of Updike's post-Vietnam-era writings that continue to deal with the Vietnam debate do not espouse the same degree of confusion, turbulence, and frustration that characterize the debate in *Rabbit Redux* and *A Month of Sundays;* yet there remains the sense that something is unresolved. Updike resurrects his anxieties over his undovishness in works like the short story "More Stately Mansions" (1982) and the novel *The Witches of Eastwick* (1984), and in doing so he reveals that the Cold War has indeed changed, but also that the transition to a new perception of the world has been difficult for him, and for his undovish characters.

"More Stately Mansions" follows what had become by 1982 a familiar plot line in Updike's fiction: a man has an extramarital affair that marks the demise of his marriage; when the affair fails, he looks back on it wistfully and reflects on his failures as a husband and as a lover. Frank, the narrator of "More Stately Mansions," is another example of an Updike protagonist who finds himself at odds with his friends, colleagues, wife, and lover on the issue of Vietnam. Yet the difference between him and Marshfield or Harry is that he has had some time to process the implications of the debate. Updike revised the story significantly between its original publication in *Esquire* (October 1982) and its republication in *Trust Me* five years later. In the *Esquire* version Frank consciously represses the debate, along with his affair; he concludes, "That was forever ago. It has taken all of the Seventies to bury the Sixties."[15] After another half-decade of processing the debate, Updike determined that the point of the story is to teach Frank a lesson about growth. As Updike gets further away from the actual debate, his perspective on it changes. It is not until he publishes "On Not Being a Dove" in 1989 that he can fully engage with it. "More Stately Mansions" represents an important link between the heated, immediate turmoil of *Rabbit Redux* and *A Month of Sundays* and the relatively cool introspection of the 1989 memoir.

Frank is a schoolteacher, which is ironic given that the point of the story is for Frank to learn something about himself through his reminiscence. He is vexed by the memory of Karen Owens, with whom he had an affair in the late 1960s. His affair with Karen coincides with the high years of the debate over the Vietnam War; he recalls, "When we did talk, Karen and

15. John Updike, "More Stately Mansions," 157.

I, it was out in the open, on opposite sides of the fence, about the war. There was a condescending certainty about her pacifism that infuriated me, and a casual, bright edge of militancy that possibly frightened me" (TM 100). The fact that Frank's attraction to Karen borders on fear in part explains both the cause for their affair and the reason it could not last. She is part of the anti-establishment camp, which intrigues Frank, yet her opinions are strong enough to threaten his self-confidence. "Why do you talk of people being *for* the war?" he questions her, "It puts you people in such a smug no-lose position, being not for the war" (TM 101). Frank's anger, which causes him to address his soon-to-be lover with the aggressive term "you people," comes from his sense that if Karen is in a no-lose position in the debate, then he is in a no-win situation.

He feels the need to defend his choice in lovers, so great is his insecurity about her "no-lose position": "There were a number of awkward, likable things about Karen in spite of the smug politics" (TM 101). Frank, who supports American intervention in Vietnam on the same grounds as Harry and Marshfield, finds that his sexual attraction to Karen is chastened by her strong opinions about the war. He emphasizes his father's working-class background, recalling how his father worked in the small-town mills that Frank's grandfather helped build, and he contrasts this world with Karen's world of million-dollar mansions in Santa Barbara and Cambridge intellectuals. Karen's husband, Alan, from the moneyed Owens family, makes pejorative references to Frank as a "townie" and a "wop." Frank's anger about the war and his feelings of relative poverty combine to cause a rift between him and his lover.[16]

Karen's anti-war attitude also threatens his role as a small-town schoolteacher, and he resorts to populist patriotism to defend his stance: "Our

16. The class consciousness that pervades the story is even more pronounced in the 1987 version published in *Trust Me;* Updike adds a number of details highlighting the class differences between Frank and the Owenses. For instance, in the *Trust Me* version Frank is initially attracted to Karen because he mistakenly thinks, "she hadn't been born rich" (TM 104) and his disillusionment with her is slightly connected to his realization that she had. Also, when Alan sends Frank out to buy more liquor during a party, Alan tells Frank to "keep the change" (113). As Updike became more distant from the debate over Vietnam and tried to explain his position on it, he was apparently most convinced it was related to his relatively poor upbringing. Frank in this story is a schoolteacher in an unaffluent town, after all, like Updike's father.

kids aren't pouring pig blood into draft-board files. Their grandparents were damn glad to get here, and when their country asks them to go fight, they go. They're scared, but they go" (TM 101). His position seems to unravel after he states this point; he cannot respond to Karen's questioning why this attitude is "right." Like many of Updike's other characters in the same position on Vietnam, Frank's gut impulse to defend American involvement in Southeast Asia evolves directly out of the simplicity of the early Cold War. He cannot help but defend the war as "right," even as he realizes the complications of his position. He resents Karen's tone, claiming that the "old Psychology major" in her "was giving up the debate and babying me" (TM 102). He doesn't want to be put in the position of a student, and he allies himself with his president as a teacher: "LBJ had been a schoolteacher as I was now, and it seemed to me that the entire class, from coast to coast, just wasn't *listening*" (TM 102).

Frank's infidelity is directly linked to the protest against Vietnam, as both unfold over the course of the narrative, and he becomes disillusioned with both the war and his affair simultaneously. The kids from Frank's hometown who once trooped off to Indochina without questioning their purpose begin to return in body bags, and Frank notices how the town's attitude toward their deaths changes quickly: "When the first local boy died in Vietnam, he got a new elementary school named after him. When the second died, they took a street intersection in his part of town, called it a square, and named it after him. For the third and the fourth, there wasn't even an intersection" (TM 102). This cool observation indicates how rapidly the tide of public opinion about the war has changed, but it also implies a simultaneous dehumanization and a loss of innocence: local boys are associated with schools, but as the boys become numbers, the schools become intersections, or less. Coinciding with this loss of innocence, his affair with Karen begins to break down as public opinion against the war becomes more pervasive; he notes, "The Movement was in the air even here now; our young Poles and Portuguese were no longer willing to be drafted unquestioningly, and the classes in government and history, even in general science [his class], had become battlefields. At Columbia and in Paris that Spring, students were rioting. Whole masses of rooted presumption were being torn up around me, but I no longer cared"

(TM 108). He becomes less discreet about his public displays of affection toward Karen, and when another teacher catches them standing suggestively close to one another in the faculty lounge, Karen says to cover up, "We were just arguing about Vietnam. . . . Frank wants to bomb South China now" (TM 110). Their arguments over the war have compromised their affair from the beginning; he recalls, "When one of my free periods backed onto the lunch hour, and we had more time, we wasted it in bickering. When LBJ announced he would not run, I told her this would bring in Nixon, and hoped she was happy. I taunted her with this while the happiness of our lovemaking was still in her eyes" (TM 107-8). After Karen confesses her affair with Frank to her husband, she tells Frank that he was shocked: "He's only ever seen us quarrel. About Vietnam" (TM 116).[17] There is no way to extricate their arguments about the war and their passion for one another; tragically, they become increasingly isolated from each other despite their attraction, and Frank is left with only the memory of an idyllic time with Karen and the turbulent debate that cut this time short.

Frank measures their affair in terms of the war even after its conclusion; he notes that Karen and her husband divorce "sometime between when Nixon and Kissinger finagled our troop withdrawal and when South Vietnam collapsed" (TM 118). Frank and Karen do not unite as a result of this breakup, though; their division over the war indicates a more fundamental difference between them that cannot be easily remedied—Frank cannot adapt to Karen's demands just as he cannot adapt to the changing Cold War. The point of his reminiscence, and the character trait that distinguishes him from Marshfield, is that he realizes his flaw, albeit years after the fact. His realization comes during a lesson to his students about a nautilus shell, a device that provides the frame tale for the story. At the beginning of the *Trust Me* version of the story he declares of the shell, "It's a killer," recalling Updike's pronouncement from "On Not Being a Dove" "to be alive is to be a killer" (SC 131). But the narrative has changed his perspective, and he concludes with a point both about the shell and his personality:

17. The brief sentence "About Vietnam" was absent from the *Esquire* version of the story.

> Thinking I should strike a more positive note, I held up the souvenir again and told the class, "There's a clear lesson here in this shape. Who knows what it is?"
> Nobody did.
> "Growth," I said "We all have to *grow.*" (TM 125)

This development is important in the Vietnam debate as it is represented in Updike's work; Frank's admission that growth is a universal necessity reveals his awareness that the Cold War world is not the same as it always was. Updike pointed out this same lesson in his 1962 memoir about boyhood: "It has taken me the shocks of many returnings [to Shillington] to learn what seems simple enough, that change is the order of things."[18] In both this memoir and in "More Stately Mansions" a nostalgic turn accompanies this realization; Frank interrupts the flow of his narrative to reminisce about the times when Karen's husband would play bluegrass music on a banjo; he tells how he would "feel so patriotic that tears would sting my corneas; all the lovely country that had been in America would come rushing back, as it was before we filled the land too full" (TM 105). America is now tainted and, as with many of Updike's renditions of Edenic bliss and innocence, the fall coincides with the disruptive debate over Vietnam.

This debate resurfaces in *The Witches of Eastwick* in the same terms of adultery, the disruption of innocence, and the need for growth. But the outcome of the debate in this novel makes it clear that Updike viewed the change to a new way of thinking about the Cold War world as a painful and wholly destructive transformation, not just a difficult lesson. In one manifestation of this debate, Felicia Griffiths accuses her husband Clyde of indifference because he doesn't share her anti-war sentiment: "You don't give a damn about the world we pass on to our children or the wars we inflict upon the innocent" (WE 162). When he suggests that his children aren't ready to accept the world, she retorts, "that's another thing you can't stand, the way Jenny and Chris have gone off, as if you can keep children home forever, as if the world doesn't have to *change* and *grow*" (WE 163). They have been discussing the town of Eastwick's decision to rename a town square after a local youth who was killed in the war; like Frank in "More Stately Mansions," Clyde defends this tribute to the boy. Fe-

---

18. John Updike, "Boyhood, Mine," in *Five Boyhoods,* edited by Martin Levin, 171.

licia presents her opposing viewpoint in no uncertain terms:"Next thing they'll want to be naming Dock Street and then Oak Street and then East-wick itself after some lower-class dropout who couldn't think of anything better to do than go over there and napalm villages" (WE 161). Felicia's terms are stronger than those in earlier debates, and the violence of Clyde's reaction is shocking, especially for the relatively placid world of Updike's fiction: he brutally murders his wife with a fireplace poker, then hangs himself. There is obviously more to this murder-suicide than the de-bate over Vietnam, but their concurrence is not accidental. Evil has been loosed in the world of Eastwick, and the debate over the Vietnam War is something more than a casual backdrop for the resulting violent disrup-tion with the domestic sphere of the novel.

The Witches of Eastwick is arguably Updike's darkest book; the familiar subject of adultery here directly results in three deaths, all of which can be construed as revenge-motivated murders. It is tempting to compare the book to *Couples:* both novels dig beneath the calm surface of coastal New England towns in the 1960s to reveal the discontent and rampant infidelity that is obscured by a peaceful and harmonious social veneer. The differ-ence in tone between the two novels can be seen as a result of this dis-ruptive change in the Cold War. *Couples,* taking place in the Kennedy years before Vietnam was everybody's business, is a book of renewal: couples re-new their energy by reconfiguring themselves, and the final chapter is en-titled "It's Spring Again."Also, the antics of the Tarbox socialites in *Couples* lead them in the direction of divorce, which presumably will come during Johnson's administration, the height of the Vietnam crisis. *The Witches of Eastwick,* by contrast, takes place in and around 1968, the most tumul-tuous year that Cold War America experienced on the home front. The book ends during the dying season of late autumn rather than spring, and the final chapter is entitled "Guilt," suggesting the everlasting taint of a fallen world. The protagonists of *The Witches of Eastwick* are already di-vorced at the beginning of the novel, which happens on the eve of John-son's announcement not to seek reelection, an event widely considered to be a turning point in the Vietnam crisis.

Why does Updike return to the Vietnam era in a 1984 novel? Just six years earlier he told an interviewer, "That was a very difficult time, the late sixties here, as in *Rabbit Redux.* Everybody had to rethink where they were and what things meant. I don't wish to return to that."[19] Perhaps he is resurrecting Vietnam-era demons in order to respond to the Reagan-era sense that the Cold War has reverted back to its early configurations. Reagan renewed 1950s rhetoric and pushed for a massive stockpiling of new weaponry and elaborate defense systems, all of which pointed America back to its early Cold War ideology. Communism was *still* a tangible threat, Reagan insisted, and he famously declared the Soviet Union an "evil empire" to be feared and mistrusted. All the change and growth that Updike had learned to accept may have been for naught if the country was simply going to revert to its pre-Vietnam Cold War mood. *The Witches of Eastwick* serves as Updike's attempt to caution America about the consequences of refusing to accept change. His own difficulty in overcoming his conception of Vietnam as more than just another Cold War maneuver translates into this cautionary tale about how all Americans must be attuned to such changes and be aware that evil might lurk in our communities rather than halfway across the world behind a rusting Iron Curtain.

The global terrorist activity that gripped America in the early 1980s has its parallel in *The Witches of Eastwick;* the shadowy group of young activists protesting Vietnam have created a mood of fear, where violence can strike at random. Walking along the Eastwick beach, Alexandra notices how even garbage looks sinister: "these unlabelled cans looked frightening—blank like the bombs terrorists make and then leave in public places to bring the system down and thus halt the war" (WE 12). We are given a closer look at one of these terrorists in the character of the Reverend Ed Parsley, who leaves his wife and Eastwick parish to join an underground anti-war movement. Sukie, Ed's former lover, comments on the shortcomings of Ed's vision:

> He wanted power. A woman can give a man power over herself in a way, but she can't put him in the Pentagon. That's what excited Ed about the Movement as he imagined it, that it was going to replace the Pentagon with an army of its own and have the same, you know, kind of thing—uniforms and speeches and board rooms with big maps and all. (WE 145)

19. Plath, *Conversations with John Updike*, 119.

The irony of Ed's desire to end a war by initiating another war is height-ened by his death in a failed attempt to carry out a terrorist act. The covert-ness of these attacks against "the System" are evidence that old Cold War thinking is not adequate to protect Eastwick in 1968 as well as Updike's America in 1984.

The difference between the world Updike is writing in and the world he is writing about is that terrorist activity in *The Witches of Eastwick* comes from within the United States, whereas in the early 1980s anti-U.S. terrorism came from abroad, especially the Middle East. Both types of ter-rorism signal again a breakdown in the unchallenged American hegemo-ny that typified the early years of the Cold War. Also implicit in both is a critique of American foreign policy as being motivated entirely by money; Ed Parsley speaks of "the connection between the present atrocities in Southeast Asia and the new little drive-in branch Old Stone Bank has next to the Superette," and puts a finer point on his argument soon after: "When Mammon talks, Uncle Sam jumps" (WE 45). Ed's ideology becomes strong enough to affect his sex life; Sukie confesses to the controversial new-comer Darryl Van Horne of her affair with Ed, "And it wasn't as if we were making love, after the first half-hour; he was going on about the wicked-ness of the corporate power structure's sending our boys to Vietnam for the benefit of their stockholders" (WE 146). This type of fervor is ulti-mately self-destructive; just as Felicia dies at the hands of her husband Clyde, who wants only to put an end to her vehement rantings, Ed dies at the hands of his own anti-war activity in an accidental bomb detona-tion. Yet their discontent with the System is reflected in other characters; Sukie Rougement's children claim that American involvement in Vietnam amounts to our "trying to create more markets for Coca-Cola" (WE 282). Sukie reports that after Clyde and Felicia Gabriel's funeral, Brenda Parsley "tried to make some connection between their deaths and Vietnam, the moral confusion of our times, I couldn't quite follow it" (WE 183). Brenda continues this theme in a sermon later in the novel, in order to link the witches' actions to the war abroad: "As we have turned outward to the evil in the world at large," she says, "turned our indignation outward toward evil wrought in Southeast Asia by fascist politicians and an oppressive capitalism seeking to secure and enlarge its markets for anti-ecological luxuries, while we have been so turned we have been guilty—yes, guilty, for guilt attaches to omissions as well as commissions—guilty of over-looking evil brewing in these very homes of Eastwick, our tranquil, solid-appearing homes" (WE 302–3).

Morality is confused in the town of Eastwick, as opinion about the Viet-nam War divides its residents and the rest of the nation. Yet *The Witches of Eastwick* indicates that this moral confusion, born in the 1960s, can have no such easy resolution in the 1980s. Things fall apart in Updike's East-wick, and instead of offering hope for renewal, as he does in *Couples,* he characterizes *Witches* with a sense of entropy. The moral confusion over America's changing place in the world is real, Updike seems to be saying, whether it manifests itself internally or externally.

Though the Cold War had changed drastically by 1984, anxiety over the potential for nuclear annihilation remained constant. Darryl Van Horne speaks of "the year one million or until we blow ourselves up, whichever comes sooner" (WE 50). He later strikes the same chord, but with Vietnam-era dissonance, claiming that "the whole damn world [is] going up in na-palm" (WE 260). Van Horne may indeed represent the rough, fatalistic viewpoint of the earlier Cold War; at one point he speaks of the "two Russkis" who bought Western art which now "sits over there in Leningrad where nobody can lay their eyes on it" (WE 98). At the same time he is the most future-oriented character in the novel, as evidenced by his avant-garde taste in art, his manic redesigning of his old Eastwick estate, and his scientific project to create a new energy source. His 1950s rhetoric and his orientation toward the future combine to make him the book's chief spokesman for the possibility of Armageddon. The witches' association with him—their turn toward acts of evil—thus finds its logical parallel in the threat of nuclear war: "it was something they had loosed on the air, like those nuclear scientists cooking up the atomic bomb to beat Hitler and Tojo and now so remorseful, like Eisenhower refusing to sign the truce with Ho Chi Minh that would have ended all the trouble" (WE 306). The subtext of this line of thinking, and of *Witches* more generally, is that we cannot return to a pastoral state once evil has been loosed upon the world.

Updike's realization that it is impossible to return to the Edenic pre-Vietnam world in which marriages withstood tribulation and Amer-icans were fighting for a common goal comes after much painful self-examination. Harry in *Rabbit Redux* and Marshfield in *A Month of Sun-*

days are poised to learn the lesson that Frank learns in "More Stately Mansions" — "We all have to *grow.*" This lesson is difficult for a writer like Updike because he never imagined its necessity. He was "so agitated and vehement an undove" during the Vietnam era because the very fabric of the American worldview that he had come to accept seemed to be unraveling. Updike's process of self-examination over the Vietnam debate is part of what makes him so compelling and enduring an author; not only is he willing to adapt to changes, but he is aware that this adaptation does not always come easily. The Vietnam debate affects his fiction profoundly as it foregrounds conflict, necessitates deep self-reflection, and places increasing emphasis on the impact historical and current conflicts have on domestic dissolution. The subject and tenor of Updike's writings changes during this period, but change, after all, is necessary.

Updike suffered a loss of privacy as a result of his response to the questionnaire in *Authors Take Sides on Vietnam,* and this loss made him a more public figure, for better or worse. The extremely localized nature of his early fiction gives way to a deeper engagement with the world at large as his career goes on. The Vietnam debate was one of the two events that contributed to the expansion of his public involvement with the larger Cold War world; the other was a state-sponsored diplomatic visit to the Soviet Union in 1964, a trip that provided Updike with a greater sensitivity to the Soviet character, but that simultaneously confirmed his distrust of communism as a viable form of government. In the next chapter, "Seeing How the Other Half Lives," I will investigate the way this trip affected Updike's writings by removing him from his limited American perspective so that he could investigate the nature of American life more effectively.

4

Seeing How the Other Half Lives

The American writer has never been much into the
political system, has always stood apart.

–John Updike, 1982 interview in "An Evening with John Updike"

IN FEBRUARY 1966—the same year Updike scrawled his hasty and ill-fated response to the questionnaire to be published the following year in *Authors Take Sides on Vietnam*—two prominent Soviet writers named Andrei Sinyavsky and Yuli Daniel were put on trial in Moscow for publishing allegedly anti-Soviet literature abroad. They were found guilty and sentenced to seven and five years in prison, respectively. This trial was a turning point in the course of literary dissent in the Soviet Union that began under Khrushchev and continued throughout the Cold War, reaching its infamous climax in February 1974 when Russian novelist Aleksandr Solzhenitsyn was expelled from his native country. Neither the Soviet government nor the Soviet Writers' Union anticipated the world's outraged response to the Sinyavsky and Daniel trial. To Westerners, it was just so much more proof of communist governmental oppression. To Western writers, the trial was even more significant because the Soviet government used it to equate the right to free expression with criminal behavior. The Western world renamed itself "the free world," and Eastern literary dissent became the most cogent example of how important freedom was.

On February 1, 1966, the *New York Times* reported that forty-nine West-

106

ern writers had signed an open letter imploring Soviet authorities to release Sinyavsky and Daniel. The list was headed by Arthur Miller, one of
the most politically active American writers of the Cold War era; it also included such prominent figures as Saul Bellow, Mary McCarthy, Philip Roth,
and William Styron. The 1966 reader would probably not have been surprised that Updike's name was absent from the list because Updike had
not yet become an active spokesperson on issues of international affairs.
But Updike's name soon began to surface in connection with the plight
of Soviet authors. Nine months after the open letter regarding the Sinyavsky-
Daniel trial, Updike and Miller together introduced the poet Yevgeny
Yevtushenko at Queens College in New York. The introduction and the
questions that followed Yevtushenko's two-hour reading explicitly ad-
dressed the Sinyavsky and Daniel trial. Such political discussion was inevitable, as Yevtushenko—whose poems Updike translated in 1967—
had been singled out as "one of the first Soviet writers to raise his voice
against the evils of Stalinism."[1] Five months after Yevtushenko's reading,
the *Times* reported that twenty-two American writers signed a letter to
the Fourth Congress of Soviet Writers demanding that they strive to allow
greater cultural freedom to Soviet Jews, who were restricted from certain
facilities for education, research, and publishing. Updike's name joined
Miller's on this list. Soviet literary dissent was a hot topic, and Updike
found himself in the thick of it at the same time that he was becoming
embroiled in the Vietnam debate. In order to understand the impact of
Soviet literary dissent on Updike's writing, we must address the crucial
question as to why Updike would have avoided protesting the widely pub-
licized Sinyavsky-Daniel trial despite his obvious sympathy for the cause
of the dissidents.[2]

1. For Updike's translations of Yevgeny Yevtushenko's poems, see *The Collected Po-
ems 1952-1990*, "Stolen Apples" (241-43), "In a Steelworker's Home" (244-46),
"Monologue of a Poet" (252-53), "Monologue of an Actress" (254-56), "A Ballad about
Nuggets" (256-58), "New York Elegy" (259-60), "Monologue of a Blue Fox" (260-62),
"The Restaurant for Two" (263-64), "Cemetery of Whales" (265-67), and "Smog" (267-
70). "Smog" is about Yevtushenko's American contemporaries, including Arthur Miller,
Allen Ginsberg, Robert Lowell, and Updike. Theodore Shabad, "Yevtushenko Opens
Tour of U.S.," *New York Times*, November 7, 1966.
2. Updike actually met Sinyavsky on October 29, 1978, in Tel Aviv. The meeting was
brief and not widely recorded, but a report from a Tel Aviv newspaper reads, "Updike

The broader question is, "What are the public duties of an American fiction writer in the politically sensitive Cold War era?" As the nation was struggling violently to define itself under Johnson's unsteady hand, Updike was rapidly becoming a major figure in American letters. Like his fictional alter-ego Henry Bech, he at times would probably have liked to be absolved of the duty "to say anything, on anything, ever" (Back 40), as we have seen in his Vietnam imbroglio. Yet the plight of Soviet writers hit close to home for Updike, as it did for many American writers who would have preferred to stay out of the messy business of current affairs. Because of his belief that politics and literature should be mixed carefully and delicately, he made sure that his responses to Soviet literary censorship and Soviet literature always had their foundation in a writer's perspective. In its most simplified form, Updike's opinion of U.S. involvement in the Vietnam War was based solely on human rights, particularly the right to self-determination. His opposition to Soviet censorship represented a similar concern; yet because he approached this topic from a writer's perspective—more like Henry Bech than Harry Angstrom—Updike managed to ally himself with other American writers on this issue. Still, he did not have the exact same role in protesting Soviet censorship as his colleagues did. He was always sympathetic to the cause of Soviet writers, but he declined to flag the attention of the Soviet government, as he would have if he had signed the letter protesting the Sinyavsky-Daniel trial. Wary of the ugly result of infusing too much politics into literature, Updike fought Soviet oppression not by shouting directly at Soviet officials, but by establishing an identity as a writer dedicated to the perfection of free artistic expression.

Updike's divergence from his colleagues on Vietnam and his alliance

---

asked what action western writers could take that would most effectively help their cause. Sinyavski answered that western writers should show constant attention to the [dissident's] situation, that perhaps it would be a very good idea to go to the Soviet Union and 'ask provocative questions' of the sensitive Soviet literary officials to establish the truth of the treatment and condition of dissidents." I asked Updike to elaborate upon their meeting in a 1998 letter, but unfortunately he didn't recall much: "I had forgotten meeting Sinyavsky and all that comes to me now is a wan smile in a wispy gray beard. I don't believe we had a common language and our exchange, if any, isn't vivid at this distance."

with them on Soviet censorship emphasizes a discernible split in his writing. His "undovish" stance on Vietnam is characteristic of the Pennsylvania farm boy who worked tirelessly to escape his hometown in pursuit of the American dream, while his responses to the Soviet literary scene are characteristic of his other side—the Harvard-educated writer whose passion for literature is as evident from the overwhelming number of reviews he has written as it is from his prodigious oeuvre of fiction and poetry. By separating these two personae as such, we can see that the division within his writing between the masterful prose stylist and the chronicler of middle-class American life grows out of the division between public and private selves exacerbated by the changing face of the Cold War. Updike's intricate and figurative prose style—one of the trademarks of his fiction—becomes more evident as his career progresses. His readings of Eastern European fiction reinforce the development of his own style; his very identity as an American writer and the evolving sense of style that accompany it can be seen as a direct response to literary dissent in the Soviet Union.

There is always the sense in Updike's fiction that a poet is commenting on the lives, thoughts, and actions of his characters. The distance between the world described in Updike's writings and the person describing it widens over the years as his style grows more complex and gradually overshadows the pastoral simplicity of his early fiction such as *Pigeon Feathers* (1962) and *Of the Farm* (1965). His later narrators are given to metaphoric and descriptive excess, and even his first-person narrators such as Marshfield in *A Month of Sundays* (1975), Ellellou in *The Coup* (1978), and Sarah Worth in *S.* (1988) add a poet's flourish to their writings, concentrating as much on visual detail and figurative language as on the plot. What has made Updike so enduring a writer with both academic and popular audiences is his ability to depict a familiar and often sordid world in dazzling language. His style and his emotional response to the world around him aren't always evenly balanced, though; whereas deep-seated emotional conflict is the most notable feature in the Vietnam works I described in the preceding chapter, wit and an artist's sensibility are more apparent in *Bech: A Book,* and an affinity for artistic beauty pervades his reviews of Soviet literature.

Updike visited the Soviet Union along with John Cheever on a state-sponsored trip in October 1964.[3] Moments before his visit and halfway through Cheever's month-long stay, Soviet officials removed their flamboyant and charismatic leader Nikita Khrushchev and replaced him with the dour Leonid Brezhnev. This was certainly a momentous time for any American to be visiting the Soviet Union, but it was especially significant for Updike and Cheever, regional writers of American suburbia who were suddenly cast in the role of literary ambassadors to a nation whose authors were about to lose what little artistic freedom they had. Updike, the younger and ultimately more prolific writer, began to develop a stronger sense of his American literary identity as a result of this trip. All of his renditions of the Soviet Union have come from a distinctly literary viewpoint, either in the guise of his fictional alter-ego Henry Bech or in his reviews, which develop a critical voice alongside his fictional and poetic voices.

Soviet dissent during the Cold War was inextricably tied to literature.[4] Ironically, Khrushchev opened the door to this dissent with his so-called "secret speech" of 1956 in which he roundly denounced the horrors of the Stalin regime. This bold political move caused government officials to soften restrictions on anti-Soviet writing even as they toughened their rhetoric on global matters. Khrushchev reportedly even cleared the way

3. In a piece called "On Meeting Writers" (PP 21–25), Updike displays his affection for Cheever based upon their first meeting in Russia: "I have seen John Cheever, for ten days we shared in Russia, turn the dour world of Soviet literary officials into a bright scuttle of somehow suburban characters, invented with marvellous speed and arranged in sudden tableaux expressive, amid wistful neo-Czarist trappings, of the lyric desperation associated with affluence" (PP 23). Updike sadly realizes, in a 1990 review of Cheever's posthumously published letters, that his affection for Cheever on the trip to Russia was far from reciprocal; Cheever wrote of Updike to Frederick Exley, "Updike, whom I know to be a brilliant man, traveled with me in Russia last autumn and I would go to considerable expense and inconvenience to avoid his company. I think his magnaminity [sic] specious and his work seems motivated by covetousness, exhibitionism and a stony heart . . . Updike and I spent most of our time back-biting one another. I find him very arrogant but my daughter tells me that I'm arrogant. We dined together at White House last Tuesday and I did everything short of putting a cherry bomb in his bug juice" (OJ 114–15).

4. For an insightful and thorough study of literary dissent in the Soviet Union, see the three-part "Reporter at Large" piece from the *New Yorker* by Ralph Blum entitled "Freeze and Thaw: The Artist in Russia" (August 28, 1965: 40–100, September 4, 1965: 32–65, and September 11, 1965: 168–217).

for the publication of the only novel Solzhenitsyn published in the Soviet Union, *One Day in the Life of Ivan Denisovich* (1962). But the reason why Soviet officials allowed the publication of this novel and others like it was that these critiques, like Khrushchev's "secret speech" itself, denounced Stalin, *not* the Soviet system of government. When it became clear that Solzhenitsyn's aim was to denounce the system in his 1967 open letter to the Congress of the Soviet Writer's Union and in his massive novel *The Gulag Archipelago* (1974), he was expelled.

The expulsion of Solzhenitsyn and the imprisonment of Sinyavsky, Daniel, and numerous other dissident writers proved that the terrorizing KGB feared the power of the written word. Historian Marshall Shatz writes that in the period between Khrushchev's secret speech and the Sinyavsky-Daniel trial, "literature, always an important vehicle of protest in Russia, played a particularly crucial role. Literature is especially well suited for the expression of moral criticism, because moral issues can best be posed in dramatic situations, and moral virtues and failings best displayed by personifying them in literary characters."[5] The connection between morality and literature may be why Soviet dissent struck such a chord for Updike, whose morality includes belief in religious freedom and in the sanctity of the rights of the individual. The spirit of Soviet writers who dared to resist their oppressive government appealed to all Americans who believed in the superiority of their nation's ideology; as Paul Cook, the Chief of Soviet Internal Affairs in the American Bureau of Intelligence and Research, notes in a 1974 forum on the Solzhenitsyn affair,

> Not too long ago it was widely accepted that Soviet psychologist Pavlov was right: people could be so conditioned that they would become virtual automatons in the service of communism—as some put it in the West, in the service of a Godless international communist conspiracy. . . . The Soviet Union exists; it is atheistic; and it still strives for world hegemony. But Pavlov was wrong. One has only to recall the names of men like [dissident scientist Andrei] Sakharov and Solzhenitsyn to give the lie to the belief that all Soviets think and act alike—are willing, eager tools ready to work for whatever the Kremlin wants at the moment.[6]

5. Marshall S. Shatz, *Soviet Dissent in Historical Perspective*, 100.
6. Ray S. Cline, *Understanding the Solzhenitsyn Affair: Dissent and its Control in the U.S.S.R.*, 2–3.

Literary dissent in the Soviet Union represented for Americans the possibility of hope that the Soviet people could resist and overcome their oppressive government. This hope, so evident from the dissident literature that challenged the Soviet system, is complemented by Updike's attempt in *Bech* and in his reviews of Soviet literature to connect two great nations that had been separated in every sense since the middle of the twentieth century. At the same time, Updike is wary of automatically lauding Soviet literature and dissident writers at the cost of overlooking American writers simply because their writing isn't as overtly "political." As the Cold War progressed, he grew more confident in his belief that writers who don't sacrifice aesthetics for politics are preferable to those who do, regardless of their country of origin. Americans were still consciously competing with Soviets during détente, but for cultural superiority rather than military strength. Updike acknowledges that Soviet dissident authors are brave and praiseworthy, but he does not heap praise upon them for those qualities alone. His literary inquiry into the mystery that was the Soviet Union is both an attempt to connect and a chance to compete.

The notion that the Soviet Union was a place radically different from the West perpetuated the Cold War as much as the arms race did. If Americans believed that Russians were essentially the same as themselves, there would have been no basis for resentment toward them. The general economic differences between Soviet communism and American capitalism—poverty and prosperity—provided the most obvious examples of the cultural differences between the superpower nations; but the American imagination stereotyped Russians as scheming, spying ideologues, emotionally colder than a Moscow winter. Furthermore, American popular culture conceived of Russians as overgrown masculine brutes—the women as well as the men. This was war, after all; America's enemy had to be portrayed as an empire of atheistic, scowling, nonsexual warriors. This depiction was, of course, willfully misdrawn, and Updike's fiction and poetry serve as a corrective to it. The Soviet *people* are not our enemies, he suggests; the Soviet *government* is what we should fear. Not surprisingly, he counters the notion that Russians are undersexed machines by portraying Russia and its people as distinctly feminine. Virtually all of Updike's fictional and poetic depictions of Russia associate it with femininity, with America as its masculine counterpart. The effect is not only to correct for America's popular misconceptions of Soviet citizens, but also to suggest that the distance between the superpowers is somehow related to the distance between the sexes. "Poem for a Far Land," first published in the *New Yorker* in 1965, is a fitting paradigm for the relationship between the gender rift and the global rift in Updike's writings:

> Russia, most feminine of lands,
> Breeder of stupid masculinity,
> Only Jesus understands
> Your interminable virginity.
>
> Raped, and raped, and raped again,
> You rise snow-white, the utter same,
> With tender birches and ox-eyed men
> Willing to suffer for your name.
>
> Though astronauts distress the sky
> That mothers your low, sad villages,
> Your vastness yearns in sympathy
> Between what was and that which is. (CP 50–51)

Updike discusses the "odd tone" of this poem and labels it an "affectionate caricature" (HS 861), but it represents a more serious topic than this assessment allows. The vastness of Russia is balanced by the vastness of America, whose astronauts "distress the sky." As in *Of the Farm*, global competition invades and alters a rustic world that tries in vain to remain static over the years ("yearns in sympathy/ Between what was and that which is"). The persistence of this competition accounts for the paradoxes of Russian femininity in this poem: this femininity breeds masculinity, Russia's mothering sky is also a battlefield, and its "interminable virginity" is difficult to reconcile with the striking image "Raped, and raped, and raped again." This far land is also a land of mystery, a concept that Updike represents through femininity rather than espionage, the most common American fictional depiction of Russia during the Cold War.

Updike writes further on the femininity of the Russian landscape in a 1987 introduction to *Nature's Diary* by Mikhail Prishvin: "The Russian landscape surprises the American visitor with an impression of feminine gentleness. Rollingly flat and most conspicuously marked by the wavering white verticals of the ubiquitous birches, it lacks the shaggy, rocky as-

sertiveness a North American is used to. It seems a young and tender landscape, without defenses. When the single-station radio in the hotel room
croons and wails its state-approved folk song, there is no mistaking what
the song is about: the 'motherland'" (OJ 196). Updike's surprise at the gentleness and defenselessness of the Russian landscape undoubtedly stems
from his nation's conception of Russia as an aggressive rival matching its
own assertiveness. In the above quotation, as in "Poem for a Far Land," femininity and reverence for the motherland are compromised by a powerful,
oppressive government signified by the terms "single-station radio" and
"state-approved folk song." When he examines Russia closely in his writings, Updike concludes that his admiration for Russia's national character
does little to temper his hatred of oppressive Communist governments.
He makes the blanket statement "Communist governments are atrocious"
in a 1983 review of a Polish novel (OJ 607). He may be able to connect
with Soviet citizens and even to sympathize with them, to a degree, but
the distance that remains between them and Americans preserved the rivalry that perpetuated the Cold War,[7] just as the distance between men
and women is the source of so much conflict in his writings.

The distance between East and West is also evident in five short poems
collectively entitled "Postcards from Soviet Cities."[8] These poems further
serve to illustrate the differences and similarities between the sensibilities
of the West and East. Leningrad's architecture, for instance, "can make Ital-
ians feel at home" ("Leningrad" 7). The speaker in this poem contrasts "the
Siege, a hell/ Of blackened snow and watered bread" with the observation,
"Some couples Twist in our hotel" (14 – 16) to show, again, how a country
so obsessed with its past is affected by the present, and by the presence

7. Even during the period of glasnost (Soviet "openness") that led to the end of the
Cold War, Updike is skeptical that the Soviet government will relinquish total control
of its citizens: "More [freedom], clearly, is to be permitted in the Soviet Union, but how
much more?" he wonders in a glasnost-era review of two Russian novels (OJ 548 – 56).
He writes of "happiness in the traditional Russian way, as something filched from the
state — a kind of spiritual sneaking, a defiant privacy and individual freedom . . . Might
the state itself change for the better? This question lies well beyond the horizon of this
novel, and we scan the daily newspapers for the answer" (OJ 556).

8. Updike is again dumbfounded to learn of Cheever's nastiness toward him; to his
dismay, Cheever describes "Postcards from Soviet Cities" as "some assinine [sic] poems
on Russian cities" (OJ 116).

of Western culture. Georgian poets in the poem "Tbilisi" "boast/ Their tongue is older than the hills" (11-12). And in "Yerevan," "the boulevards . . . lead from slums of history/ Into a future stripped of swords" (6-8). The sense is that "Far Russia" ("Moscow" 11) is a vague, distant, ancient land whose traditions are far removed from those of the West. Yet connections and echoes exist throughout these poems which link the realities of the East to the West. Updike connects the two spheres in the last quatrain of "Yerevan," the last poem of "Postcards from Soviet Cities:"

> Mount Ararat, a conscience, floats
> Cloudlike, in sight but unpossessed,
> For there, where Noah docked his boat,
> Begins the brutal, ancient West. (CP 45)

The West, like the East, is ancient and brutal, and they are separated at least partially by history and mutual misconceptions. The connections between them are tenuous and ephemeral; the misconceptions that distance them are as daunting as the misconceptions that separate the sexes in much of Updike's fiction.

Updike takes these representations of the theme of separation much further in *Bech: A Book*. In "Rich in Russia," Bech, like Updike, travels to Russia in 1964; the fictional memoirist who narrates this story describes the year, from the perspective of five years later, as "a thaw or so ago" (Bech 4). Updike acknowledges the connection between himself and Bech and also the connection between his literary self and Russia in a 1971 interview: "When I returned from the Soviet Union and Eastern Europe in '64 I had a number of impressions that only a writer could have collected. So, in trying to utilize some of them I invented Henry Bech, just to serve as a vehicle for my own impressions" (PP 486). Given the strength and obviousness of this connection, it is surprising that even post-Cold War criticism of the Bech stories, such as Sanford Pinsker's article in *Modern Fiction Studies* (spring 1991), virtually ignore the fact that the character of Henry Bech was conceived in the Soviet Union, and that his identity, like Updike's, was shaped by the Cold War milieu. Three of the stories in *Bech* and the appendix, "Bech's Russian Journal," grew directly out of Updike's impressions of the Soviet Union. It is no coincidence that *Bech* is Updike's funniest book; its wit and irreverence contrast sharply with the bleak, serious communist world, the "glum Soviet surroundings" (OJ 112) that characterize his memories of his trip to Russia. These stories show how even a temporarily blocked writer like Bech has far less to worry about than communist writers who must either contend with the surveillance of hard-line officials—a condition sure to make their prose stiff, awkward, and falsely patriotic—or publish underground *samizdat* that could land them in a Siberian prison.

Updike contrasts Eastern and Western writers to demonstrate that, on many levels, the contest between capitalism and communism was an uneven match. Yet Bech's superiority is complicated by his nagging feeling that the communist world contains something profound and heroic, something that capitalism has obscured. In an early unpublished draft of "Bech's Russian Journal," Updike writes about an encounter between Bech and his Russian counterparts in which the Russians sing a teary "God Bless America" in honor of Bech: "And Bech did retain, from those chaotic luminous hours embittered by the taste of tomato, a strange sense of literature, foreign to the weary quarterlies that littered his apartment, as a heroic endeavor manly, comradely a war carried forward against a wordless wilderness that extended, somehow, to the east."[9] Updike reiterates this position in an uncollected piece published in 1977 titled "The Cultural Situation of the American Writer" in which he writes, "During a month, spent many years ago, in the Soviet Union, almost exclusively in the company of literary personnel, I did, through the haze of translation, gather some impressions of the situation of the Soviet writer. It is one I do not envy." Updike goes on to describe the merits of inheriting Russia's "noble literary tradition," but concludes, "I present this picture in a spirit of anthropological dispassion, not to condone the stifling, farcical repressiveness that murdered Mendelstahm and Isaac Babel, sent Sinyevshy [*sic*] and Daniel to jail, and condemned Pasternak and Solzhenitsyn for the crime of winning the Nobel Prize."[10] Like Updike, while Bech develops a stronger sense of his country's benefits, he confronts himself as a writer when he is removed from his country.

9. By permission of John Updike and the Houghton Library, Harvard University, 81M-51 (649).

10. Updike, "The Cultural Situation of the American Writer," 22, 23.

Along with the contrast between Soviet and Western societies, *Bech: A Book* is characterized by Henry Bech's identity crisis that is manifested in his lost sense of his innocent past, his writer's block, and his difficulty with women. The narrator describes the year after Kennedy's assassination nostalgically; relations between the United States and the Soviet Union in the mid-1960s were indeed more amicable than they had been since the start of the Cold War, despite American involvement in Vietnam. The narrator of "Rich in Russia" writes:

> Russia, in those days, like everywhere else, was a slightly more innocent place. Khrushchev, freshly deposed, had left an atmosphere, almost comical, of warmth, of a certain fitful openness, of inscrutable experiment and oblique possibility. There seemed no overweening reason why Russia and America, those lovable paranoid giants, could not happily share a globe so big and blue; there certainly seemed no reason why Henry Bech, the recherché but amiable novelist, artistically blocked but socially fluent, should not be flown into Moscow at the expense of our State Department for a month of that mostly imaginary activity termed "cultural exchange." (Bech 4)

1964 is seen as a period of innocence between tense events of the war; Bech's visit takes place "in Russia five years ago, when Cuba had been taken out of the oven to cool and Vietnam was still coming to a simmer" (Bech 6). The jaded attitude of the narrator in 1969 as well as Bech's placement in a relatively relaxed 1964 setting are crucial to an understanding of "Rich in Russia" because they underscore the fact that Bech's world is a volatile place with an uncertain future.

Bech is destined to confront his past during his visit. He is reminded of his youth from his first contact with Russia: "Entering the Aeroflot plane at Le Bourget, Bech thought it smelled like his uncles' backrooms in Williamsburg, of swaddled body heat and proximate potatoes, boiling" (Bech 4-5). In Russia Bech is able to confront a suppressed part of his past: "Bech did find a quality of life . . . reminiscent of his neglected Jewish past. Virtue, in Russia as in his childhood, seemed something that arose from men, like a comforting body odor, rather than something from above, that impaled the struggling soul like a moth on a pin" (Bech 6). In Bech's mind, Russia is a place of innocence and virtue where he can free his struggling soul. He is liberated from the culture that has caused him to lose this innocence, and, ironically, he is finally rich, but in a country where monetary wealth does not mean as much as ideological commitment.

Bech's wealth in Russia provides the story's primary conflict; he makes Kate, his translator-escort, a foil to his own situation: "'Kate,' he said, displaying his rubles in two fistfuls, letting some drift to the floor, 'I have robbed the proletariat. What can I do with my filthy loot?' He had developed, in this long time in which she was always with him, a clowning super-American manner" (Bech 7). The story becomes a quest to get rid of the rubles, and an ideological rift develops between Bech and Kate as a result of his jocularity. When she solemnly advises him to deposit his money in a Russian bank, his response, meant as a light joke, reveals the anxieties common in his country: "'What?' said Bech, 'And help support the Socialist state? When you are already years ahead of us in the space race? I would be adding thrust to your rockets. . . . No, Kate, we must spend it! Spend, spend. It's the Keynesian way. We will make Mother Russia a consumer society'" (Bech 9). Bech's idealistic view of the relationship between capitalist and socialist countries is complemented by Kate's cartoonish impressions of America, comically mixed with the language of American science-fiction that she translates. Their attempts to understand each other's culture are balanced by an inability to communicate, based on their deep-seated impressions of the other culture. Bech's lighthearted attempt to "make Mother Russia a consumer society" fails; immediately after his comment, he "received a haunted impression—that [Kate] was locked into a colorless other dimension from which only the pink tip of her nose emerged. 'Is not so simple,' she ominously pronounced" (Bech 10). Kate's tone is ominous because the distance between them has become greater despite Bech's attempt to bridge the gap, just as the two nations have become colder toward one another after the "momentary Khrushchevian thaw" of 1964 (OJ 115).

The rest of the story underscores the awkwardness of this mix of cultures and their mutual misunderstandings, like Bech's inability to become emotional at Soviet-produced war movies juxtaposed with Russian writers "who uniformly adored Gemingway" (Bech 10), or Bech observing Russians "Twisting to Voice of America tapes" coupled with the silence that greets Bech's assertion that Nabokov is America's best living writer (Bech 11). Another more fundamental conflict arises from the inability of these

cultures to mix: the inability of Kate and Bech to unite sexually. The failure of these two characters to have sex develops out of the belief systems
of their respective countries; Kate "could not imagine that Bech did not,
like herself, loathe all officials" (Bech 11). In her effort to keep Bech apart
from an American diplomat, she resorts to "another weapon. She squeezed
his arm smugly and said, 'We have an hour. We must rush off and *shop*'"
(Bech 12). Her own beliefs cause her to misunderstand Bech and resort
to what she thinks he wants. The shopping is unsatisfactory because there
are no quality goods to be bought; Kate says, "I know what you have in the
West. I have been to Science Fictions Writers' Congress in Vienna. This
great store, and not one leather suitcase. It is a disgrace upon the people"
(Bech 12). Their shopping excursion together, as if they were involved ro-
mantically, is marred by the poor quality of the shopping and by Bech's
attempting to trade on the black market. The episode ends in a reaffir-
mation of Kate's fear of officials and of Bech's disregard for her feelings instead of in sex, the logical culmination of the obvious attraction between
them: "She told him in tears, 'Had the authorities witnessed that scene we
would all be put in jail, biff, bang'" (Bech 13). Bech tries to cheer her up
with empty praise of Socialist realist art, and she reacts to his condescending tone: "'It is stupid stuff,' she said. 'We have had no painters since
Rublyov. You treat my country as a picnic'" (Bech 14). The conflict is based
on the cultural differences that separate them, but Bech is also frustrated
as a man unable to comfort a woman, tied up with feelings of a lost innocence: "'Kate, I *mean* it,' Bech insisted, hopelessly in the wrong, as with a
third-grade teacher, yet also subject to another pressure, that of a woman
taking sensual pleasure in refusing to be consoled" (Bech 14). This "pressure"—the simultaneous wish to antagonize and comfort the opposite
sex is characteristic of Updike's writing, and the recurrent Cold War
metaphor of global division used to illustrate it is fully realized here.

This pressure gives way to further frustration and wistfulness about
missed opportunities. Bech hears Kate bathing in the bathroom in his
hotel and wonders with clear sexual interest, "how could such a skinny
woman be displacing all that water?" (Bech 15). But this acknowledgement
of his desire is immediately replaced by the original conflict between the
economic systems of their countries: "Bech counted his rubles. He had
spent only a hundred and thirty-seven. That left one thousand two hundred

and eighty-three, plus the odd kopecks. His heart sank; it was hopeless" (Bech 15). His attempt to convert Mother Russia to consumerism is as hopeless at his repressed sexual desire for Kate because, like their countries in general, they do not understand each other. After another argument over the best way to spend Bech's rubles, Kate obliquely inquires if Bech is homosexual, and the narrator observes, "How little, after a month, these two knew each other!" (Bech 18). Bech defends himself by insisting to Kate that his books are "*all* about women" and she responds, "Yes . . . but coldly observed. As if extraterrestrial life" (Bech 19). The analogy between Bech's inability to understand both the East and Kate (or women in general) is complete; Bech has only to accept the consequence of his shortcomings, which he does as he is about to depart: "He went to kiss Ekaterina on the cheek, but she turned her face so that her mouth met his and he realized, horrified, that he should have slept with her" (Bech 20). This realization is a pretty obvious one for Bech to have overlooked, and it is linked not only to the lack of understanding between their cultures but to his failure to recapture the innocence of his youth: "'Oh Kate, forgive me; of course,' he said, but so stumblingly she seemed not to have understood him. Her kiss had been colorless but moist and good, like a boiled potato" (Bech 20-21). This simile connects Bech's taste of sexual connection with Kate to his early comparison between Russia and the "proximate potatoes, boiling" from his youth in Williamsburg. Bech has failed all around; he has not succeeded in the "cultural exchange" that is ostensibly the reason for his visit, nor in the sexual tryst that would have redeemed the visit, nor in recapturing the repressed part of his youth. The opportunity has been lost, as a "cultural freeze-up" (Bech 21) follows Bech's visit. The implications of this lost opportunity are enormous; if we follow the associations the story makes, Bech's failure to sleep with Kate connotes a failure to recapture innocence and a failure of Russia and America to come to terms with one another.

The innocence associated with Russia in "Rich in Russia" is altered in the next story in *Bech*, "Bech in Rumania." As Bech travels through this country—a mere pawn to Russia's king—the narrator perceives a difference from Bech's situation in Russia: "Yet there had been a tough and heroic naïveté in Russia that he missed here, where something shrugging and effete seemed to leave room for a vein of energetic evil" (Bech 39). Perhaps this difference is due to the obscurity, from an American's perspective, of the non-Russian Soviet countries; Bech feels comfortable defining himself in absolutes against Russia since its history, literature, and culture are somewhat familiar to him. Yet he knows nothing about Rumania, and he must question his definition of himself.

Bech's identity is clear and facile in the previous story: "Russia seemed Jewish to him, and of course he seemed Jewish to Russia" (Bech 5). By contrast, his identity is muddled from the first sentence of "Bech in Rumania": "Deplaning in Bucharest wearing an Astrakhan hat purchased in Moscow, Bech was not recognized by the United States Embassy personnel sent to greet him, and, rather than identify himself, sat sullenly on a bench, glowering like a Soviet machinery importer, while these young men ran back and forth conversing with each other in dismayed English and shouting at the customs officials in what Bech took to be pidgin Rumanian" (Bech 22). Bech refuses to play the "super-American" here as he did in Russia because this country is but a shadow behind the Iron Curtain. Confused about his true origins and his role within this country, he tries initially to be more Russian than American: "After five weeks of consorting with Communists, he felt himself increasingly tempted to evade, confuse, and mock his fellow Americans" (Bech 22). His cocky impressions of Russia give way to confusion about this tiny Slavic country—both its role in the Soviet scheme and his role as a visitor in it. Even the cuisine takes Bech by surprise: "waiters brought them soup and veal a continent removed from the cabbagy cuisine of Russia" (Bech 28). The narrator fully acknowledges Bech's ignorance: "Bech knew little about Rumania. From his official briefing he knew it was 'a Latin island in a Slavic sea,' that during World War II its anti-Semitism had been the most ferocious in Europe, that now it was seeking economic independence of the Soviet bloc" (Bech 29). Bech finds himself in a limbo between East and West, and in puzzling over the identity of this place he loses touch with his own identity. He has stepped behind the Iron Curtain to confront on some level the realities of the global other, but in this story his quest has become complicated by the size and complexity of the Soviet Union.

As in "Rich in Russia," Bech is accompanied by a translator-escort in this story, Petrescu, and this character is essential to the conflicts Bech faces. Like Kate, Petrescu has a murky perception of America based on odd translations of American literature, and he speaks in a comical idiom that highlights the distance between him and Bech. There is even less common ground between Petrescu and Bech than there is between Kate and Bech because while Bech knows Russian authors such as Tolstoy and Pushkin, he is almost entirely unfamiliar with Rumanian literature; the head of the Rumanian Writer's Union asks Bech,

> "You are a literary man. Do you know the works of our Mihail Sadoveanu, of our noble Mihai Beniuc, or perhaps that most wonderful spokesman for the people, Tudor Arghezi?"
> Bech said, "No, I'm afraid the only Rumanian writer I know at all is Ionesco."
> The exquisite white-haired man nodded eagerly and emitted a length of tinkling sounds that was translated to Bech as simply, "And who is he?" (Bech 26)

The inadequacies of translation are tied up with Bech's disoriented identity; shocked that the only Rumanian writer he knows is unknown in Rumania, Bech takes up the issue with Petrescu:

> "And Ionesco? Is he really a non-person?"
> Petruscu smiled. "The eminent head of Writers' Union," he said, "makes little jokes. He is known here but not much produced as yet. Students in their rooms perhaps read aloud a play like *The Singer Devoid of Hair.*" (Bech 30)

The play in question is of course known to Bech as *The Bald Soprano;* such slight mistranslations exacerbate the cultural differences that Bech cannot seem to penetrate as he could in Russia. Language remains a game between Bech and Petrescu:

> "And how did you like Mr. Taru [the head of the Writers' Union]?" Petrescu asked on the way.
> "He's a doll," Bech said.
> "You mean—a puppet?"
> Bech turned curiously but saw nothing in Petrescu's face that betrayed more than a puzzlement over meaning. Bech said, "I'm sure you have a better eye for the strings than I do" (Bech 28).

In a culture that Bech finds so unfamiliar, translation is essential, and the breakdown in communication that he experiences serves only to feed his identity crisis.

Though Bech amuses himself by toying with Petrescu's imprecise English, untranslatable customs bespeak a danger that makes Bech anxious. Notably, the erratic driving of their chauffeur (the alternate title of the story is "The Rumanian Chauffeur") is a source of constant worry for Bech. He repeatedly confesses his anxiety to Petrescu, calling their driver "sick and dangerous" (Bech 31). He is suspicious of the chauffeur, wondering "if the man did not understand English a little" (Bech 33). Petrescu acknowledges later, "that man our driver. Not all is well with him" (Bech 40). Bech's final failure is that he forgets to tip the chauffeur, and his initial guilt gives way "to a vengeful satisfaction and glad sense of release. . . . He realized that for four days he had been afraid" (Bech 48). The driver's erratic behavior is the sinister counterpart to Petrescu's faulty translations; both Rumanian men represent to Bech the distance between his culture and theirs, but the driver represents the potential danger of such misunderstanding—the threat to Bech's security when diplomacy and communication break down.

Bech gradually discovers that his role in Rumania is less an agent of cultural exchange than the literary equivalent of a Central Intelligence agent. Phillips, the U.S. ambassador, tells him over the telephone, "I know damn well this line is bugged, but here goes. This country is hot. Anti-Socialism is busting out all over. My inkling is they want to get you out of Bucharest, away from the liberal writers who are dying to meet you." Reflecting Updike's skepticism of his own ability to effect political agitation, Bech asks, "Are you sure they're not dying to meet Arthur Miller?" (Bech 24). Bech has unknowingly become a Cold War literary spy; Phillips tells him, "Kidding aside, Bech, there's a lot of ferment in this country, and we want to plug you in" (Bech 25). For Bech, this literary espionage is silly and anticlimactic as well as dehumanizing. Yet his eventual meeting with a Rumanian writer does help him resolve the identity crisis that pervades the story. As he finds Rumania more confusing he feels his grasp on his sense of self slipping. The Rumanian nightclub he visits with the writer and two translators is characterized by a confusion of nationalities and cultures; the performers are Polish, Czech, Bulgarian, Chinese, and East German. The East German performer sings, "in English, 'Dip in the Hot of Texas' and 'Allo Cindy Lou, Goodbye Hot.' She pulled guns from her hips and received much pro-American applause, but Bech was on his third Scotch and needed his hands to hold cigarettes" (Bech 43). Though still trying to distance himself from his American identity, Bech is confused by this microcosm of the Communist world. Trying to gain some stability, he focuses on the idea of home, rejecting the carnivalesque spectacle. Before they go to the nightclub, he suggests, "'Shouldn't [the Rumanian writer and his wife] go home?' It worried him that Communists never seemed to go home" (Bech 41). As the nightclub spectacle overwhelms him, he exclaims, "My God . . . isn't this ever going to be over? Don't you Communists ever get tired of having fun?" (Bech 44). This disorienting meeting with the Rumanian writer causes Bech to begin to resolve the differences between their cultures, differences that he has become unable to discern.

As they leave the club Bech feels compelled to perform his duty as a literary spy; he experiences a revelation about his identity in relation to the differences between his culture and Rumania's culture:

> He felt duty-bound to confront the other writer. They stood, the two of them, on the cobbled pavement, as if on opposite sides of a transparent wall one side of which was lacquered with Scotch and the other with vodka. The other's rimless glasses were misted and the resemblance to Teddy Roosevelt had been dissipated. Bech asked him, "What do you write about?"
>
> The wife, patting her nose with a handkerchief and struggling not to cough, translated the question, and the answer, which was brief. "Peasants," she told Bech. "He wants to know, what do *you* write about?"
>
> Bech spoke to him directly. "*La Bourgeoisie,*" he said; and that completed the cultural exchange. Gently bumping and rocking, the writer's car took Bech back to his hotel, where he fell into the deep, unapologetic sleep of the sated. (Bech 45)

Bech is sated because he has discovered who he is during this visit. The Iron Curtain dissolves into "a transparent wall," nearly a mirror, that Bech peers through to find himself. He regains his identity as an American as he focuses on his role as an American writer. Besides the differences in the class of people they write about and their choice of liquor,[11] the two writ-

11. The imagery for this section of "Bech in Rumania" almost certainly derives from Yevtushenko's poem "In a Steelworker's Home," which Updike translated in 1967:

ers are essentially alike. Bech is finally able to speak "directly" to a Rumanian who is not a translator, and the "cultural exchange" that ensues makes the visit valuable for him. The Cold War equivalent of this exchange is also deemed valuable by Phillips:

> "You spent the evening with *him?* That's fabulous. He's the top of the list, man. We've never laid a finger on him before; he's been inaccessible. . . . For our money he's the hottest Red writer this side of Solzhenitsyn. He's *waaay* out. Stream of consciousness, no punctuation, everything. There's even some sex."
>
> "You might say he's Red hot," Bech said. (Bech 47)

There was, of course, no profound exchange of ideas between the two writers, nor anything akin to the subversive connection Phillips had in mind, and Bech mocks the attempt to involve him in international affairs, invoking the Gary Powers incident: "I think of myself . . . as a sort of low-flying U-2" (Bech 47). Though Bech's meeting serves no clear benefit to the U.S. Embassy, it seems that a connection was all that was necessary for the job to be successful. The connection is also crucial to Bech's temporary resolution of his identity crisis, which he has apparently resolved, as the story ends in his admission, *"Je suis Americain"* (Bech 48). The conflict between the United States and the Soviet Union is a barrier in both

---

> I love America,
>   the America who swam
> the Maytime Elbe
>   holding aloft whiskey
> with a tired right arm,
>   paddling with the left;
> yes, and Russia swam to meet her in
> the Maytime Elbe,
>   holding aloft vodka
> with a tired left arm,
>   paddling with the right,
> as vodka and whiskey—
>   neat!—without translation
> understood
>   each other perfectly,
>   goddamnit,
> on the waters where victories met! (1-17)

Collected Poems, 244-46.

of the first two stories in *Bech;* in both cases, Bech's status as a "blocked" writer is related to the block in his development as an individual, represented metaphorically by the global conflict (or the attempt to confront the "bloc"). Whereas he fails to recapture his past and to fulfill his sexual desires in "Rich in Russia," he ultimately succeeds in coming to terms with his identity in "Bech in Rumania."

Yet both his romantic and his identity crises resurface and blend together in the next story in *Bech,* "The Bulgarian Poetess." In this story the Iron Curtain fully becomes a mirror for Bech, one that reflects the inadequacies of his life as he stares into it: "At times, indeed, Bech felt he had passed through a mirror, a dingy flecked mirror that reflected feebly the capitalist world" (Bech 52). Bulgaria seems to mirror the West despite the fact that Bech's mission is to travel "to the other half of the world, the hostile, mysterious half" (Bech 50). He becomes conscious that the mirror that separates East from West exists as a barrier in addition to a reflector: "If there was one thing that irked Bech about these people behind the mirror, it was their assumption that, however second-rate elsewhere, in suffering they were supreme" (Bech 68). This sentiment foreshadows Updike's sometimes unfavorable reviews of Soviet literature, which at its worst tends to emphasize suffering in order to make up for its aesthetic flaws.

Bech, a narcissist, is sexually aroused by mirrors; he recalls his excitement in the Moscow Ballet School as he sees a roomful of young girls dancing in front of a "floor-to-ceiling mirror" (Bech 60). Viewing a play in Bulgaria, he experiences a similar sensation: "Bech found it oddly ecstatic when, preparatory to her leap, [the actress] would dance toward the mirror, an empty oval, and another girl, identically dressed in pink, would emerge from the wings and perform as her reflection" (Bech 65). This mirror-play fans Bech's desire for Vera, the Bulgarian poetess, with whom he flirts; he describes to her an essay he wrote on the "'orgasm as perfect memory. The one mystery is, what are we remembering?' She shook her head again, and he noticed that her eyes were gray, and that in their depths his image (which he could not see) was searching for the thing remembered" (Bech 68). Vera becomes for Bech a mirror, like the Eastern world is a mirror for the West. Sex is now intertwined with Bech's quest to find himself, a quest based on the fusing of perceived opposites—East and West, men and women—which he increasingly views in terms of their similarities.

At the end of the story Bech's attempt to connect with Vera breaks down, as does his metaphoric attempt to see into the culture of the Soviet Union:"He was surrounded by America: the voices, the narrow suits, the watery drinks, the clatter, the glitter. The mirror had gone opaque and gave him back only himself" (Bech 70). He at first blames his feelings for Vera on "romantic vertigo" (Bech 60), but later comes to feel he is truly in love. The impediment to this love is partially a function of his inability to see beyond the mirror, and thus to bridge the gap between Eastern and Western cultures. He acknowledges the tragedy of his situation in the final lines of the story, his inscription to Vera on a book he gives to her: "It is a matter of earnest regret for me that you and I must live on opposite sides of the world" (Bech 70). Bech again blames his failure to fulfill sexual or romantic desire on the separation between his culture and that of the country he visits. His attempt to come closer to an understanding of both himself and the world behind the Iron Curtain has again failed.

Bech's identity crisis may also stem from his feelings that his writing is valued much less than the political writings of Soviet authors, even in his own America. Updike sensed that Soviet writers may have overshadowed their American counterparts for a time simply because they wrote under oppressive circumstances. There was such a fervor in the United States over the plight of Soviet dissident writers in the late 1960s and early 1970s that American literature was in danger of being overlooked. Ironically, American access to Soviet literature was limited; there was a great disparity between the number of American books published in the Soviet Union (6,305) and the number of Soviet titles published in the United States (405) between 1946 and 1972. In 1977 and 1978 two conferences were held, the first in Moscow and the second in New York, to bring Soviet and American writers together to discuss literary matters. The conversations were more political than strictly literary, focusing on the status of the Soviet dissident writer, the imbalance of access to books from the other nation, and the prevalence of pornography in American society and writing. Updike was a guest at the New York conference and was the first American speaker. He used the opportunity to emphasize human spirituality and truth in response to a comment by the first Russian writer to speak at the conference, Felix Kuznetsov, who argued "that the conquest of hunger and poverty in the Soviet Union has not produced a corresponding increase in spiritual and human values." Endorsing the subject of his own fiction, Updike not only argued that the rise of the novel was "concurrent with the rise of capitalism," but went on to say that "the novel cannot exist without adultery." The Russians reacted with shock to this comment, according to Norman Cousins, rejoining "that there is much more to life than love." This exchange reflects Updike's growing belief by the late 1970s that American suburban bourgeois life is the proper subject for fiction, and that American writers need not bother themselves with political propaganda simply because their Soviet counterparts seemed noble in doing so. In 1998 Updike recalls the conference this way: "Censorship and the gulag were always in the back of American minds at such meetings but there seemed no point in durmming on the dissidents to the exclusion of all else. We weren't going to change policy at the top in any case."[12]

In a 1982 interview with Updike, Robert Boyers quotes Saul Bellow as saying, "The only trouble [with writing my latest novel] is that now and then, I pull a volume of Solzhenitsyn from the shelf and feel how utterly insignificant everything I've written has been." In a response so pertinent that I must quote it at length, Updike speaks out as vociferously as in any interview he has given, on any subject:

> It is very like Saul Bellow (and I'm sure Norman Mailer and others) to have this anxiety about not being Solzhenitsyn. I, myself, am not sure that the Soviet oppressions of writers should be encouraged in this country as a way of making our writers write better. I think that for every Solzhenitsyn, who wrote both under the system and outside of it, there are an awful lot of gifted writers whose powers are crushed and forever distorted by the Soviet system. Bob Boyers' friend, and mine, George Steiner, harks to this point often in his writings, saying how frivolous, how *domestic* and trivial American, Free World writing is and how *admirable* is

12. Summaries of the 1977 and 1978 conferences can be found in the *Saturday Review*, both written by Norman Cousins: "When Writers Meet (September 17, 1977: 8-10, 58-59) and "When American and Soviet Writers Meet" (June 24, 1978: 42-45). Also see Leo Gruliow's article in the *Christian Science Monitor* (June 14, 1978) and Isabella Zorina's article in *Inostrannaya Literatura* (no. 2, February 1978: 195-98). Kuznetsov's argument appears in "When American and Soviet Writers Meet," 42. Updike is quoted from a letter to the author, August 10, 1998.

this stuff which the giants of the Soviet culture have squeezed out around the censors and the commissars. I find this a horrendous point because it does imply that we'd all be better off if we were oppressed, and seems to disregard the fact that most of these writers have expressed themselves by going underground or out of the country. I don't want to dwell on the obvious for long except to say that there *is* a kind of American liberal mind which honestly believes we'd be better off with the police sifting through our works-in-progress all the time. I don't believe that. I believe we are blessed in this country, not only as writers but as human beings. . . . I must say that I don't find Solzhenitsyn all *that* readable—I'd rather read Bellow, even if he *is* only writing about a kind of disturbed, philosophical guy who keeps getting into run-ins with cops and former wives. I find that Bellow tells me more about life as I see it than any other American writers. But sure, we have a bad conscience, and of course there's this effort now by organs of review like the *New York Review of Books* to emphasize this by saying, "Why isn't American writing more political? Let's get those political muscles *going,* guys and gals!" It drives me . . . well, I'm getting indignant! But it's important to be honest about this. The American writer has never been much into the political system, has always stood apart.[13]

There is a value judgment implicit in this final sentence; certainly *some* American writers can be said to be "into the political system." He defines American writers as apolitical both as a reaction to the accolades of Soviet dissident literature and as a defense of his own writing. The voice of novelist and critic merge here, and speak in defense of the type of writing that values aesthetics and attention to middle-class American life over politics. In "The Cultural Situation of the American Writer" he states, "The American writer, surprising to say, is rather typically baffled and disgusted by what would seem his prime subject, the daily life of his society."[14] Refusing to compromise the significance of his own carefully wrought works, he feels that Americans should praise the accomplishments of Soviet literary dissidents, but that they should *not* romanticize literary bravery at the expense of undervaluing American literature.

As a way of gaining authority on the subject, he uses his reviews to speak out on the way Cold War concerns have impacted literature from both

13. Robert Boyers (moderator), "An Evening with John Updike," 48–49.
14. Updike, "Cultural Situation," 27.

sides of the Berlin Wall. Eastern-bloc writers hold a more prominent place in Updike's reviews as the Cold War develops; *Assorted Prose* (1965) contains only one review of Eastern-bloc literature, but the number increases to ten in *Picked-Up Pieces* (1975), fifteen in *Hugging the Shore* (1983), and twenty in *Odd Jobs* (1990). (These numbers include Russian exiles, notably Nabokov and Solzhenitsyn; there is also a stray review in the *New Yorker* entitled "Behold Gombrowicz" [September 23, 1967, 169–76] that Updike did not collect in *Picked-Up Pieces,* or anywhere else.) We learn from these writings that although the Cold War was hottest in the late 1950s and early 1960s in terms of the threat of nuclear war and official Soviet-American relations, writers such as Updike were engaged in an ongoing battle on the human rights front throughout the rest of the Cold War. This ideological opposition kept the Cold War going along traditional lines even as the global rivalry became fragmented and obscured throughout the 1970s and 1980s with the advent of nontraditional Cold War fronts such as Vietnam, Iran, and Afghanistan. Updike's status as a *literary* Cold Warrior reveals both a sympathy for the citizens of the rival East and a firm conviction that communist governments are responsible not only for dehumanization and alienation but also for bad prose.

In short, even though Updike's stance on Vietnam causes him to acknowledge the changes in the Cold War in the 1970s and 1980s, he also concludes through his investigation of Soviet writers that the American way is still a cause worth fighting for. We clearly see in Updike's reviews of Soviet literature his tendency to "get indignant" about fiction that aims to be only political. He praises those Soviet works in which political propaganda takes a back seat to the search for truth. The two are obviously intertwined, but the difference between success and failure is a matter of emphasis. In his own writings, history provides a backdrop for very real domestic conflict; as he writes in a 1985 *Esquire* piece titled "The Importance of Fiction," "Romances safeguard the importance of our sentiments amid the uncontrollable large-scale surges that constitute history; the inner lives of the obscure, as Erich Auerbach points out in his *Mimesis,* have been, from the New Testament on, the peculiar and precious burden of the *Western* narrative imagination" (OJ 86, emphasis added). Retelling the lesson that Bech learned in "Bech in Rumania," Updike asserts, "The novel and the short story rose with the bourgeoisie, as exercises in democratic feeling and in individual adventure" (OJ 87). The examples he cites in this article are all from the Western tradition, but as a nonfiction writer and reviewer of Eastern European fiction, Updike prefers these same qualities to what he deems "bad propaganda, like the boy-meets-tractor novels of socialist realism" (PP 46).

Nevertheless, he is quick to give praise where it is due. He is wary of the negative effects that propaganda and censorship have on fiction, but he recognizes true talent and acknowledges that Soviet writers do face far greater difficulties than their American counterparts do. He realizes the relatively easy circumstances of the American writer in "The Cultural Situation of the American Writer":

> The American writer, in many respects, is conspicuously fortunate. He is the citizen of a wealthy, literate country where "the freedom of speech, or of the press," as the Constitution puts it, has been a vigorously defended right for two centuries of national existence . . . no American writer, to my knowledge, has ever gone to jail for anything he has written. Whatever the inhibitions and limitations cultural circumstances set upon him, governmental censorship is not one of them, and for this he should be grateful.[15]

In a 1998 letter to me he recalls his encounters with Soviet writers: "The writers I knew best were Yevtushenko and Vosnisensky [*sic*], who were establishment figures relatively, but what I glimpsed of their situations didn't make me want to swap political systems. I enjoyed the Soviets, even some of the staunch partyliners, but came away more pro-American than ever."[16] He concludes a 1967 *New Yorker* "Notes and Comment" article, "To speak and write honestly in the Soviet Union is still a more difficult enterprise than an American can imagine" (PP 27). This essay, "Voznesensky Met," is a candid assessment of the dangerous conditions Soviet writers face, but it is also another instance of his indignation at the unnecessary burdens American writers saddle themselves with in an effort to be as noble as their Eastern counterparts. "Thaw cannot be imported from the West" (PP 26), he declares; if Americans are to fight the Cold War on the battlefield of artistic freedom, their best bet is to read and appreciate Soviet literature, not to make noise about it.

15. Ibid., 19.
16. Updike, letter to the author, 1998.

"Voznesensky Met" is ostensibly an account, based on Updike's 1964 visit, of his impressions of the Soviet poet; but the central of the essay's three paragraphs indicates exactly why Updike's name did not appear on the list of American writers who opposed the Sinyavsky-Daniel trial. It is clear that he defines his role more as the liaison between American and Soviet literary life than as the voice of solidarity between American and Soviet authors. Voznesensky wrote a letter denouncing the Soviet Writers' Union, even though the authors' organization had tried, according to Updike, "as far as its fundamentally anti-artistic function permitted, to cherish him" (PP 26). Updike writes, in the first-person plural typical of "Notes and Comment" articles, "We worry that our side might do him in. Introducing him at a poetry reading in this country last May, Robert Lowell confided to the audience that he thought both he and Voznesensky had 'really terrible governments.' Such a remark could not hurt Lowell but would certainly arrest the attention of the Russian Embassy watchdog who invariably attends displays of Russo-American cultural exchange" (PP 26). In other words, it's not up to Americans to fight the cause for Soviet dissent;

> a poet of Voznesensky's fame and genius is not defenseless . . . along with the censorship there are the summer dachas and assured incomes and pleasant dining halls and erratic indulgences. Stalin sheltered the maverick Mayakovsky; Khrushchev let Yevtushenko keep writing. The Sinyavsky-Daniel trial was carried to its foregone conclusion, but a petition of dissent was signed by Russia's best writers. . . . If Voznesensky carries his point, it will not be thanks to indignant editorials in this country or petitions signed by writers smug in their pre-bought freedom. If he cannot carry his point, let him at least survive. (PP 26–27)

Here, in late 1967, Updike has decided that his role in the Soviet dissent movement is to do what he does best—to read and write about Soviet literature. Knowing this, we can understand how Updike's identity as a writer was influenced by his conception of the changes in Eastern European literature during the latter half of the Cold War.

Picked-Up Pieces contains many statements that are consistent with this sentiment, notably on Solzhenitsyn and Nabokov, both Russian exiles to America. Updike again isolates his writing self from other facets of his personality in a 1974 speech entitled "Why Write"; after confessing that his fiction isn't motivated entirely by his potential to improve social conditions, he writes,

> To be sure, *as a citizen* one votes, attends meetings, subscribes to liberal pieties, pays or withholds taxes, and contributes to charities even more generously than—it turns out—one's own President. But as a writer, for me to attempt to extend my artistic scope into all the areas of my human concern, to substitute nobility of purpose for accuracy of execution, would certainly be to forfeit whatever social usefulness I *do* have. It has befallen a Solzhenitsyn to have experienced the Soviet labor camps. . . . But a writer's witness, surely, is of value in its circumstantiality. Solzhenitsyn's visible and brave defiance of the Soviet state is magnificent; but a novel like *The First Circle* affords us more than a blind flash of conditioned and—let's face it—chauvinistic indignation; it affords us entry into an unknown world, it offers a complex and only implicitly indignant portrait of how human beings live under a certain sort of political system. (PP 48)

He also describes *The First Circle* in a review of Marge Piercy's *Dance the Eagle to Sleep* as "a masterpiece, as magnanimous as it is devastating, of political disaffection" (PP 384). In both cases, Updike uses Solzhenitsyn as a yardstick against which to measure his own writing and that of other novelists. By extension, his identity as a writer during this period is defined against the writings of Soviet dissidents. Emphasis on resistance to government and awareness of the dangers of free expression characterize Solzhenitsyn's novels, but they also indicate what Updike's novels are *not*. Just as Bech realizes that the only difference between himself and the Soviet writer he encounters in "Bech in Rumania" is that they write about different classes of people, Updike too does not apologize for the difference between himself and a writer such as Solzhenitsyn. He praises the Soviet writer to a point, but he is aware that an implicit competition exists between them and therefore feels free to criticize him even to the point of highlighting his "chauvinism," a touchy subject in reviews of his own fiction. Too much praise for Solzhenitsyn undercuts the value of his own style of writing, which he feels is just as conscious of social issues as Solzhenitsyn's is, if not as politically explicit.

Updike's connection to Nabokov is markedly stronger than his connection to Solzhenitsyn. He dedicates more space in *Picked-Up Pieces* to

Nabokov than to any other single author, making no secret of the fact that his feeling for the master stylist is of abject worship, as opposed to the competition between himself and Solzhenitsyn. Nabokov was in Updike's words "a rabid Soviet-hater" (PP 218) who lived with the fact that he had produced "a precious *oeuvre* unpublishable in the Soviet Union" (PP 195). What separates Nabokov from Solzhenitsyn is his emphasis on style rather than politics, a trait that earns Updike's respect. Yet Nabokov's attunement to America—something Solzhenitsyn never even pretended to attempt in all of his years in Vermont—ingratiates him to Updike, who confidently declares that Nabokov "is now an American writer and the best living" (PP 220). He also writes, "To my taste his American novels are his best . . . In America his almost impossible style encountered, after twenty years of hermetic exile, a subject as impossible as itself, ungainly with the same affluence. He rediscovered our monstrosity" (PP 192). In a sense, Nabokov shares Updike's sensibilities—his stylized prose and his attention to America's troubled identity—but he has the added benefit of a Russian perspective. Nabokov is Updike's first and most lasting link to the mystery of the Soviet mind, a link possible only because of Nabokov's understanding of America. Updike feels betrayed when he senses that Nabokov became nostalgic for Russia in his old age, and in a review of Nabokov's 1966 revision of his autobiography *Speak, Memory,* Updike describes this betrayal in Cold War terms: "If [Nabokov] devotes the rest of his days to fond rummaging in the Russian attic of his mind, the loss is national, and sadder than *Sputnik*" (PP 192). This attitude epitomizes Updike's attitude toward Soviet dissident and exile literature in the late 1960s and early 1970s: on the literary front, America loses ground when an imaginative writer such as Nabokov forfeits his American identity in an attempt "to rejoin, by some sparkling future rivulet beyond the grim hydroelectric dam of Sovietism" (PP 194), the main current of Russian literature. Again, Soviet exiles and dissident writers should be praised, but American writers should not be overshadowed by them.

Nabokov, who died in 1977, is accorded a slightly less prominent position in Updike's next collection of nonfiction, *Hugging the Shore.* Nevertheless, he is still a presence, and Updike is still haunted by the master's dual allegiances; he notes with some concern, "The posthumous publication of [Nabokov's] *Lectures on Russian Literature* comes as a bracing reminder of his original and deepest cultural allegiance" (HS 237). Nabokov's allegiances are no longer the hot issue, though; the high period of Soviet literary dissent was over by the mid-1970s, when Updike collected *Picked-Up Pieces*. *Hugging the Shore* reveals that in the aftermath of both the Solzhenitsyn affair and the turbulent Vietnam era Updike spoke out even more loudly on how censorship by totalitarian governments negatively affects art, and on how the Western reader should be wary of propaganda disguised as fiction. His growing confidence in this fact coincides with his increasingly stylized fiction.

A cursory glance at even the table of contents of *Hugging the Shore* shows that Updike was concentrating more on the global literary scene in the late 1970s and early 1980s than he ever had before. He devotes considerably more space to foreign writers than to Americans, including sections on "Eastern Europeans" as well as "The Far East" and "The World Called Third" in addition to the customary sections on Western Europeans. It is clear from this collection as much as from his novel *The Coup* that Updike widened his focus beyond the claustrophobic worlds of Olinger, Pennsylvania, and the North Shore of Massachusetts in the late 1970s. Such a shift required a redefinition of the artist's identity but *not* a radical revision of the artist's themes. *The Coup* seems on the surface far removed from Updike's other work because of its setting in an imaginary African country, but its themes and the motion of its plot are quintessentially Updikean, and its main character, Colonel Ellelloû, shares the basic sensibilities of a Tom Marshfield, a Harry Angstrom, or any number of Updike's short-fiction protagonists. Though Updike turns his attention to a foreign landscape in *The Coup* and to foreign literature in *Hugging the Shore,* he continues to value the same features that he has always looked for in Western literature, and that he has attempted to embody in his own writings. In the case of Eastern-bloc literature, this translates into a continued disdain for fiction whose sole purpose is to criticize "the system" at the expense of investigating basic human emotional responses and relationships.

Certain East German novels seem to bear the brunt of Updike's distaste for this type of literature. In a review of Reiner Kunze's *The Wonderful Years,* Updike begins by acknowledging that dissident writers are to be lauded for their bravery; this novel, Updike writes, embodies "a set of presumptions and grievances which awakened in the apologetic breast of your reviewer another brand of impatience. Publication of this book in West Germany, it should be stated at the outset, cost the author his passport and his membership in the East German Writers' Union and represented an act of courage of a sort that American writers are not asked to perform" (HS 446). But this unfortunate circumstance alone is not cause enough for celebration. Kunze's novel is nothing new to Western readers who have already formed opinions about "the unlovely process of growing up in a Communist state" (HS 446); Updike writes, "The biases of our own news, unfortunately, so condition us that these brave writers from behind the Iron Curtain appear quaint. . . . Why be astounded that a state— the German Democratic Republic—founded by an army of occupation and maintained by a barb-wired wall should be oppressive and hypocritical? 'I am not an enemy of the Republic,' Kunze has stated; 'I am an enemy of lies.' To his own government, this position appears menacing; to a Western reader, it seems disingenuous" (HS 447–48). Updike has a similar gripe against Hans Joachim Schädlich, another East German writer. He begins with the same disclaimer that he grants Kunze: "all honor is due yet another writer who has struggled against the inane censorship of a Communist state. However, the American publication of his courageous work under the title *Approximation,* may afford its American readers satisfactions more political than aesthetic; Herr Schädlich's style is as bleak as his themes, and the ingenious strategies of expression under tyranny can seem rather spindly out in the open" (HS 453). This is a polite way of saying, "I know I'm supposed to admire it, but it's not a very good book!" Updike clearly won't stand for books that tip the balance toward politics when it is possible, as he claims of his own writing, for fiction to have "more history in it than history books" (PP 482) without sacrificing beauty, and a sense of humor. When reviewing *Approximation* and another East German novel, Updike admits, "I took [them] with me on a week in the Caribbean and must confess that, brief as both are, it took all the bracing counter-effects of sun, sea, and shuffleboard to get me through them. . . . A world where no one is at home seems deducible from these evidences of the human spirit's atrophy" (HS 456). This confession reads like an advertisement for the American bourgeois life; it is clear that Updike sensed in 1981—also the year he published *Rabbit Is Rich,* which describes the closest Harry Angstrom comes to realizing the American dream of excessive wealth—that Western capitalism was emerging as the winner.

Yet Updike felt that even some Western literature was dealt a blow by the ongoing need for fiction writers to foreground politics, which he posits as diametrically opposed to aesthetics in the reviews of Schädlich and Kunze. In a 1982 review he writes, "Those who urge upon American writers more social commitment and a more public role should ponder the cautionary case of Günter Grass. Here is a novelist who has gone so public he can't be bothered to write a novel. . . . It is hard to imagine an American writer of comparable distinction publishing a book so unbuttoned in manner, so dishevelled in content" (HS 482, 484). Here is another advertisement for the American way; the style of our literature has reached a higher plane than literature written behind or near the Iron Curtain. Like the ongoing reminders in our popular culture and journalism that life in America was simply better than life in Russia, Updike contends that American writers, free from the political burdens of their Eastern counterparts, have become superior to them.

Freedom is the issue that topped Updike's list, and that of many Americans, of the reasons to hate and fear Soviet Communism. American capitalism is about nothing if not choice, and, the American bourgeoisie believes, such choice raises our standard of living to a level far surpassing that of Soviet-bloc countries. Updike uses the differences between American and Soviet standards of living to denigrate New York City: "[New York], like the Soviet Union, has this constant usefulness: it makes you glad you live somewhere else. As in the Soviet Union, nothing is easy: there are lines at the bank and the post office, there is nowhere to park, everything is an exhausting walk away, the restaurant has no tables, the theatre has no seats, and carbon monoxide ubiquitously offers an invitation to succumb" (OJ 56). All of the Soviet Union, according to this passage, is like the worst elements of our most overcrowded city. The unspoken distinction between the two is that Americans are free to live someplace other than New York; Soviet citizens, on the other hand, must remain in the Soviet Union. Creative expression is also limited by communist governments; Updike is somewhat awestruck by the ability of Soviet artists to render Lenin variously as Western artists from bygone eras would represent Jesus on the crucifix; yet his "rapture was slightly dulled, [in 1964] when he was taken through a Lenin factory, a clattering place where identical busts of the sacred agitator came down an assembly line" (OJ 850). Repetitive mass production takes precedence in the Soviet Union over individual expression. Compare this assessment to a piece he wrote on architecture in which he observes Levittowns—those 1950s American suburban housing developments in which all of the housing units look exactly alike—and extols the spirit of the American individual, noting how the Levittowns "turned, decade by decade, less tacky and boxlike as proud owners made additions and improvements, and trees and shrubs matured in a pervasive softening" (OJ 51).

At the end of the 1980s, Updike, in the introduction to *Odd Jobs,* acknowledges the startling end of the Cold War; in compiling the collection, he apologizes that "no attempt has been made to bring the historical background—the contemporary temperature of the Cold War . . . up to date. Most of the pieces belong to an already slightly bygone era when Ronald Reagan reigned over the United States" (OJ xxii). One cannot fault Updike for failing to account for changes in the structure of the world in September 1990, for he was writing during a time when geopolitical changes were so rapid that to update old reviews would have been an exercise in futility. He expresses his shock, shared with nearly all Americans, at the speed and completeness of the Cold War's end in a footnote to a review of a novel by Thomas Bernhard: "Little did any of us dream that, within a few months of this review's publication, the Wall would come down, and East and West would be no more" (OJ 615). *Odd Jobs* represents, among other things, Updike's last candid writings on the state of America's place in the world as he had come to know it. The final years of the Cold War revealed no major changes in the way he construed the Soviet Union and its relation to the United States, but one senses a turn toward the nostalgia that characterizes his later works. It is as though the rivalry between the superpowers isn't as real or as exciting as it used to be, even though anti-Soviet rhetoric was renewed vigorously under Reagan.

The nostalgic tone of *Odd Jobs* is evident from the first lines of the body of the text: "As I get older, my childhood self becomes more accessible to me, but selectively, in images as stylized and suspect as moments remembered from a novel read years ago. In one of my first memories, I am lying

on the floor reading newspaper headlines . . . and the cartoon on the editorial page shows a little fellow on skis defiantly standing up to a huge
bear, who is wearing bandages and has the cartoon symbols signifying
dizziness and pain scattered about his head. The bear is Russia" (OJ 3).
Though the subject of the cartoon is the Russo-Finnish "Winter War" of
1939–1940, this image from Updike's memory says much about his attitude toward Russia in 1987, the year the memoir was written. He senses
Finland's "potentially oppressive closeness" (OJ 9) to Russia, but also notes
a Russian desire for more expensive Western goods. The Soviet Union is
still essentially a place where an enormous, oppressive government denies
its citizens the objects of their desire — consumer goods — and the citizens
are thus pitiable from a Westerner's perspective.

The Soviet Union has failed, from Updike's late-1980s standpoint, because of such denial of individual human rights. After comparing "the
bourgeois, capitalist world" to "the Communist hierarchies that would
supplant it," he muses rhetorically, "What is important, if not the human
individual?" (OJ 87). Updike's critique of Soviet oppression runs deepest
in a section of reviews from *Odd Jobs* entitled, not altogether tongue-in-
cheek, "The Evil Empire." The first set of three reviews (entitled "How
the Other Half Lives") begins with a lament for the politically oppressive
nature of Soviet fiction: "Wouldn't it be nice to forget about the dreary
old Iron Curtain and to read fiction from the Communist countries for
its aesthetic and informational charms?" (OJ 511). The mock-naive tone
of this sentence underscores the seriousness of Updike's opinion of the
diminished quality of Soviet literature in the 1980s — his insinuation that
"fiction from Communist countries is to be read as prisoners' outcries"
(OJ 511). Updike sees in Soviet-bloc authors a yearning to be free from
their oppressive system, and speculates that the Western reader will
marvel "at the courage still alive after sixty years of the Soviet system"
(513) — courage, that is, to put into print critiques of the Soviet system
and of Eastern-bloc culture. In these reviews Updike emphasizes the differences between American freedom and Soviet oppression; he points
out, "Written within and for a society controlled by Communists, [Milan
Kundera's novel] *The Joke* contains none of the frivolous bitterness and
nihilism common in the West; its bitterness has been hard-earned and is
presented at risk" (OJ 514). At the end of the three reviews in this sec-

tion, Updike reminds us that all three books have been banned in their respective homelands, and he concludes with a strong statement denouncing Soviet censorship:

> The absurd cowering by Communist governments in the face of honest and questioning art is one of the wonders of the world, a fertile source of embarrassment to its enforcers and an apparent declaration of bad faith, for from such fear of the truth we can only deduce a power that believes itself to be based upon lies. (OJ 519)

Updike's view of the Soviet Union has not altered much since the early years of the Cold War; the Soviet Union is still a real enemy, in 1982, because of its refusal to grant free expression to its citizens. This refusal remains odious to American authors who believe strongly in the rights of the individual and in the kind of society that grants artistic expression the freedom it deserves.

The next section of reviews in *Odd Jobs*, called "Out of the Evil Empire," reflects another aspect of Updike's perception of Russia in the waning years of the Cold War. Though he is still firmly against Soviet totalitarianism and bitter over the loss of individual freedom, he also acknowledges that Russia does not appear to be the absolute threat it once was. He begins the reviews,

> The Russians seem to be receding. It is not just that our President cracks jokes about outlawing them and calls them an evil empire; their own chiefs of state, from the sickly late Brezhnev to the sallow and infirm Andropov to today's far from entirely healthy Chernenko, have become wan, and the Russian global presence is signified by a muffled, stubborn war in Afghanistan and by non-appearance—at the Olympics, at the conference table. One remembers with a perhaps soft-headed fondness the old days of Khrushchev in America, banging his shoe at the U.N. and waggling his hips at Disneyland. And one turns to some contemporary Russian fiction with genuine curiosity as to life in our recessive fellow superpower's territory. (OJ 519–20)

Two aspects of this quotation are striking: one is Updike's "soft-headed fondness" for the old days of the Cold War when a volatile Khrushchev provided a visible justification for American fears of Soviet Russia. The other striking aspect is Updike's curiosity to confront, again, the man behind the

Iron Curtain. Yet Updike's tone in 1984 is nearly one of pity; the Soviet leaders are "sickly . . . sallow and infirm," and the country as a whole is "recessive" — that is, receding from its once prominent position on the world stage. What may be bothering Updike most at this point is the diminishment of real competition, something Rabbit Angstrom might feel playing one-on-one against an unworthy opponent. The Cold War, we once believed, was not really meant to be "won"; the only two possibilities for its end were the unthinkable (nuclear war), and the only slightly more likely (ideological concession). Updike sensed in the mid-1980s that the possibility for Soviet concession to Western ways was becoming more likely, and his renewed "curiosity as to life in our fellow superpower's territory" must have been brought about by this ideological waffling — similar to the thaw that allowed for his travels in the Soviet Union twenty years before.

The four sets of reviews within "Out of the Evil Empire" are tinged with a sort of dissatisfaction; to return to the basketball analogy, it is as if the better player, having knocked his weak opponent to the floor, is now offering his hand to help him up. Updike maintains that the Soviet government is evil and oppressive, but he also goes to great lengths to reveal how these four books of Russian fiction are essentially like Western fiction, and all the better for this similarity. As Bech discovered twenty years earlier, there are important differences, such as "the seriousness with which work is taken" (OJ 529); yet Updike's newfound pity for a weakening opponent causes him to admit, at the end of the reviews, "A life-loving trait . . . has helped make the Soviets, for these forty years of ragged truce, tolerable partners in power" (OJ 534). Updike's decision to emphasize similarities rather than differences between Soviet and Western culture in these reviews and his somewhat startling reference to Soviets as "partners" signify a rapid change in his attitude; as he said in a 1995 letter, "The thing about the Soviets was we never really hated them, the way we hated the Axis powers in WWII."[17] The competitive Updike who yearns for the old days of Khrushchev gives way to the humble Updike who refuses to gloat when the enemy/partner-in-power seems to be weakening. Like many "patriotic citizen[s] of the free West" (OJ 540), including himself, Updike appears in these reviews not quite prepared for the Cold War to end. In a review

17. Updike, letter to the author, 1995.

of *Alone Together,* an account of the Sakharov affair, he continues to denounce the Soviet government's tactics to oppress its people (OJ 544); yet
he reiterates that the Soviet system is in decline, and that the Soviet threat
to America is no longer prominent:

> In these last years, even under a conservative administration and in spite
> of the usual Cold War spy cases and murderous international meddling,
> there has arisen the sensation that the Soviet Union is not the enemy. Its
> political religion has fallen flat; free enterprise is creeping in even into its
> own sluggish system; as a nation, it is soggy with internal problems, and
> some of them resemble ours. Perhaps radical Islam is the threat, or, from
> another angle, Japan; but Russia, like a gruff old chess foe who has grown
> corpulent and distracted over the years, seems an almost comfortable
> neighbor in the global village. (OJ 546)

Updike's admission that "the Soviet Union is not the enemy" is coupled
with an immediate search for another global enemy—perhaps Japan for
economic reasons, or Islam for ideological ones. It could not be otherwise;
Updike's definition of American identity is so dependent upon global competition that when one enemy bows out of the ring, another must instantly
take its place.

In his most recent and most ponderous collection of essays and criticism, *More Matter* (1999), Updike wistfully addresses his status as a reviewer in the post–Cold War era; he writes, "In a strange way, the passing
of the Cold War has made it harder to frame a literary opinion; the polari-
ties of right versus left and red versus free lent a tension to aesthetic questions miles removed from the Manichean global struggle" (MM xx–xxi).
Updike is understandably surprised by the impact of this tension on him
because the Cold War did not seem likely to end, ever. *More Matter* sees
Updike the reviewer branching out into unexplored territory, from bi-
ographies of Helen Keller and Isaac Newton to longer meditations on literary predecessors such as Melville and Wharton. When Updike does address the Cold War in this collection, he is nearly nostalgic for it, as in an
essay written for the official souvenir program of the 1992 Olympic Games
that begins, "Ever since the revival of the modern Olympic Games in 1948,
the Cold War has framed and accentuated their competition" (MM 121).
After meditating on this idea and tracing its history, he writes, "with the
old Communist-capitalist dualism no longer present to lend drama, what

use will the world have for the Olympic Games? They will serve, I suggest, as a quadrennial source for televised images of humanity at its most physically exalted" (MM 122). This optimistic observation is an analogue for his own reviews: essentially, the Cold War lent drama and sharpness to their meaning, but something purer might emerge after the drama has ended.

Therefore, when Updike does review an Eastern European novel in *More Matter,* he treats it as an artifact. In a review of Ivan Klíma's *Love and Garbage* he notes, "Klíma's novel seems to arrive from long ago, since it predates the fall of the Iron Curtain and originates within the weird and warped circumstances that Communist governments imposed upon would-be practitioners of the arts" (MM 377). In a review of another novel by Klíma, he describes communism as "something we'd rather not think about" because it "ended mired in the world's economic mud, humiliated by its own poverty and beggary. The empire was worse than evil: it was inefficient. A rather majestic enemy became a pitiable failure" (MM 380).

There are other references in this collection to the Cold War as a thing of the past, notably a review of a pair of novels by Romanian dissident Norman Manea (MM 386–94). But the rivalry is undeniably over by this point, and there is no satisfaction that the West has "won." In an essay entitled "Freedom and Equality" Updike even problematizes the lessons that we have learned from the Cold War and the value of our national idea of freedom: "The Soviets' gulags and purges and show trials, their absurd censorship and xenophobia, their military invasions of the supposed allies, and finally their stubbornly backward economy all made us feel good about ourselves, and told us what freedom was. It was being not-them. . . . But now they and their former satellites are reaping the mixed and difficult results of 'a free market,' whose most visible benefits seem to be near famine for many and the rapid rise of affluence of former criminals" (MM 12). Perhaps it is because the Cold War wasn't a war in the traditional sense, but the euphoria of victory here is clearly supplanted by a tinge of cynicism: is anyone better off now? Updike's doubt is evident: the phrase "seems to" pervades this final collection and he is both unsure about his role as a reviewer and almost apologetic for publishing "my fifth such collection and—dare we hope?—my last" (MM xix). Consistent with the fiction he has published in the post–Cold War era, his nonfiction turns increasingly away from today and toward the past.

During the period from his Soviet visit in the high years of the Cold War to his reviews in its waning years, Updike's identity as a writer solidified. His belief in the dehumanizing and artistically damaging effects of totalitarian governments is rooted in early Cold War attitudes, but unlike his stance on Vietnam, this belief didn't pose a problem for his public self. These divergent reactions to the Cold War world had profound effects on his career: without the Vietnam debate, his writings might have lacked some of their conflicted tension, and without Soviet dissent they might have downplayed the narrative excesses that make them so compelling. His unwillingness to envy Soviet writers their political circumstances helps to distinguish him from his contemporaries, and thus enables us to locate him in an American tradition in which the American writer can "stand apart" from "the political system" while still being aware of it. This is the ideal for Cold War writing, in Updike's eyes: the danger, the structure, and the rhetoric of the global rivalry are all there, but if the writing is any good, the reader's attention should be elsewhere.

Yet as should be evident by now, the Cold War is so ubiquitous in Updike's writings that one can scarcely imagine them apart from it. As I have suggested, his response to a dying world order is nostalgia, evident even from the titles of his post–Cold War works of fiction (*Memories of the Ford Administration* [1992], *The Afterlife* [1995]). This nostalgia is characteristic of much of his writing, from his yearning for small-town simplicity and values in *The Centaur* (1963) to his frustrated imagining of an early twentieth-century America that had faith in his more recent novel *In the Beauty of the Lilies* (1996). Yet one might be surprised by a writer's desire to return to the dangerous and volatile early Cold War. The next and final chapter will demonstrate how it could not have been otherwise, in Updike's case.

5

A Reason to Get Up in the Morning

The Fifties—Cold-War years *par excellence*—
Loom in memory's mists as an iceberg, slow
In motion and sullenly radiant [. . .]
A certain breathlessness
Was felt; perhaps the Bomb, which after all
Went *mu*SHROOM! as we entered puberty,
Waking us from the newspaper-nightmare
Our childhoods had napped through, was realer then;
Our lives, at least, were not assumed to be
Our right.

–**John Updike, "Apologies to Harvard," 1973**

THE NOSTALGIC TONE of this excerpt from "Apologies to Harvard" seeps into Updike's writing in the early 1970s and saturates it throughout the rest of his career. Critics have argued with good reason that Updike's early works about Pennsylvania (*Olinger Stories, Of the Farm,* and *The Centaur*) are also characterized by nostalgia, but it is different from the nostalgia that characterizes his later work. His early work yearns for an idealized pastoral rural world; his later work yearns for the heady fifties, the decade that made Americans anxious about a well-armed nuclear enemy and paranoid about domestic communist subversion. Though the 1950s were prosperous years, they were also precarious; according to Updike in this poem, "the Bomb . . . was realer then," and humanity's very existence on the planet was tenuous because of the standoff between the super-powers. The threat of nuclear annihilation was no less real in the 1970s, but it seemed less immediate, partly because of détente and the SALT talks, and partly because the world had survived thirty years with the Bomb. Fur-thermore, the easy distinctions between "Us and Them" in the 1950s—the division of the world into the Red and the free, to use the terms of King Edumu in *The Coup*—had become blurred by the 1970s when the battle-grounds shifted from the shadowy halls of the Kremlin to the less familiar if more palpable landscapes of Vietnam, Afghanistan, and Iran. Many of Up-dike's characters become nostalgic for the early Cold War not because life in 1950s America was necessarily better than life in late Cold War America, but because it was so much easier to read. Updike's writings during the 1970s convey a sense of confusion about the way American attitudes to-ward world politics were evolving, and a longing to return to those "Cold-War years *par excellence*," if only to remove the burden of trying to sort through the events of the 1970s and 1980s—the conflicting tensions, the unexpected fronts, and the increasing sense that if American identity were threatened, the American individual would be powerless to change it. As he says in a 1985 interview, "If a new McCarthy should arise, would I stand up against him?—I would have my doubts if I could achieve much."[1]

Late Cold War America found the future difficult to predict. The year 1984 came and went, and Orwell's famous projection of an invasive total-itarian Western government was not significantly more accurate than it had ever been. Despite Soviet President Gorbachev's progressive policies of glasnost (openness) and perestroika (restructuring), Presidents Reagan and Bush tried to renew early Cold War rhetoric in order to paint Ameri-ca's beleaguered enemy as a real threat. Popular writers such as Tom Clancy, Robert Ludlum, and John le Carré churned out international spy thrillers that cast the Russians in the same cold, malignant light they had been in since Khrushchev pounded his shoe on a U.N. negotiating table years before. In short, Updike was not the only one looking back fondly on the days of sockhops and Sputnik, but his backward glance is note-worthy because it lingered and took hold of the latter half of his oeuvre, providing a way to classify even his experimental novels like *The Coup*

1. Plath, *Conversations with John Updike*, 174.

(1978), *Brazil* (1994), and *In the Beauty of the Lilies* (1996) in the way that sexual frankness and the modern quest for spirituality have been used to categorize his earlier work. Critics and reviewers who are baffled by these later projects need only look at the impact of the Cold War on all of Updike's writings to explain why this nostalgic turn is a perfectly understandable development. The consistency of his nostalgic response underscores the enduring influence of early Cold War thinking on his writings and on the American mind-set more generally.

The young Updike who tried to avoid the Cold War gives way in the mid-1970s to a writer who realized how impossible it was to do so. Although history has always been one of his focuses, it becomes nearly an obsession in his later works, as one can easily see from *Buchanan Dying* (1971), *Memories of the Ford Administration* (1992), and *In the Beauty of the Lilies*—fiction as carefully researched as history books. To read through the newspaper clippings, history articles, letters from experts, and other research matter related to *In the Beauty of the Lilies* deposited in Updike's files at the Houghton Library would take much more time than it would take to read the novel itself. This increased emphasis on history undoubtedly stems from the passing of a historical era along with the uncertainty of what would follow it. By the 1970s Updike had developed into a writer obsessed with chronicling the American present, but with the collapse of the Soviet Union, he retreated into the past. The end of the Cold War seemed like "the end of history," to borrow the title from Francis Fukuyama's controversial 1989 study. Updike confirms this idea in a 1990 interview when he says that Harry Angstrom in 1989 is plagued by the idea "that the postwar world is surely ending."[2] Updike's focus on the past as the Cold War waned was consistent with contemporary American thought and with a pattern in American history; according to cultural historian Tom Engelhardt,

> The loss of boundaries beyond which conflict could be projected and of an enemy suitable for defeat in those borderlands meant a collapse of story. The post-Vietnam War years have so far represented only the afterlife of this societal crisis, the playing out of storylessness. It is hardly surprising that, after 1975, the basic impulse of America's political and mil-

2. Ibid., 226.

itary leaders (as well as many other Americans) was not to forge a new
relationship to the world but to reconstruct a lost identity of triumph.[3]

The early Cold War, for all of its terror and paranoia, had provided Americans with a kind of unified meaning and opposition to an other that they
had always leaned on for their national identity, according to Engelhardt.
This identity began to break down during the Vietnam era for Updike and
for many Americans like him. If America were to continue to prosper, it
would have to find some replacement for the shattered Cold War consensus that opposed the monolith of communism.

Nostalgia in Updike's later work is a response to the uncertain future,
but it is also a tribute to Cold War America, which managed to live through
a volatile recent past based on the strength of its national character developed in the fifties. Updike began in the 1970s to gaze back fondly on
his salad days because he felt that America's development into the only
real superpower had something to do with a set of core values more evident in the Eisenhower era. Updike felt that Americans were happier before Vietnam because, in spite of McCarthy and the Bomb, they had a sense
of appreciation and a unified goal to be the last one standing in the ring.
"Our lives . . . were not assumed to be/ Our right," he declares, and he sees
the struggle to fashion a national identity by establishing a Cold War consensus as the trait that allowed America to flourish while rust spots were
becoming visible on the Iron Curtain. In "The Fifties: Each Man Was an Island," a revealing essay he wrote for *Newsweek* in 1994, Updike apologizes
for the years that "got a bad rap from their successor decade" (MM 26); he
writes, "I was happy in the Fifties. . . . Many Americans were happy in the
Fifties—but not as happy, looking back, as we should have been" (MM 25).
After Americans exercised their collective concern about the future in the
form of social unrest and activism during the 1960s and 1970s, Updike's
characters begin to romanticize the past, as Updike himself does in 1994
when he writes, "the hectic Sixties, hot and (in my mind's eye) a psychedelic red, would wreck our Fifties marriages, shatter our faith in the anti-
communist crusade and leave scarcely a hero standing" (MM 29). While acknowledging that those years of simmering discontent were not without

3. Tom Engelhardt, *The End of Victory Culture: Cold War America and the Disillusioning of a Generation,* 15.

their problems, Updike chooses to emphasize their potential for growth and prosperity. America's eventual emergence as the Cold War winner validates such a perspective; yet we can see the origins of this perspective in Updike's fiction as early as the Nixon era.

Updike's nostalgia for the fifties began well before the Cold War actually ended. Vietnam bifurcated the Cold War for him, and when Nixon began to pull U.S. troops out of Indochina, Updike began to look back wistfully at a bygone era. Through Updike's eyes, the fifties are a mythical, romantic time, and they are invariably years of prosperity, growth, and marital bliss. The narrator of "When Everyone Was Pregnant" (1971), collected in *Museums and Women,*[4] is nostalgic for the old Cold War and for its attendant happiness. Yet there is a strong sense of loss from the moment he introduces himself: "I'm in securities, but I read a lot, on the train. Read yesterday that the Fifties were coming back. All through the Sixties writers kept knocking them: Eisenhower, Lester Lanin, skirts below the knee, ho-hum. Well, turns out Eisenhower was a great non-war President. Rock is dead. Skirts have dropped to the ankle. But *my* Fifties won't come back" (MW 91). His possessiveness of the decade causes us to wonder what the difference is between *his* fifties and the *actual* fifties. There is certainly a split between him and the "Sixties writers" who "knock" the previous decade. The 1960s counterculture was united in its rejection of the previous decade as a time of complacency and intellectual and artistic stagnation. Liberal writers of Updike's generation were allied with the younger generation on this issue; Robert Lowell refers to the decade as "the tranquillized Fifties,"[5] for instance. For the narrator of Updike's story, the fifties

4. Separation is a prominent theme in *Museums and Women,* and these stories are characterized, like *Rabbit Redux,* by marital strife, infidelity, and the specter of divorce. The narrator of "One of My Generation" tries to elicit the gratitude of the younger generation by reverently discussing Ed, a former roommate who begins as a headstrong, ineffectual student of poets and ends as a pawn in the Cold War game—a minor CIA agent. The narrator treats it as a way to understand the world and his place in it. The narrator of "The Witnesses" points out that his story takes place during "the high noon of the Eisenhower era" (MW 71), and recalls how he and the other characters discuss such events as "McCarthy's fall" and Dulles's "brinkmanship interview." In both of these stories, the consequence of nostalgia and the inability to change one's worldview results in isolation from the rest of the world.

5. Robert Lowell, "Memories of West Street and Lepke," in *Selected Poems* (New York: Farrar, Strauss, and Giroux), 91.

were not so much tranquillized as tranquil, or in his own words, "Not only kind but beautiful years" (MW 91). Women in the flush of youth cavort around beaches with children and men admire them, shuffling off from time to time to make money. This is, of course, the stereotypical vision of 1950s America, and on the surface it seems as though this narrator is completely sincere and secure in his nostalgic bubble. He characterizes this 1950s world by its bravado, and its opposition to the Soviet other, describing himself and his generation as "young, newly powerful, born to consume. To procreate greedily. A smug conviction that the world was doomed. Beyond the sparkling horizon, an absolute enemy. Above us, bombs whose flash would fill the scene like a cup to overflowing" (MW 93). This narrator shares with the narrator of "Packed Dirt" a "knowledge of an immense catastrophe," and he is convinced as Piet Hanema is that sexual licentiousness is connected to the certainty that the world could be destroyed by nuclear war instantaneously.

The difference between this scenario in "When Everyone Was Pregnant" and in the other stories is that this narrator treats the early Cold War milieu as a cause for celebration, ignoring or dismissing the fear and turmoil of the times. There is a single "absolute enemy" in the 1950s, and the narrator contrasts the old way of thinking to the new way: "Korea seemed the best bargain we could strike: extremities of superpowers tactfully clashing in distant cold mud. The world's skin of fear shivered but held. Then came Eisenhower and gave us a precarious peace and sluggishly rising market and a (revokable) license to have fun, to make babies. Viewed the world through two lenses since discarded: fear and gratitude. Young people now are many things but they aren't afraid, and aren't grateful" (MW 93). The final sentiment echoes Harry Angstrom's debate with Jill in *Redux* about fear versus love; in both cases, fear and the natural opposition to an enemy are evils necessary to keep people in motion. Fear is just a thin skin stretched over something volatile, something "precarious." Nostalgia is justified, it seems, because the license to have fun was at some point revoked, presumably during the social upheaval of the 1960s; this generation had to grow up, and to yield to the next generation. The narrator reluctantly does so as he concludes his story: "Now: our babies drive cars, push pot, shave, menstruate, riot for peace, eat macrobiotic. Wonderful in many ways, but not ours, never ours, we see now" (MW 97).

This passage is just part of his earlier recognition that his youth "won't come back."

The narrator's yearning for the 1950s is more than just a lament for lost youth, though; it is evidence of the psychological impact that the Cold War had on Updike and his generation. The early years of the Cold War, with their disregard for the future combined with fear and gratitude, render the past so inviting that Updike's narrators tend to forget that the fifties were anything but fun. Yet the narrator of "When Everyone Was Pregnant" casts a shadow of doubt on the reality of his vision, wondering, "Did the Fifties exist?" (MW 97). Earlier he says of the parties he is describing, "Should remember them better" (MW 93). He also obliquely admits his guilt: "Can never be revisited, that time when everyone was pregnant guiltlessly. Guiltlessness. Our fat Fifties cars, how we loved them, revved them: no thought of pollution. Exhaust smoke, cigarette smoke, all romantic" (MW 92). There is a pang of regret here, and more than a pang of guilt, but nostalgia helps the narrator to feel less guilty. "Everyone" was doing it, as the title suggests. On the other hand, the narrator has claimed that they are *his* fifties.

The narrator of "When Everyone Was Pregnant" also contrasts marital bliss and innocence in the 1950s with deceit and treachery in the 1960s, and he suggests a parallel between the domestic sphere and the Cold War situation. During the fifties couples dance and squeeze hands, "all innocent enough" (MW 95). He describes the fifties as "a house decade, never ventured into the streets. Cuba, Sputnik, Tibet" (MW 95). In 1960, he notes, "The parties got wilder. . . . Over the ocean, riots. Assassinations, protests, a decade's overdue bills heaped like surf thunder on the sand bar. We were no longer young" (MW 95–96). Nor were they innocent; the certainty of an absolute enemy allows them to be content with their day-to-day existence, but the narrator associates the uncertainty of the 1960s with infidelity, and even dates the first wild, licentious party at the turn of the decade: "might have been 1960" (MW 95). All that remains from the decade he yearns to return to is his unaltered response to the Cold War world; he concludes the story by realizing, "I am still afraid. I am still grateful" (MW 97). Nostalgia becomes a mechanism to preserve a stable sense of self. It does not matter whether one's recollection of the past is accurate or not; the impression of the past as a better time makes the present more bearable, though inferior.

This type of nostalgia is far from uncomplicated, though. Updike is aware that it can be dangerous to become too firmly entrenched in the past, as is illustrated by Tom Marshfield's inability to adapt to the new Cold War in *A Month of Sundays*. He is finally isolated from his community because of his inability to update his views and cope with the changes of the geopolitical situation. The danger of Marshfield's unbending 1950s ideology is taken to greater extremes in *The Coup*.[6] Like Marshfield and Harry Angstrom, Colonel Ellelloû thrives on competition, thinks differently about world politics than those around him do, and is ultimately exiled as a result of these beliefs. This pattern is more obvious in *The Coup* than in the other novels; perhaps more clearly than any of Updike's other works, *The Coup* describes a world whose very basis is the global conflict between the United States and the Soviet Union.

Even though *The Coup* is undeniably Updike's most political book, critics have attempted to depoliticize it, focusing on spirituality instead of contemporary history. Updike has described the book as "a kind of global parable," and it is clear that the reader is to learn something about the current state of the world from Ellelloû's tale.[7] One prominent lesson is that the inability or unwillingness to adapt to changes in global conflicts can prove catastrophic to nations and individuals alike. As is the case in Up-

6. "God Speaks" (1965), collected in *Museums and Women,* is a noteworthy precursor to *The Coup.* It is Updike's first story that takes place on international Cold War territory, and describes a central Asian country named Nuristan which is a focal point for the struggle between the United States and the Soviet Union. The leader of this nation is assassinated in 1962; the assassination is "so ambiguous in its effects that both the Russians and the CIA were rumored to have been responsible" (MW 182). The narrator's friend, Gish Imra, is the son of the assassinated leader and returns to his country, trying to convert it to an autonomous state. The narrator recalls a conversation they had about a class they had taken at Harvard called "Cross-Currents in Nineteenth Century Thought." The narrator, a Lutheran, allies himself with Heidegger and Gish Imra allies himself with Marx, perhaps against the trends of his father's reign, which was influenced by "perhaps excessive helpings of American advice and French cuisine" (MW 184). The narrator sees Gish's attempt to convert his country to a state of "cultural autonomy" as an extension of his God-like status; the narrator's feelings of inferiority are related to his inability to escape the power struggle between Russia and America, which is something Gish is ultimately able to do.

7. One such attempt to depoliticize *The Coup* is Malini Schueller, "Containing the Third World: John Updike's *The Coup,*" 113. For Updike's description of the book, see Plath, *Conversations with John Updike,* 169.

dike's other books written during the 1970s, *The Coup*'s underlying conflict is more complicated than a simple polarization of the East and West.
The Cold War front has in essence been fragmented; America and Russia
confront each other covertly on African soil. Both superpowers exploit
Kush and its people economically and militarily, attempting to disguise
their presence all the while. In Ellelloû's eyes, the Soviet presence in Kush
is less overt than the American one. This disparity can be explained partially by the fact that his vendetta against America runs much deeper than
his problems with the Soviet Union do because he feels that America has
betrayed him. He also senses that America is winning the larger war, and
the battle for Kush in particular; American economic exploitation has the
upper hand over Soviet military exploitation by the end of the novel.

The status of Kush as a battleground for Soviet and American forces is
clear enough; yet critics still overlook this conflict. Malini Schueller's article, "Containing the Third World: John Updike's *The Coup*," is a conscious
attempt to discuss the book in the context of politics and history. Schueller
fails to mention the Soviet Union even once in the article, though, and
instead sees the conflict between the United States and Kush as the primary one: "The plot of *The Coup* is a narrative of the Third World well
rehearsed in the Western imagination. . . . The historical plot is a thinly-
veiled fantasy of expansionism, disguised as the familiar rationalization of
the inability of the Third World natives to govern themselves."[8] I suggest
rather that the operative rationalization in *The Coup* is the domino theory that controlled American ideology throughout the Cold War—that if
"we" fail to establish control within a small, economically underprivileged
country, "they"—the Soviets—will succeed. There is evidence in the novel (as well as in Cold War history) that this fear is more than "fantasy."

The so-called Third World, and Africa in particular, was a hotbed of Cold
War activity in the late 1970s, setting up that decade's dramatic Cold War
finales in Iran and Afghanistan. The African continent during this period
was riven by a series of clashes between countries that tended to be
aligned with either the United States or the Soviet Union. African nations
were likely to see-saw in their alliances during these precarious years, serv-
ing as puppet states and battlegrounds for Cold War maneuvers. Despite

8. Schueller, "Containing the Third World," 115.

President Carter's initial intent to negotiate and reduce the global nuclear arsenal, this new phase in Cold War history was characterized by a return to the pre-détente way of thinking about the Cold War. This condition un-doubtedly compelled Updike to examine the effects of Cold War threats and tensions in their most apparent location. His files on *The Coup* in the Houghton contain dozens of articles detailing military upheavals in African nations in the mid-1970s. Most of the articles from both academic journals and the popular press articulate the idea that coups d'etats such as the one described in *The Coup* had more to do with the superpowers than with the smaller, powerless, individual African nations.[9]

Soviet and American presence is felt throughout the novel; Schueller's claim that Updike's representation of Kush is "the third world as Other" fails to acknowledge that the primary Other is still the Soviet Union. Kush is a void between the two—what Updike calls "the emptiest part of the world I could think of"—which serves as a Cold War battlefield.[10] Ellellou's struggle to achieve an identity as well as his constant revisions of this identity are emblematic of his country's identity crisis. Ellellou summarizes this crisis succinctly in a one-sentence paragraph: "But who, in the world, now, does not live between two worlds?" (Coup 73). Despite his resistance to the worlds represented by the superpowers, Ellellou cannot imagine his existence without them. Furthermore, he is constantly "between" them—not entirely with one against the other—because in the 1970s the once-clear border between the two worlds has become fuzzy.

The Coup begins with Ellellou's perception of Kush as a small country "landlocked between the mongrelized, neo-capitalist puppet states of Zanj and Sahel" (Coup 13). This description is a paradigm for the remainder of the novel; Ellellou's project is to define himself and his country against other people and countries that have given in to U.S. influence. As the novel

9. Some of the titles of these articles and their sources are: "Soviet Running a Protection Racket" (*Boston Herald American,* Professor John P. Roche, May 29, 1977), "U.S. Bides Time, Beds Down with Strange Comrades" (*Boston Globe,* James O. Jackson, January 2, 1977), "Somalia Trying to Live by Both Koran and *Das Kapital*" (*New York Times,* John Darnton, October 11, 1977), and "U.S. Loses Old Friend in Africa: Ethiopia Looking Toward Marx and Moscow" (*Boston Globe,* Crocker Snow, Jr., November 19, 1977).

10. Schueller, "Containing the Third World," 118. Updike's statement is in Donald Greiner, *John Updike's Novels,* 30.

progresses, it becomes increasingly clear that Kush is, like its neighbors, a puppet state; yet it is a puppet tossed back and forth between Soviet and American hands. As Ellelloû continues his initial definition of Kush, he places his country in opposition to "America, that fountainhead of obscenity and glut" (Coup 13). Indeed, his original depiction of Kush casts it as the antithesis of America; Kush embodies "The pure and final socialism envisioned by Marx, the theocratic populism of Islam's periodic reform movements" (Coup 17). In the early stages of the novel Ellelloû believes firmly in his wide-eyed view of Marxism, and he allies himself in early Cold War fashion with the idea that America is diametrically opposed to the Soviet Union, which includes, by extension, his own country.

Yet the conflict between the superpowers in the 1970s was more complex than Ellelloû believes it to be. America spread its global influence in this decade economically as well as militarily. The ineffectual King Edumu points out this fact to the high-minded Ellelloû:

> "Your friends the Russians," he said, "are generous exporters of spies and last year's rockets. They themselves buy wheat from the Americans."
> "Only to advance the revolution. The peasantry of America, seeing itself swindled, seethes on the verge of riot."
> "The world is splitting in two," said the king, "but not in the way we were promised, not between the Red and the free but between the fat and the lean." (Coup 26–27)

Ellelloû's inability (or refusal) to see the king's wisdom arises from his will to see the world in terms of early Cold War oppositions. This inability ultimately proves to be Ellelloû's flaw; the Cold War has changed since Ellelloû's college days in 1950s America, and his belief in the persistent reality of early Cold War oppositions renders him unable to cope with the problems posed by new Cold War configurations. As a result, Ellelloû, like the protagonists of Updike's other 1970s fiction, destroys the world around him, and he is ultimately exiled from his native land.

The events of the first section of the novel detail Ellelloû's fall from power. He visits a Soviet military bunker set up covertly in his own country and wonders privately at its decadent decor. He supervises the murder of a US-Aid representative named Gibbs, who is burned alive while standing atop "a pyramid of crates, sacks, and barbarically trademarked boxes. USA USA USA, they said, *and Kix Trix Chex Pops*" (Coup 47). Assaulted by American materialism, he takes decisive action by publicly executing the king who, after being tortured, "hurled at [Ellelloû] an absurd litany of American trade-names—'Coca-Cola! Polaroid! Chevrolet! IBM!'" (Coup 82). All of his anti-American actions and his alliance with the Soviets stem from a fierce refusal to accept that the world has changed, as the king told him; the force that polarizes the world is now economics, not ideology. Ellelloû's refusal to accept that fact loses him his dictatorship and his identity. He falls out of favor with the Soviets, who undermine his power by stealing the executed king's head and transforming it into a mechanized prophet in a distant mountain region.

Feeling alone, once he has commenced his quest to confront the talking head in the mountains, Ellelloû can finally begin to narrate his experiences in the United States. We discover that his time in America began in 1954, at the height of the old Cold War. This thread of Ellelloû's narrative is the most candid segment of the novel; in telling of his experiences with Candace in Wisconsin (at the pointedly named McCarthy College), he seems more human and more vulnerable than when he is president of Kush. Ellelloû describes McCarthy College in the 1950s in careful detail. It is a world characterized by middleness; Updike's readers are in recognizable territory for the first time during the novel: "Everything in America, through that middle bulge of the Fifties, seemed to this interloper fat, abundant, and bubble-like, from the fenders of the car to the cranium of the President" (Coup 145). Ellelloû paints his years at McCarthy College as an innocent time, all ice-cream sodas and football games; but the Cold War tensions are apparent. He notes of Esmeralda Miller, "she claimed she was a Marxist, in these days when that was a deadly serious thing to do" (Coup 152). Contention, an idea that Ellelloû has come to accept as part of human nature, is all around him in Wisconsin, usually in the form of racism or debate about race. Yet even in a lengthy discussion with Candace's racist father the Cold War atmosphere is apparent. Ellelloû responds to one of Mr. Cunningham's points about African Americans with a remark about American individualism and enterprise, and Cunningham replies, "Christ, if that's enterprise, let's give it all over to the Russians. They've got the answer. Concentration camps" (Coup 170). Cunningham goes on with his tirade using the rhetoric of the atomic age, claiming that Black Americans have "done to Newark what we did to Hiroshima" (Coup 170).

In this atmosphere, Ellell3 begins to form his philosophy, which does not change once he returns to Africa. During these formative years he senses the injustices of history and he critiques both American culture and Marxism, which, he feels, has failed to address the reality of the contemporary Western world. He tells Esmeralda, "Your Communism is such a failed gesture. In the industrialized countries of Western Europe, where Marx reasoned the uprising must come, the Communist party officials wear suits with vests, and sidle forward for their share, as you Americans say, of the pie" (Coup 190). Workers in America, he claims, "are thoroughly enrolled in consumerism, making junk and buying junk, drinking junk and driving junk," and this condition amounts to "a kind of poisonous mush abroad in the planet" (Coup 189). This period in Ellellou's intellectual development explains in part his wide-eyed idealism once he becomes president of Kush. He embraces a pure version of Marxism, one that he sees no evidence of in the Western world.

Ellellou's intellectual development is complicated by his sexual experiences, and his feelings of hatred toward Candace's world. "There is a tension that screwing her relieves" (Coup 187), he tells Esmeralda, and this tension is obviously generated partly from the cultural baggage carried by their different races, and partly from his difficulties in dealing with women in general. Yet Cold War tensions also affect the tension he associates with sex. His sexual encounter with Esmeralda at the Young Communist Club becomes symbolic for him as he enters a new phase in his life, both sexually and ideologically:

> [Esmeralda] had no climax, and he had been distracted by the giant red poster of Lenin, goateed and pince-nezed, staring upwards with the prophetic fury of a scholar who has just found his name misspelled in a footnote. "She ain't even taught you how to screw," Esmeralda said, pleased to have an additional score on Candy, and depressing her lover with the hint that their fornication, in such romantic surroundings, had been merely an extension of a propaganda campaign. To an extent, it worked; he looked more kindly upon Marx thereafter, as Marx, from a poster on the other wall, grandfatherly and unfoolable, had looked kindly down upon the heaving buttocks of the future Ellellou. (Coup 194)

This passage clearly demonstrates Ellellou's position on both Marxism, which seems benevolent to him, and Soviet-style communism, which is intimidating to the point that it distracts him from sex. This moment serves to explain further Ellelloû's reluctance to shed his old beliefs once the Cold War changes in the 1970s. Marx approves of Ellelloû, in his mind, and although Leninism frightens him, it is the next best thing to the type of socialism he desires. The red and furious poster of Lenin represents power to Ellelloû, the type of power that has been taken away from him by virtue of his status as a Black man in 1950s America and by Esmeralda's comment about his poor sexual performance. He sees sex as part of a "propaganda campaign"; the Cold War has affected even the most private aspect of his life.

Ellelloû leaves America with a greater understanding of history, world politics, and philosophy, but also with a confused sense of his role (and, by extension, Kush's role) within the world. He takes his leave of Dr. Craven, a professor of government at McCarthy who teaches a course entitled "U.S. *vs.* U.S.S.R.: Two Wayward Children of the Enlightenment" (Coup 213). Not entirely enlightened himself, Craven reveals his racial prejudices when he tries to dissuade Ellelloû from bringing Candace back to Africa. Ellelloû responds in terms of now-familiar Cold War rhetoric: "distinctions in tint of skin have no priority in the world that my professors, you foremost, have taught me must be welded into one, lest the nuclear holocaust transpire" (Coup 216). Ellelloû sees Craven as just another representative of American ideology; he retrospectively notices a resemblance between Craven and Gibbs, the martyred USAID agent, and as a parting shot in his interview with Craven, he says, "Good luck in your Cold War, your battle against Sputnik" (Coup 218). This moment is his final impression of America, and it serves as a capstone for his experiences there. America fails to welcome him and treats him as an outsider in the 1950s; his persistent hatred of Western values and his misguided alliance with the Soviet Union are based on this experience.

Having established the basis of his ideology, Ellelloû's narrative returns to his confrontation with the mechanized head of King Edumu. The head, rigged by the Soviets and (ironically) used to make money as a tourist attraction, urges its spectators to overthrow Ellelloû; it says,

> This man, while proclaiming hatred of the Americans, is in fact American at heart, having been poisoned by four years spent there. . . . He has grown weary of seeming to hate what he loves. Just as nostalgia leaks into his reverie, while he dozes above the drawing-board of the People's

Revolution so vividly blueprinted by our heroic Soviet allies, so traces of decadent, doomed capitalist consumerism creep into the life-fabric of the noble, beautiful, and intrinsically pure Kushite peasants and workers. (Coup 228)

There is some truth in this allegation, made apparent by Ellelloû's narrative of his formative years in America, which create in him romantic nostalgia for the beauty of America and, simultaneously, hatred of America for rejecting him. Even as he describes the scene in the cave, he criticizes Soviet technology and speculates that the Americans could do better. Despite his struggle to achieve and maintain an identity in the Cold War world, he realizes that he cannot succeed if he removes himself from the struggle between the superpowers. After revealing to the crowd that he is Ellelloû, he concedes, "my identity was unsettled until one of the Soviets came forward and shook my hand" (Coup 233). The Soviets' attitude toward him is condescending at best. As an explanation for the Soviets' manipulation of the king's head, Colonel Sirin says, "It is very boring, in the bunker. As part of *détente,* our government has instructed us to mingle more freely with the local population" (Coup 234). At this point Ellelloû's fervent struggle to form his own and his nation's identity is proven futile, since he is clearly still a mere pawn for the superpowers. He notes, "The wires leading into my head were as many as those into the dismantled king's" (Coup 235). He continues his quest to see the Americanized town of Ellelloû in the Ippi Rift, but he does so with "the weariness of the destined, who must run a long track to arrive at what should have been theirs from the start: an identity" (Coup 235). When Opuku fails to carry out his orders to machine-gun the tourists at the site of Edumu's head, Ellelloû's rhetoric is lacking in spirit. Betrayed by his loyal assistants, and fearing for the safety of his wife Sheba, he is finally able to acknowledge the realities of the new Cold War; he tells Opuku, "You will be Xed out by Exxon, engulfed by Gulf, crushed by the U.S., disenfranchised by France" (Coup 241). Ellelloû no longer speaks in terms of 1950s Cold War rhetoric, which shows that he recognizes at last the wisdom of Edumu's words and that he admits defeat.

The Ippi Rift,[11] where the city of Ellelloû is located, serves as a geo-

11. In a note to himself contained in his file on *The Coup* at the Houghton Library, Updike refers to the Ippi Rift as "the Hippie Rift." I took this slip to reveal that the place

graphical metaphor for Ellelloû's tardy recognition of the way the world is developing: "the Rift marks the line along which Africa will eventually break in two—not, as would seem from a human standpoint sensible, along an east-west axis" (Coup 250). The "human standpoint" that Ellelloû speaks of is that of recent history, born of early Cold War thinking. When he observes that the town which bears his own name resembles exactly a small town in the United States, he claims, "Where money exists, there must have been pillage: Marx proves this much. There must be capital, exploitation, transmutation of raw materials. In a word, industry" (Coup 253). The war, signified by the word "pillage," has become economic at last for Ellelloû, and he attempts to work within its context, donning American-style clothes instead of his traditional orange-peddler's disguise. But his knowledge of America is inextricably linked to the 1950s; when he asks a clerk for a drink from a soda fountain, the clerk points him to a soda can dispenser, observing, "You are living in the past" (Coup 255). Ellelloû makes a final attempt to update his thinking; in his speech exhorting the workers in the town of Ellelloû to destroy the oil refineries, he says, "The battle now in the world lies between the armies of necessity and those of superfluity" (Coup 271). His cries fall on uncaring ears, though; the war has been fought and won on this front, and Ellelloû retreats, once again, into nostalgia. He takes a job as a short-order cook in a luncheonette and becomes, more completely than ever before, an American. Working happily to the tunes of a jukebox that contains records straight from "America of the Fifties" (Coup 276), he internalizes the message of the music: "Even the grill grew hotter, the fast food came faster. And when the whistling section of 'The River Kwai March' penetrated us, we knew, knew in our bones, that we would win the Cold War. Freedom, like music, rolled straight through the heart" (Coup 277).

Ellelloû's transformation from a demagogue resistant to change to an American wage worker is far from happy. His change reflects a change in the world, but not necessarily one for the better. Klipspringer, the Ameri-

---

underscored the 1960s as a dividing time in American history, which makes perfect sense in terms of Ellelloû's experience: he is trying to recapture the relatively unscathed America that existed in the 1950s before the "Hippie rift" ensued. In a 1998 letter, Updike assured me that the slip was unconscious: "No, Ippi was meant to be a pun on Mississippi, one of the many allusions that make Kush a disguised U.S. The African rift and the central American river [are] doppelgangers."

can emissary to Kush who is sent to restore ties, proposes a toast: "Here's to 'er, Mother Change. A tough old bitch, but we love 'er" (Coup 283). When Ellelloû enters soon after this scene, Ezana observes, "Would that change, so bumptiously saluted by our American emissary, were all there were to the world. As well, there is a deadly sameness" (Coup 285). There are echoes in this passage of the post-Vietnam stories discussed in chapter 4: both "More Stately Mansions" and *The Witches of Eastwick* are violent, gradual acceptances of the principle of change. In *The Coup* it is clear that the Cold War has changed, but in some ways it has merely disguised itself. The problems Ellelloû has in trying to keep up with the changes are shared by many Americans, and the difficulty adapting to change has taken its toll; Candace tells Ellelloû, "But it's boring back home [in America] now. The Cold War is over, Nixon's over. All that's left is picking up the pieces and things like kissing OPEC's ass. You'd be depressed. It turns out the Fifties were when all the fun was, though nobody knew it at the time" (Coup 289). The Cold War is not over at this time, but the version that Candace and Ellelloû knew in the 1950s is. The "fun" is also over, she maintains, and Ellelloû agrees; it is impossible to return to "those Cold War years *par excellence*," though, and the difficulty of this transition into the new Cold War explains the state of mind of Updike's protagonists in the 1970s. These characters are alike in their dismay with the world around them and their inability to find ideological common ground with others. The new Cold War does not provide the same type of structure for thinking about the world that the old Cold War did. Since the globe is no longer as clearly divided as it once was, these characters retreat into nostalgia, isolation, and paranoia. The fifties were "when all the fun was," and not coincidentally, there was an absolute enemy to serve as the scapegoat. The complications of the new Cold War leave Updike's characters scrambling for a cause, or a new structure with which to order the world.

In the years between the publication of *The Coup* and *Rabbit at Rest* (1990) Americans simulated the early Cold War, most notably by electing as president a 1950s screen actor. Reagan charmed the nation into believing that it needed elaborate defense systems to guard against the evil empire that lurked, as ornery as ever, on the other side of the world. Magazine advertisements for scotch whiskey touted the good things that always come back in style—the perseverance of short hair, gray flannel

suits, and corned-beef-on-rye sandwiches despite some wild and taste-
less fads in the 1960s and 1970s. Reagan-era Americans, who lacked the
postwar prosperity of their 1950s predecessors while sharing their ideology, spent money as though debt were simply a fact of life. The Cold War
couldn't be ending, they insisted; it had been too *good* to them. And how
would they construct the future? The enemy was now a faceless terrorist
blowing up American planes over Scotland rather than a harsh army general glowering over maps in the Kremlin.

Harry Angstrom is obsessed with the bombing of Pan Am flight 103 and
with other terrorist activity in the last book of the Rabbit tetralogy. Americans in the late 1980s and early 1990s were not psychologically prepared
to cope with global terrorism as the replacement for the Cold War. Although the threat of terrorism was not the same as nuclear annihilation,
it was a real threat: the Soviet Union did not kill any Americans during the
Cold War, but more than one hundred people died when Pan Am flight 103
exploded over Scotland. Moreover, the threat of terrorism is random, unlike the obscure but definite spy-vs.-spy calculations of the CIA and the
KGB during the Cold War. It is understandable, in these terms, why Harry
would become nostalgic for the early Cold War. In his article "Appropriating the Scene: The World of *Rabbit At Rest,*" Dilvo Ristoff links Harry's nostalgia for the early Cold War to an editorial by Peter Tarnoff ("Bizarre Nostalgia for the Cold War") published in the *New York Times* in 1989.
Tarnoff's essay was published on the same day that Senate Majority Leader
George Mitchell accused the Bush administration of nostalgia and "ambivalence . . . about the dramatic transformation now under way in the
Eastern bloc." Mitchell continues: "This ambivalence is difficult to understand." The Bush administration's will to preserve the old Cold War even
as the Soviet Union was reconfiguring itself may have been belligerent and
backward, but it is not difficult to understand. Reporting on Mitchell's
comments, Thomas Friedman refers to "Administration officials who seem
to prefer the *certainties* of the cold war over the *uncertainties* of Mr. Gorbachev's changes" (emphasis added).[12] Tarnoff quotes Secretary of State

12. Ristoff's citation for Tarnoff's article is incorrect; the article appears on page
A25 of the *Times,* not A14. Thomas L. Friedman, "Senate Leader Asserts U.S. Fails to
Encourage Change in East Bloc," *New York Times,* September 19, 1989.

Lawrence Eagleburger, who described the old Cold War as "characterized by a remarkably *stable* and *predictable* set of relations among the great powers" as contrasted with the present "in which power and influence is diffused among a multiplicity of states" (emphasis added).

In short, the early Cold War, despite its anxiety, was preferable because it was more stable, more certain than the unsettled present or the potentially chaotic future. Tarnoff warns against the dangers of this nostalgia as a potential romanticizing of the past: "Are memories so short that the days of the Berlin airlift, Cuban Missile Crisis and bloody regional conflicts in Vietnam and Afghanistan as well as murderous phases of Soviet internal repression are remembered as preferable to the current, albeit uncertain, state of affairs?" He concludes, "the Administration should look to the future, not the past."[13] He was probably right, but the solution wasn't necessarily that easy for the Bush Administration or for Americans like Harry who had no way of imagining anything beyond the Cold War. Four years after Mitchell's comments and Tarnoff's editorial, Americans were still wrestling with this identity issue, as we can see in a *New York Times Magazine* piece by Friedman entitled "Cold War Without End": "For the past 40 years, the Federal bureaucracy was largely shaped by the confrontation with Moscow. Who *we* were was in many ways defined by who *they* were, and what *we* were about was in many ways defined by what *they* were up to. . . . All of this makes for a very odd twilight moment. While some agencies are quickly adjusting to the end of the cold war, others hang on to the past, not so much because they believe it is coming back but because no one has yet come up with anything to replace it."[14] This attitude trickled down from the U.S. government to its citizens, and in Harry's case hanging onto the past was a way of avoiding the future, which contained the possibility that whatever replaced the Cold War would be worse.

Updike seals the coffin on Harry and on the Cold War simultaneously, suggesting that his most enduring anti-hero is ill-equipped to cope with the changing face of world politics. Nostalgia functions in *Rabbit at Rest* as a means of regaining a lost period of happiness; it is the alternative to

13. Peter Tarnoff, "Bizarre Nostalgia for the Cold War," *New York Times*, September 19, 1989.

14. Thomas L. Friedman, "Cold War without End," *New York Times Magazine*, August 22, 1993.

a meaningless present devoid of religious faith. The consequences of Harry's poorly lived life are evident by his decline; his nostalgia cannot compensate for his failing health and peace of mind in the way that religion could. He makes a bald pronouncement of his attitude toward the monumental shifts in the world in 1989: "'I miss it,' he says, 'The cold war. It gave you a reason to get up in the morning'" (Rest 293). He reiterates this idea as his death approaches: "Without the cold war, what's the point of being an American? Still, we held out. We held off the oafs for forty years. History will remember that" (Rest 367). The most relevant source of Harry's identity—his status as an American citizen, underscored by his dressing as Uncle Sam in a Fourth of July parade—dissipates as the Cold War ends. His life becomes part of "history" even before it is over, and he takes pride in the fact that his generation will not be forgotten. Yet he cannot go on living because, as he says in this passage, "what's the point?" The Cold War is all he has known; the remainder of his life, except for his memory, will be insignificant. The monumental changes in the world in 1989 thus explain Harry's newfound interest in history books, or his thrill at watching a documentary about Russians battling Nazis during World War II, back when he collected scrap metal for the allied cause, "a ten-year-old participant in actual history" (Rest 244).

Stacie Olster acknowledges Harry's nostalgia for the early Cold War, but argues that "the absences that pierce his heart most deeply he expresses with respect to less monumental things" such as the minutiae of his youth: movie stars, songs, even candy.[15] His romantic view of these icons reflects his general unwillingness to accept the younger generation. The last two Rabbit novels are increasingly about Harry's conflict with Nelson, who is fighting, he senses, to replace him. This sense of approaching death becomes a dominant motif in *Rabbit at Rest;* to understand Harry's fear of his own mortality—his hatred of Nelson, his existential angst—we must understand how his view of the world, based as it is upon Cold War tensions, is slipping from under him in 1989. Americans could scarcely imagine a peaceful end to the Cold War. Harry, who always lacked imagination, has not prepared himself for the fall of the Soviet Union. He is so steeped

15. Stacey Olster, "Rabbit Rerun: Updike's Replay of Popular Culture in *Rabbit at Rest,*" 48.

in the Cold War mind-set that even a flowering suburban tree causes him
to think of "those old photos of atomic bomb-test clouds in the days when
we were still scared of the Russians" (Rest 264). Far from a cause for re-
joicing, the Cold War's abrupt conclusion is, for Harry, a tragedy.

There are post–Cold War parallels to Harry's domestic battles with his
son; speculation surrounding the terrorist bombing of Pan Am flight 103
pervades the novel, as does renewed economic competition with Japan.
Yet Harry seems too weary to participate in the new geopolitical games,
finding it easier to turn back into his memory. His cynicism about the present state of the world links the end of the Cold War to his own mortality:
"Vocations drying up, nobody wants to be selfless any more, everybody
wants their fun. No more nuns, no more rabbis. No more good people, waiting to have their fun in the afterlife. The thing about the afterlife, it kept
this life within bounds somehow, like the Russians. Now there's just Japan,
and technology, and the profit motive, and getting all you can while you
can" (Rest 226). Just after this observation Harry examines a picture of his
failing heart through an x-ray machine. Though he doubts the existence
of an afterlife, it suddenly becomes all too real for him. According to this
observation, the end of the Cold War signifies the end of meaningful existence for Harry; without it, life amounts to a game without rules. The waning of the Cold War has caused him to realize, as he has suspected all along,
that his life has been pointless: "the whole point of his earthly existence
has been to produce little Nellie Angstrom, so he in turn could produce
Judy and Roy, and so on until the sun burns out" (Rest 38). Without the
Russians and the afterlife to keep him in bounds, Harry begins a series of
pathetic attempts to regain his youth—seducing his son's wife, reassert-
ing his authority at Springer Motors, and playing a round of basketball
against a kid forty years his junior that results in his cardiac arrest. In his
waning months, desperately following a lifelong pattern, Harry tries to recapture lost youth, yearns for the Cold War, and initiates an active interest
in history. Given his anticlimactic death, these nostalgic activities seem futile and pathetic. The past is only a temporary shelter.

Given the late-1980s climate of history's ostensible end, it is not surprising that history becomes a concern of Harry's in 1989, nor is it surprising that history becomes the very subject of Updike's next novel. The
title alone of *Memories of the Ford Administration* emphasizes Updike's

continued fascination with the most confusing years of the Cold War in terms of the way the simple oppositions of the 1950s disappeared. The book's narrator, Alfred Clayton, a historian at Wayward College, is asked to contribute to a written symposium on the Ford years; like all of Updike's first-person narrators, Clayton is self-involved to the point of narcissism, and his account becomes more about himself (and his fascination with James Buchanan) than about Ford. In order to justify his ultra-subjective approach to history, Clayton apologizes to the editors of *Retrospect,* who solicited his contribution: "When I first received NNEAAH's kind and flattering request to contribute to its written symposium, I ventured to the library and flipped through a few reference books, the kind of instant history that comes from compiling old headlines, and was struck by how much news is death, pure and simple. . . . Surely, *Retrospect* editors, you don't want this sort of thing, which any sophomore with access to a microfilm reader that hasn't broken its fan belt can tote up for you. You want *living* memories of those of us fortunate enough to have survived . . . the Ford administration. . . . Enough time slides by, we're all history, right?" (MFA 8–9). Clayton is arguing for a living, cultural history here, and his motivation for producing such a history mimics that of Harry in the last books of the Rabbit tetralogy, or Ellelloû in *The Coup:* he is seeking to recapture a lost time of innocence, which corresponds with both his first romance and with the early (simple) years of the Cold War. He falls into a reverie about the early 1960s: "Salad days! Days of blameless leafing out! I had all the equipment of manhood except a grown man's attitude. My queen, my palely freckled and red-headed bride, still had her waist then, her lissome milky legs, and an indolent willingness to try anything. Lyndon Johnson's supercharged Sixties were about to break upon us like a psychedelic thunderstorm" (MFA 5). The point of disruption occurs for Clayton, as it did for Updike, during the high years of Vietnam, when innocence and the sense of American hegemony simultaneously ended.

The measurement of personal history against public history in *Memories of the Ford Administration* mirrors the disruption in Clayton's life and the sense that the Cold War is changing. Thinking back to a 1975 party, Clayton locates that moment in history as a crossroads for Americans, and he explicitly associates it with the loss of our earlier innocence. He concludes, like the narrator of *Couples,* that the peaceful end of the Cold

War was nearly a letdown for Americans who tended to live for the moment, and like Harry in *Rabbit at Rest,* he emphasizes the need for limitations to our free-spirited lifestyle of the kind posed by the presence of the Soviet Union:

> It was a great month for Americans: a Soviet pilot defected with an advanced MiG-25 . . . our Space Shuttle was unveiled. . . . I cannot hear any of this in the rumble of the party, though it all would have been fodder for our swelling hilarity; what I hear instead is a certain mid-Seventies disappointment that the sky had not fallen, that we as a nation, a faculty, a circle of aging adults were obliged to plod on. We had worn love beads and smoked dope, we had danced nude and shat on the flag, we had bombed Hanoi and landed on the moon, and still the sky remained unimpressed. History turned another page, the Union limped on, the dead were plowed under, the illegitimate babies were suckled and given the names of wildflowers and Buddhist religious states, the bad LSD trips were being paid for by the rich parents who covered the bills from the mental institutions. Young American men and women, sons and daughters of corporation lawyers, had sinned against the Holy Ghost and got up the next morning to take a piss and look in the mirror, to see if there was a difference. There didn't seem to be. Everything was out of the closet, every tabu broken, and still God kept His back turned, refusing to set limits. A President had been shot, a war had been lost, our empire had been deemed evil, our heavenly favored-nation status had been revoked, the air had been let out of our parade balloon, and still we bumped on, as we had in 1865, with wandering steps and slow, as out of Eden we took our solitary way. (MFA 247 – 48)

Clayton's reflection says much about the time in which he wrote it — the years just following the end of the Cold War in 1989. Looking back, he is able to locate a day of reckoning in American history that coincides with the end of his own promiscuous behavior. The Ford years — not usually a period of history associated with monumental significance — are positioned crucially in terms of Updike's version of the Cold War. The aftermath of Vietnam, the triumphs of the Space Race, and the self-indulgence of the Baby Boomers were rapidly becoming "history" and Clayton sees that Americans during this period were coming to terms with the way the world was changing. Like Adam and Eve emerging shamed from their state of innocence, Americans were able to continue on their path in the waning years of the Cold War, but there was a cost.

This cost, according to Clayton, was a lack of self-confidence, a compli-
cation of the way things are that plunges him into nostalgia. "A fellow historian called ours a culture of narcissism," Clayton writes, "The Ford era
was a time of post-apocalyptic let-down, of terrifying permissiveness"
(MFA 248). This permissiveness allows Clayton to escape the horror of the
post-apocalyptic let-down that he describes in the above passage. Like Piet
Hanema or any of the other swinging suburbanites in *Couples,* Ford-era
promiscuity was a way for Clayton to avoid confronting the possibility of
the apocalypse, and also a way to assert his American right to freedom. At
the moment he decides to commit his fatal error of sleeping with the
mother of one of his students, thereby ruining his chance for eternal happiness with Genevieve (the "Perfect Wife") he muses, "as de Tocqueville
was among the first to point out, Americans prize freedom above all other goods. Tied though I was, to two women, five children, a mother, and
an unfinished book, did I have no rights of movement? Was this the Soviet Union, where one needed a permit to go from Omsk to Tomsk?" (MFA
217). Clayton must invoke the old Cold War threat of totalitarianism in order to justify the way he misuses the licentiousness of the times; but, we
must keep in mind, he is writing from a nostalgic perspective when fears
of Soviet governmental control have subsided. He longs as Harry does for
the days when a competitive global structure would help him to explain
or justify his actions, when the Russians would keep things within bounds.

Looking back on the Ford years from an early 1990s perspective, Clayton associates profound loss with the luxury to free himself from the responsibilities of monogamy and of thinking about the implications of the
Cold War. During a three-day tryst with his mistress Genevieve he is able
to escape these pressures, if only temporarily. Not coincidentally, he and
Genevieve are in New York so that he can attend a conference entitled
"Cold-War Deformations of Developing-World Economies and Elites" (MFA
168). Throughout the three days of this affair he attempts to escape history metaphorically by avoiding the conference and by spending the entire time eating and having sex. "Life must now and then be allowed to take
precedence over history—else there will be no new history" (MFA 168),
he declares with a flourish of bravado; yet he cannot escape history. While
buying a souvenir for one of his children on this trip, he is reminded of a
souvenir his parents had bought for him from the 1939–1940 World's Fair,

when he was four years old: "It lit up, somehow, and had a curving ramp of many tiny bas-relief people, streaming into the future, which was now. No—which had never been. World war, Holocaust, cold war, oil spills, famine, massacre, serial killing, man the vermin of the planet: the innocent future I had seen in that glowing souvenir, with a helicopter in every garage, had never come" (MFA 169). This litany of terrible developments in Western history after 1940 shows that Clayton cannot escape history, especially as it is associated with a loss of innocence. His attempt to escape history is futile, but, like his nostalgia in 1990, it is the only alternative he has when his world seems to be falling apart. He declares to his first mistress, whom he refers to as the Queen of Disorder, "I'm trying to lead an orderly life" (MFA 11); Clayton's increasing inability to maintain such order in his life is related to his sense that history is falling apart in front of his eyes. His impulse to use the article for *Retrospect* as a chance to record an apology for his life links his desire for order to his desire to have things the way they used to be, before the simple order of the old Cold War fell apart entirely.

Updike again returns to a bygone era—the late 1960s and early 1970s— in *Brazil,* and he again combines the impulse to retreat from history with the theme of a lost innocence. He removes himself from the American landscape altogether, but unlike *The Coup, Brazil* is nearly devoid of references to America or contemporary Western history in general. In this novel Updike escapes the sense of history that is so prominent in his later writings; he digs into myth and uses the techniques of magical realism to weave a narrative of two young lovers who try to stay together despite various forces that conspire to keep them apart, notably opposition from Isabel's father. The novel confronts contemporary history for the first time during a debate about Marxism versus bourgeois values reminiscent of the debate between Ellelloû and his classmates in *The Coup.* The debate takes place when Isabel is at college, in 1966; just as the discussion is heating up, and it seems that Isabel will become involved, her lover Tristao arrives and the two of them escape into a mythical world that renders time irrelevant. Once their journey leads them back to Brasília, though, the novel locates itself within the context of the Cold War. Upon their return, we are informed that Isabel's "father was no longer Ambassador to Afghanistan, where King Muhammad Zahir Shah had been deposed by a group of young military officers increasingly subject to Soviet influence" (B 218). He tells the lovers how he has become assistant minister of Interior Development, assistant to a minister "whose sole authentic passion is spying on the Argentines and Paraguayans to make sure they have no rocket or supersonic jet fighter in their arsenals that we do not also have. He is quite paranoid about it, and imagines that Castro is getting all sorts of wonderful Russian goodies which our alignment with the Western imperialists is denying him" (B 222–23).

In short, the isolated world Tristao and Isabel left as children has become influenced by the superpowers. This change sets up the tragic end of the novel. Tristao, who has survived enslavement as well as a host of other human indignities, has remained essentially the same during his journey with his lover through Brazil's interior; but upon return to the changed world of Brasília he becomes thoroughly bourgeois, and though he and Isabel live happily for a while, he wakes one day to find that he "craved the old innocence" (B 253). Innocence is once again associated with a time before the radical changes of the late 1960s; the material results of conforming to the world he encounters when he returns to the city of his youth—his expensive clothes and Rolex watch—have made Tristao an easy target for muggers, who are more vicious than he had been as a mugger during his youth. The book comes full circle; Tristao falls victim to street criminals as an adult just as he victimized others when he was young. There is a period of lost innocence and an attempt to escape history during the late 1960s and early 1970s. These parallels between *Brazil* and *Memories of the Ford Administration* serve to highlight how nostalgia functions in Updike's post–Cold War novels; the end of contemporary history as he knows it leads to a reflection on the time when history becomes disrupted.

Reviewing Updike's career throughout the Cold War and during the dozen years that have passed since its end, one can easily see why it would inform his identity as an author to such a degree. As the most prominent Protestant American writer of his generation, he is in some senses the heir apparent to the Puritan ethos, particularly John Winthrop's profession of America as "a citty upon a hill." Updike himself acknowledges this connection in "The Cultural Situation of the American Writer": "The United States was settled by Protestants, and its expansion has continued, right up to the moon shots, in the ethos of Protestantism. . . . Luther and Calvin freed men to be independent, competitive, and lonely; and so Americans are."[16] Yet the city upon a hill concept had different implications during the Cold War. The leaders of the city on the hill had the power to destroy the city, the hill, and everything surrounding it. Placed in such a position of power, Cold War Americans ran the risk of losing sight of their mission and their faith in God. This is precisely the point of *In the Beauty of the Lilies;* we see a progressive loss of faith traced over four generations reach a brutal climax in the early 1990s. But this is also the point of *Couples, Rabbit, Run,* and virtually every story, poem, and novel discussed in this study. In one form or another, God punishes Updike's Americans for getting off track, for losing their humility. In many cases, this punishment occurs as Americans drift away from their early Cold War ideals: their fear of a threatening other and their gratitude for the bounty God has given them.

For Updike, the end of the Cold War represents this loss of fear and gratitude. As Harry Angstrom says in his dying years, the Russians, like the afterlife, kept America within bounds somehow (Rest 226). Without predetermined boundaries, Updike's Americans will have to set their own. This prospect is not comforting. During Vietnam, the last time Updike's characters had to define their national identity, the result was chaos and domestic strife. The same is true of *In the Beauty of the Lilies:* the violence and tension that would once have been channeled toward a national ideology are now directed inward. In place of consensus, we have a house divided against itself, as was the case during the Vietnam war. Post–Cold War Americans fight their own government with the blind rage of the faithless; religion becomes nothing more than a vehicle for anger. Updike's version of the American dream, with one eye on the afterlife and the other on the cornucopia of the present, has become an apocalyptic nightmare. The loss of faith in modern America has always been one of his favorite topics, and *In the Beauty of the Lilies* underscores this theme and showcases his augmented awareness of the forces of history and the powerful turn toward nostalgia in his later work.

Though *In the Beauty of the Lilies* spans four generations leading back to the 1910s, the final apocalyptic tragedy is set up in the third and most compelling section, which takes place during the 1950s. Essie's screen ca-

16. Updike, "Cultural Situation," 25.

reer gets off to a shaky start when she bungles her answer to the question, "How would you make the world a better place?" during a beauty contest. "Some of the girls wanted to talk forever, about the Iron Curtain" (IBL 278), but Essie responds by stating that she would end the communist witch-hunt in Hollywood. When the m.c. pauses menacingly and asks her, "Do I understand you to say, Esther, that you don't believe there is a Communist threat?" she realizes her mistake and falters, ruining her chances at early stardom: "There is," she responds, "but it's b-being exaggerated, and b-being used by politicians to get themselves p-p-publicity" (IBL 282). Her family tries to comfort her after her performance, all except for her fourteen-year-old brother Danny, who declares, "I hate Communists. . . . They don't play fair. They steal elections. They put everybody who disagrees with them into concentration camps" (IBL 283). Danny goes on to become a CIA agent who weathers the changes of the Cold War admirably while Essie's life becomes pathetic. Her fault is that she appreciates the country she lives in, but she isn't grateful for it; "She didn't really mean to defend Communists. She couldn't even picture one, or imagine why anybody would want to overthrow the American way of life, with its football and cheerleaders and hollyhocks and soda fountains and new Studebakers" (IBL 283). Her problem is that, unlike Updike, she doesn't recognize that someone has to pay for the American cornucopia. Even so, her starry-eyed appreciation for "the American way of life" clearly contains elements of Updike's own nostalgia; her sentiment clearly reflects his post–Cold War longing for "the innocent Fifties" (A 223).

The narrator of *In the Beauty of the Lilies* constantly reminds us that he is looking back at bygone days rather than projecting us into them; he rattles off litanies of news events, or speaks of the "smoldering Fifties discontent" (IBL 332) of certain films that Essie sees to remind us that he knows what will follow. The perspective of this novel encourages us to locate meaning in the past, whereas Updike's early books concentrated more on the ephemeral present. We look back on each generation of the Wilmots to discover the cause of their faithlessness, which leads by extension to the faithlessness that plagues our contemporary world. It is no accident that Essie's faith in herself falters during the Red scare; her mediocre success as an actress and her wayward son both seem linked to her unwillingness to embrace the Cold War consensus. Her brother Danny represents the opposite extreme; he becomes increasingly passionate about politics as she concentrates on her career. When their grandmother praises Essie for her films, he reminds us of the national concerns of the times: "Danny, as if hearing himself slighted, came into the kitchen from the living room, where he had been watching the six o'clock news on television. 'Well, the Soviets have successfully tested their intercontinental ballistic missile,' he announced aggressively. 'So they have one, and we don't'" (IBL 344). The siblings have a symbiotic relationship, mediated by their attitudes toward America: "The more [money] she made . . . The more the government took to pay people like Danny to fight the Cold War" (IBL 347). They argue during one of her rare visits home about the relative worth of each other's career. She defends herself by saying, "the movies have never pretended to be anything except entertainment. But what you're doing pretends to be a good deal more. 'It pretends to be history,' he said quickly. 'It *is* history. Cast of billions. The future of the globe at stake. I kid you not'" (IBL 347). Danny's severe stance on the global rivalry counters Essie's flippant attitude toward it, and suggests that her flaw may be her lack of gratitude toward the country that has given her so much.

Her attitude in the 1950s carries over to the book's tragic final section when her career and her son Clark are both in decline. We learn that she "wanted North Vietnam to win, which seemed strange to Clark, since America had been pretty good to her" (IBL 365). The anti-American rhetoric of Jesse, the leader of the cult that draws Clark into its folds, is also linked to the still-open wounds of Vietnam: "I was there [in Vietnam] to descend into Hell," he tells Clark, who responds, "My uncle's in the CIA" (IBL 384), as if to continue the opposition the novel has set up between Clark's mother and his uncle. Danny is nearly an emissary trying to sway Clark away from Essie's lack of support for her country, a condition that sets the stage for his joining the cult. Clark recalls Uncle Danny's visits fondly, remembering how they drove around Los Angeles listening to classical music and talking politics. When Clark asks Danny how the United States could have made such a mistake by getting involved in Vietnam, Danny questions this viewpoint:

> "It got us into China," Uncle Danny told him. "It got us the two SALT agreements. We've got Mao and Brezhnev each trying to kiss our ass. Nobody's

supposed to say this, but Vietnam impressed the right people. The superpowers all agree, the North Vietnamese are pricks. . . . What the kids
don't seem to see is that their freedom to grow long hair and smoke pot
and shit on poor Tricky Dick is based on the willingness of someone else
to do their fighting for them." (IBL 393)

This is familiar rhetoric from Updike's Vietnam-era books, but placed as it
is in this novel it carries the weight of history. That is to say, the fact that
Updike still chooses Vietnam as the turning point for a nation that has lost
its faith underscores how powerful his nostalgia has become. "I love this
crazy, wasteful, self-hating country in spite of itself" (IBL 394), Danny tells
Clark, and we hear Updike's voice echoing this statement. Updike believes
that when Americans failed to appreciate their nation's achievements in
the 1960s—the decade that "shatter[ed] our faith in the anti-Communist
crusade" (MM 29), we lost something that was fundamental to our national
character.

This idea follows its logical path to tragedy in the novel's conclusion.
The CIA sends Danny to Cambodia and Clark is left with only his self-
involved mother as a role model. We hear periodically about Danny's re-
assignments to East Germany in 1983 or back to Washington when the
Cold War comes to its startling conclusion in the late 1980s. But the damage to Clark's personality has been done by Danny's absence; the anti-
government fervor that seized America in the years just after the Cold
War—most evident in recent national tragedies like the war between the
FBI and the Branch Davidian cult or the related bombing of a government
building in Oklahoma City—have their foundations in the breakdown of
the Cold War consensus, according to this novel. Clark tells the deputy
who attempts to arrest the cult leaders for not paying taxes, "we live independent here, and ask no services" (IBL 425), and the deputy replies,
"You ask to be protected from the Russians. There's a lot you people ask,
without knowing it" (IBL 426). Danny, the consummate Cold Warrior, sums
up America's post–Cold War dilemma when he declares, "We beat the
Communist pricks and now the world is full of other pricks" (IBL 489).
The West's seeming victory over the communists doesn't offer any real security. It is even possible to argue just the opposite; the "other pricks" who
fill Danny's world are cult leaders and terrorists who are especially dangerous because they are so unpredictable. The "other pricks," certainly,

provide a more sinister kind of opposition than the "Communist pricks" did. Soviet communism and American democracy, though not always amicable, seemed like well-matched opponents; but anti-American terrorism and American democracy do not even seem to be playing the same game. Americans will not be able to forge a new identity simply by defining their nation against anyone who hates it. Updike is obviously distressed by the disturbing events of recent years such as the incident at Waco, and he digs back into the past in this novel to locate the reasons behind what he sees as a national identity crisis.

He suggests, in his writings from "When Everyone Was Pregnant" on, that this crisis would not have occurred if Americans could have kept living as they did in the 1950s. It was the best of times, in his memory; he writes, "The Fifties in my mind's eye are a waxy blue-white, a shining cold-war iceberg drifting by in the wake of the khaki-brown Forties and the grit-gray Thirties" (MM 25). This idyllic post–Cold War nostalgia for the decade when fidelity and prosperity reigned supreme is complicated by his concession in *The Coup* and *Rabbit at Rest* that people had either to adapt to changes in the Cold War or be left behind. Nostalgia lends form to his most recent works, and it highlights how important the Cold War has always been in his writing. The question that Updike, like all Americans, must ask now is, "What's next?" Without a clearly defined opponent to lean against, where will America turn for self-definition? Nostalgia, after all, can only last so long before it becomes a trap. As Updike acknowledges in a response to an interviewer's question about *Memories of the Ford Administration,* "neither history (the determined study of past events) nor memory (in the form of nostalgia) can really bring back the past."[17] The problem for Updike, as for all post–Cold War Americans, is to find a strategy to prepare for the future.

Tom Engelhardt in *The End of Victory Culture* argues that the unnerving end of the American tale of victory during Vietnam leaves a narrative void; he sees a trend in the post–Cold War era toward diverse and multicultural stories, "the attempt to uncover, express, and in some sense celebrate experiences and points of view previously ignored within the boundaries of the story." Although these stories "seemed initially to

17. Plath, *Conversations with John Updike,* 233.

promise a future revised and far more 'diverse' yet inclusive national tale,"
Engelhardt does not see how this fragmentation can approximate the type
of American story that fell apart during the Cold War; "implicitly or explicitly, [these stories] remain part of the breaking down of one story, not
the building up of another. Without the larger story—or at least a memory of it to play off of—they may have no national existence."[18] In trying to
write about life in America after the Cold War, Updike is caught within the
same kind of quandary: what will be the larger story that provides a background for all of his smaller stories? He does have the memory of the Cold
War "to play off of," and that memory becomes the powerful force behind
the nostalgia that characterizes his latest fiction. His recent short fiction
collected in *Licks of Love* (2000), which takes its title from a story called
"Licks of Love in the Heart of the Cold War," continues to use the fifties as
a setting, suggesting that Eisenhower's presidency was, as Candace tells Ellellou in *The Coup,* "when all the fun was" (Coup 289). It was also when
domestic stories had a relationship to national identity, when "the violence
and tension that does exist beneath even the most peaceful seeming life"
could be explained in terms of the overwhelmingly dominant national ideology that reached a disconcerting fever pitch during the McCarthy years.

Following Updike as he crosses and recrosses the boundaries of ideological consensus over the course of the Cold War, we see a conflicted
writer who is torn between emotional reverence for the country that has
given him so much to be thankful for and intellectual distance from the
countrymen who have disappointed him through their failure to show
their appreciation for their great if troubled nation. Yet throughout his career, whether he was sounding a warning against nuclear catastrophe or
defending his stance on Vietnam, he has shown his willingness to examine the changing face of American identity. His disposition "to take contrary positions and to seek for nuances within the normal" (SC 146) gives
him an edge as a social commentator. He will ultimately prove that he is
not *exclusively* a Cold War writer. For now, Updike has the memory of the
Cold War to contend with. But, if history is any guide, the remainder of his
career will locate some new structure that will contextualize "the daily do-
ings of everyday people" (PP 482) that serve as the basis for his fiction.

18. Engelhardt, *End of Victory Culture,* 301.

Conclusion

End of Time or Afterlife?

The thing about the afterlife, it kept this life in
bounds somehow, like the Russians.

-John Updike, *Rabbit at Rest*, 1990

THE RUSSIANS, in Harry Angstrom's poignant observation, set limits for Cold War Americans in search of an identity. American life after the Cold War is potentially chaotic, or even meaningless, like life without an afterlife. Updike elaborates upon Harry's sentiment by naming his first post-Cold War collection of stories *The Afterlife* (1994). Continuing the trend discussed in the previous chapter, the "afterlife" of the Cold War in these stories is characterized by a bittersweet return to earlier, better years. Nostalgia is evident to even a cursory reader of this collection. Virtually every story in the collection takes the perspective of an aging, adulterous man who longs to recapture a period of lost innocence, and who is conscious of his own mortality. Like Harry, these characters struggle in the wake of the Cold War for a reason to get up in the morning. Updike turns his gaze toward the quotidian in these stories; post-Cold War developments in history and culture do enter the stories, but they simply do not have the lasting impact that the Cold War did. The narrator of the title story notes about Carter, the protagonist, "There were, it had recently come to him, vast areas of the world he no longer cared about—Henry James, for example, and professional ice hockey, and nuclear disarmament" (A 15). Nuclear disarmament—*The Portrait of a Lady* and the Boston Bruins aside—had been an issue that Carter, like all of Updike's characters, was forced to think about all his life. We again have the sense that Updike's characters are at a loss for what to do in the wake of the Cold War. This postwar scrambling for order leads Jay Parini to conclude, in a review of *The Afterlife,* "One argument consistently made against Mr. Updike is that he often ignores history or merely uses it as a backdrop for his otherwise claustrophobic tales. This is true enough; in fact, one sorely misses in his work some consciousness of the larger web in which families, and individuals, operate."[1] I would, of course, argue with the assessment that Updike ignores history, or even that it functions as merely a backdrop, and I am surprised that anyone could reach such a conclusion just two years after the publication of *Memories of the Ford Administration,* a novel that foregrounds history to as great a degree as any contemporary American novel I have read. What Parini may be responding to is Updike's turn toward the daily lives of his protagonists as an alternative to the Cold War nostalgia his works embody during the post-Vietnam era.

History is in fact the driving force of Updike's works, yet his view of history is always a way of commenting upon the present. His excavations of our nation's history over the past century in *In The Beauty of the Lilies* or his return to the Buchanan presidency in *Buchanan Dying* and *Memories of the Ford Administration* are means of exploring some past conflict that complicates present-day America. His nostalgic return to the pre-Vietnam era in the works I discuss in the previous chapter represents a similar impulse. Yet with the Cold War decidedly over, it is not surprising that he has turned to another era in his most recent works. It is also not surprising that this era is the near future.

After the end of the Cold War, the present is almost maddeningly unknowable for Updike, whose worldview has been so permeated by the ongoing rivalry between the global superpowers. Predictions about the future amount to the same thing as nostalgia for the past: both offer alternative ways of considering the present by playing around with possibility. In "Bech and the Bounty of Sweden," the final story in his recent collection *Bech at Bay,* Updike finally allows Henry Bech to break away from his own

---

1. Jay Parini, "All His Wives Are Mother."

CONCLUSION   179

experiences. Bech has followed Updike through the Soviet Union, through book tours and college lectures, and through Updike's tenure as the president of the American Academy of Arts and Letters, but in this story Updike projects a couple of years into the future and awards Bech the Nobel Prize. The incident is humorous and ironic, but it is significant in that it allows Updike to break free from the nostalgia for the Cold War era that has dominated his most recent works. Updike's characters are still alive in the future, the author seems to be saying; there is an afterlife.

Yet there is also an obsession with endings. Bech's acceptance speech is his final comic display: he scrambles around trying to get his words together, then ends up bringing his infant daughter onto the stage with him and letting her communicate a speech they have together worked out: "The Nature of Human Existence," which consists of the young girl's saying "hi" into the microphone followed by "the gentle clasping and unclasping motion that signifies bye-bye" (Bay 241). Bech, in his obsession with his own ending, his own mortality, is like Updike's other post–Cold War protagonists. Harry in *Rabbit at Rest,* various narrators in *The Afterlife,* and especially Ben Turnbull in *Toward the End of Time* (1997) are preoccupied with death and with the ephemerality of life. The past may have so much meaning because the future is difficult to predict, more so than usual in the absence of a stable global configuration.

This other characteristic of Updike's most recent work—his focus on the mysterious future in addition to nostalgia for the past—is a direct result of the vacuum left by the end of the Cold War. When Americans speculated about the future during the Cold War, the outcome was predictable: the Soviet Union, that hostile enemy, had initiated the unthinkable: the world was a post-apocalyptic nightmare of totalitarian mind-control. The future was horrifying but imaginable. The current post–Cold War mindset, fueled by millennium fever, renders the future more difficult to envision. As a result, the present is inscrutable. Beginning his acceptance speech for the Nobel Prize, Bech says, "I could talk to you about the world . . . as it exists in this year of 1999, waiting for the odometer to turn over into a new millennium, watching to see if Islamic militants will lock ever more of its surface into a new Dark Age, or if China will push the United States aside as a top superpower, or Russia will spit out capitalism like a bad fig, or the gap between those who ride in airplanes and those who drive ox-carts will widen to the point of revolution or lessen to the point of Disneyfied, deep-fried homogeneity—but what, my distinguished friends, do I know of the world? My life has been spent attending to my inner weather and my immediate vicinity" (Bay 238 – 39). Bech is only a fictional and fantasized version of his author, though. Updike may have wanted to spend his life attending more to his "inner weather" and his "immediate vicinity," but he does in fact know something of the world, and he has relentlessly explored America's place in that world through his fiction. Despite its backward glances, his work has always found a way to look at the present, to write, as Dilvo Ristoff says, "with a map of the socioeconomic and political concerns of America in mind."[2]

Updike's fiction is about the intersection of history and the present, and despite its projection into the future, *Toward the End of Time* is no exception. Ben Turnbull is obsessed with time, and his experiences include not only nostalgic reveries characteristic of Updike's other post–Cold War writings but also entrance into parallel universes. The reader enters these universes along with Ben; we are abruptly in ancient Egypt, or accompanying St. Paul in Rome, or listening to a monk in medieval Ireland, or hearing the perspective of a guard in a Nazi concentration camp. These parallel universes seem to be a blend of the narrator's imagination, memory, and fantasy, but it is possible that they are also literally the fracturing of time into a new dimension. *Toward the End of Time* is further complicated by its setting in the future: the novel takes place in 2020, after a Sino-American conflict has made the world a radioactive dump, depleted the population, and rendered the U.S. government obsolete.

Updike projects a future based on one of the very scenarios about which Bech refuses to speculate. In 1995 Updike wrote, "The global other these days seems divided between the Arabs and the Chinese"[3] rather than the Russians. *Toward the End of Time* alludes to a war between the United States and China, but the effect of this war is essentially to weaken America by breaking down its already weak consensus. There is no more federal government; the police barely exist, and there is not even a currency to unite the country. Artificial insects called "metallobioforms"

2. Ristoff, *Updike's America,* 10.
3. Updike, letter to author, 1995.

threaten to devour humanity, a "torus" floats on the horizon like another moon, causing wonder and fear about the possibility of extraterrestrial life, and the only security comes from adolescent thugs who demand protection money from individual citizens.

The future as Updike imagines it is clearly not a comfortable or happy place. Yet much of the novel is recognizably the present, and there is a glimmer of hope that comes in two entities: nature, and the next generation. Ben's wife Gloria is obsessed with her garden, and her attendance to it, with Ben's help, bespeaks a faith that nature, despite the destroying effects of humanity, will survive. The younger generation is an emblem of the future. The final sentences of *In the Beauty of the Lilies,* describing the survivors of a Waco-like siege of a cult, foreshadows Updike's sentimental attachment to the youngest Americans as the hope for the future: "Then a concluding zoom of the four or so women with smoky faces coming out of this storm hutch like they're scared they're going to be shot, then stepping into the open, squinting, blinking as if just waking up, carrying or holding on to the hands of their children, too many to count. The children" (IBL 491). Bech similarly returns to the Romantic wisdom of his infant daughter in his Nobel acceptance speech, and Ben Turnbull is revived and rejuvenated not through his sexual forays with the young Dierdre or the even younger Doreen, but through his visits to his ten grandchildren. He sums up his own life, and recent history, in the following passage:

> Though some grandparents looked ten years younger than I, and some as many or more years older, I was basically among members of my own generation. We had experienced birth in the conformist Fifties, adolescence in the crazed and colorful Sixties, and youth in the anticlimactic drug-riddled, sex-raddled Seventies. We had by and large dodged our proud nation's wars, the Cold War skirmishes and then the hideous but brief Sino-American holocaust. . . . It was amazing to me how many we were: white-haired and arthritic, we were like the specialized plants that spring up a week after a forest fire has apparently swept all life into ashes. And our multitudinous grandsons were there to carry mankind deeper into the twenty-first century, to the brink of the unimaginable twenty-second. (TET 145–46)

The future is "unimaginable" here, even as Updike has projected a future world. Yet the hope for the future is expressed in terms that unite the novel's regenerative strains: nature in the form of "the specialized plants that spring up a week after a forest fire," and the younger generation. When a gang of shiftless adolescents squats on his property and demands protection money, Ben takes the opportunity to instruct them in the ways of American business ethics, entreating them to create a structure of trust and encouraging them to negotiate rather than to intimidate. Despite the breakdown of his country's values, he believes there is still something essential in the American character that will prevail; he says, "At least that much was left of the United States after the Chinese war—a belief in fairness, rudimentary rights guaranteed to everyone regardless of creed or color" (TET 168). This simple belief in the goodness of his democratic American life coupled with his faith in nature's power to renew itself and in his grandchildren's potential to pick up where he has left off makes Ben's twilight somehow bearable. He is preoccupied with the recent collapse of the world and with the ultimate collapse of the universe, but he manages to hang onto a glimmer of hope. Contemplating the collapse of the universe and the end of time, he encounters an epistemological quandary: "But *can* time end? Space can be obliterated with the matter that measures it, but can time excuse itself from the grammar of sequence? It *was* implies a present that still *is*. . . . My own mind quails. The blue shift is tens of billions of years from heating the interstellar space by so much as a degree Fahrenheit. I am safe in my nest of local conditions, on my hilltop in sight of the still-unevaporated ocean. . . . The very short view alone is bearable" (TET 328–29). This sentiment is something like Henry Bech's assertion that he does not know anything about the world, that he has enough to do to keep up with his inner weather and immediate surroundings. In both cases, Updike's characters realize their limitations with regard to the future. Trying to imagine what the world will be like is ultimately unbearable. Yet the fact that two of Updike's most recent fictions take place in the near future implies a willingness to move into that future. The near future is only *toward* the end of time, and, for the time being, that may be enough.

Bibliography

Adams, John G. *Without Precedent.* New York: W.W. Norton, 1983.

Anisfield, Nancy, ed. *The Nightmare Considered: Critical Essays on Nuclear War Literature.* Bowling Green, Ohio: Bowling Green University Popular Press, 1991.

Atwill, William D. *Fire and Power: The American Space Program as Postmodern Narrative.* Athens: University of Georgia Press, 1994.

Bacon, Jon Lance. *Flannery O'Connor and Cold War Culture.* Cambridge: Cambridge University Press, 1993.

Bloom, Harold, ed. *John Updike.* New York: Chelsea House, 1987.

Boyer, Paul S. *By the Bomb's Early Light: American Thoughts and Culture at the Dawn of the Atomic Age.* New York: Pantheon, 1985.

Boyers, Robert (moderator). "An Evening with John Updike." *Salmagundi* 57 (summer 1982): 42–56.

Broer, Lawrence R., ed. *Rabbit Tales: Poetry and Politics in John Updike's Rabbit Novels.* Tuscaloosa: University of Alabama Press, 1998.

Burchard, Rachael. *John Updike: Yea Sayings.* Carbondale: Southern Illinois University Press, 1971.

Calleo, David. *Beyond American Hegemony: the Future of the Western Alliance.* New York: Basic Books, 1987.

Campbell, Jeff H. "'Middling, Hidden, Troubled America': John Updike's Rabbit Tetralogy." In *Rabbit Tales: Poetry and Politics in John Updike's Rabbit Novels,* edited by Lawrence Broer. Tuscaloosa: University of Alabama Press, 1998.

———. *Updike's Novels: Thorns Spell a Word.* Wichita Falls, Texas: Midwestern State University Press, 1987.

Caputi, Jane. "Psychic Numbing, Radical Futurelessness, and Sexual Violence in the Nuclear Film." In *The Nightmare Considered: Critical Essays on Nuclear War Literature,* edited by Nancy Anisfield. Bowling Green, Ohio: Bowling Green University Popular Press, 1991.

Cline, Ray S., ed. *Understanding the Solzhenitsyn Affair: Dissent and its Control in the U.S.S.R.* Washington, D.C.: Center for Strategic and International Studies, 1974.

Cousins, Norman. "When American and Soviet Writers Meet." *Saturday Review* (June 24, 1978): 42–45.

Derrida, Jacques. "No Apocalypse, Not Now: Full Speed Ahead, Seven Missiles, Seven Missives." *Diacritics* 14, no. 2 (summer 1994): 20–31.

Detweiler, Robert. *John Updike.* New York: Twayne, 1972.

Dorris, Michael, and Louise Erdrich. "The Days after Tomorrow: Novelists at Armageddon." In *The Nightmare Considered: Critical Essays on Nuclear War Literature,* edited by Nancy Anisfield. Bowling Green, Ohio: Bowling Green University Popular Press, 1991.

Edsall, Thomas. *Chain Reaction.* New York: Norton, 1991.

Engelhardt, Tom. *The End of Victory Culture: Cold War America and the Disillusioning of a Generation.* New York: Basic Books, 1995.

Friedman, Thomas L. "Senate Leader Asserts U.S. Fails to Encourage Change in East Bloc." *New York Times,* September 19, 1989.

———. "Cold War without End." *New York Times Magazine* (August 22, 1993): 28–31.

Fukuyama, Francis. "The End of History?" *The National Interest* 16 (summer 1989): 3–18.

Gillon, Steven M., and Diane B. Kunz. *America during the Cold War.* Fort Worth, Texas: Harcourt Brace Jovanovich, 1993.

Greiner, Donald J. *John Updike's Novels.* Athens: Ohio University Press, 1984.

Halberstam, David. *The Fifties.* New York: Villard, 1993.

Hayward, Max, ed. *On Trial: The Soviet State versus "Abram Tertz" and "Nikolai Arzhak."* New York: Harper and Row, 1967.

Hodgson, Godfrey. *America during the Cold War.* Fort Worth, Texas: Harcourt Brace Jovanovich Publishers, 1993.

Hoffman, Stanley. "Revisionism Revisited." In *Reflections on the Cold War,* edited by Lynn H. Miller and Ronald W. Preussen. Philadelphia: Temple University Press, 1974.

Howard, Jane. "Can a Nice Novelist Finish First?" *Life* 4 (November 1966): 74–82.

Levin, Martin, ed. *Five Boyhoods.* New York: Doubleday, 1962.

Levy, David W. *The Debate over Vietnam.* Baltimore: Johns Hopkins University Press, 1991.

Luscher, Robert M. *John Updike: A Study of the Short Fiction.* New York: Twayne, 1993.

McNally, J. M., and Dean Stover. "An Interview with John Updike." *Hayden's Ferry Review* 3 (spring 1988): 102.

McNamara, Robert S. *In Retrospect: The Tragedy and Lessons of Vietnam.* New York: Times Books, 1995.

Markle, Joyce B. *Fighters and Lovers: Theme in the Novels of John Updike.* New York: New York University Press, 1973.

Matusow, Allen. *The Unraveling of America: A History of Liberalism in the 1960s.* New York: Harper and Row, 1984.

May, Elaine Tyler. *Homeward Bound: American Families in the Cold War Era.* New York: Basic Books, 1988.

Miller, D. Quentin. "Updike's Rabbit Novels and the Tragedy of Parenthood." In *Family Matters in the American and British Novel,* edited by Andrea O'Reilly Herrera, Elizabeth Mahn Nollen, and Sheila Reitzel Foor. Bowling Green, Ohio: Popular Press, 1997.

Neary, John. *Something and Nothingness: The Fiction of John Updike and John Fowles.* Carbondale: Southern Illinois University Press, 1992.

Newhouse, John. *War and Peace in the Nuclear Age.* New York: Alfred A. Knopf, 1988.

O'Connell, Mary. *Updike and the Patriarchal Dilemma: Masculinity in the Rabbit Novels.* Carbondale: Southern Illinois University Press, 1996.

Olster, Stacey. "Rabbit Rerun: Updike's Replay of Popular Culture in *Rabbit at Rest.*" *Modern Fiction Studies* 37, no. 1 (spring 1991): 45–60.

Parini, Jay. "All His Wives Are Mother." *New York Times Book Review* (November 6, 1994): 7.

Pinsker, Sanford. "John Updike and the Distractions of Henry Bech, Professional Writer and Amateur American Jew." *Modern Fiction Studies* 37, no. 1 (spring 1991): 97–111.

Plath, James. *Conversations with John Updike.* Jackson: University Press of Mississippi, 1994.

Podhoretz, Norman. *Why We Were in Vietnam.* New York: Simon and Schuster, 1982.

Ristoff, Dilvo I. "Appropriating the Scene: The World of *Rabbit at Rest.*" In *Rabbit Tales: Poetry and Politics in John Updike's Rabbit Novels,* edited by Lawrence Broer. Tuscaloosa: University of Alabama Press, 1998.

———. *Updike's America: The Presence of Contemporary American History in John Updike's Rabbit Trilogy.* New York: Peter Lang, 1988.

Ruthven, Ken. *Nuclear Criticism.* Portland, Oreg.: Melbourne University Press, 1993.

Samuels, Charles Thomas. "Updike on the Present." *New Republic* (November 20, 1971): 29–30.

Schaub, Thomas Hill. *American Fiction in the Cold War.* Madison: University of Wisconsin Press, 1991.

Schlesinger, Arthur, Jr. "The Historical Mind and the Literary Imagination." *Atlantic Monthly* (June 1974): 54–59.

Schueller, Malini. "Containing the Third World: John Updike's *The Coup.*" *Modern Fiction Studies* 37, no. 1 (spring 1991): 113–28.

Shatz, Marshall S. *Soviet Dissent in Historical Perspective.* Cambridge: Cambridge University Press, 1980.

Simons, Thomas W. *The End of the Cold War?* New York: St. Martin's, 1990.

Sokoloff, B.A., and David E. Arnason. *John Updike: A Comprehensive Bibliography.* Norwood, Pa.: Norwood Editions, 1972.

Solzhenitsyn, Aleksandr I. *The Gulag Archipelago 1918–1956.* Translated by Thomas Whitney. New York: Harper and Row, 1974–1978.

———. *One Day in the Life of Ivan Denisovich.* Translated by Ralph Parker. New York: Time, Inc., 1963.

Stein, Gertrude. "Reflection on the Atomic Bomb." In *Reflection on the Atomic Bomb, Vol. 1 of the Previously Uncollected Works of Gertrude Stein,* edited by Robert Bartlett Haas. Los Angeles: Black Sparrow, 1973.

Suchoff, David. "New Historicism and Containment: Toward a Post–Cold War Cultural Theory." *Arizona Quarterly* 48, no. 1 (spring 1992): 137–61.

Tarnoff, Peter. "Bizarre Nostalgia for the Cold War." *New York Times,* September 19, 1989.

Taylor, Larry E. *Pastoral and Anti-Pastoral Patterns in John Updike's Fiction.* Carbondale: Southern Illinois University Press, 1971.

Updike, John. *The Afterlife*. New York: Knopf, 1994.

———. *Assorted Prose*. New York: Fawcett Crest, 1965.

———. *Bech: A Book*. New York: Knopf, 1970.

———. *Bech Is Back*. New York: Knopf, 1982.

———. *Bech at Bay*. New York: Knopf, 1998.

———. "Behold Gombrowicz." *New Yorker* (September 23, 1967): 169–76.

———. *Brazil*. New York: Knopf, 1994.

———. *Buchanan Dying*. New York: Knopf, 1974.

———. *The Centaur*. New York: Knopf, 1963.

———. *Collected Poems 1953–1993*. New York: Knopf, 1993.

———. *The Coup*. New York: Fawcett Crest, 1978.

———. *Couples*. New York: Fawcett Columbine, 1996.

———. "The Cultural Situation of the American Writer." *American Studies International* 15, no. 3 (spring 1977): 19–28.

———. *Facing Nature*. New York: Knopf, 1985.

———. *Hugging the Shore*. New York: Vintage, 1984.

———. *In the Beauty of the Lilies*. New York: Knopf, 1996.

———. *Licks of Love*. New York: Knopf, 2000.

———. "Licks of Love in the Heart of the Cold War." *Atlantic Monthly* (May 1998): 80–90.

———. *Memories of the Ford Administration*. New York: Knopf, 1992.

———. *Midpoint*. New York: Knopf, 1969.

———. *A Month of Sundays*. New York: Fawcett Crest, 1975.

———. *More Matter*. New York: Knopf, 1999.

———. "More Stately Mansions." *Esquire* (October 1982): 142–57.

———. *Museums and Women*. New York: Knopf, 1972.

———. *The Music School*. New York: Knopf, 1966.

———. "Notes and Comment." *New Yorker* (September 26, 1959): 33.

———. "Notes and Comment." *New Yorker* (October 24, 1959): 34.

———. "Notes and Comment." *New Yorker* (June 5, 1965): 31.

———. "Notes and Comment." *New Yorker* (November 6, 1965): 43.

———. *Odd Jobs*. New York: Knopf, 1991.

———. *Of the Farm*. New York: Knopf, 1965.

———. *Olinger Stories*. New York: Knopf, 1964.

———. *Picked-Up Pieces*. New York: Fawcett Crest, 1975.

————. *Pigeon Feathers.* New York: Knopf, 1962.

————. *The Poorhouse Fair.* New York: Fawcett Crest, 1959.

————. *Problems.* New York: Fawcett Crest, 1979.

————. *Rabbit at Rest.* New York: Fawcett Crest, 1990.

————. *Rabbit Is Rich.* New York: Fawcett Crest, 1981.

————. *Rabbit Redux.* New York: Fawcett Crest, 1971.

————. *Rabbit, Run.* New York: Fawcett Crest, 1960.

————. *Roger's Version.* New York: Knopf, 1986.

————. *S.* New York: Knopf, 1988.

————. *The Same Door.* New York: Fawcett Crest, 1959.

————. *Self-Consciousness.* New York: Knopf, 1989.

————. *Too Far to Go.* New York: Fawcett Crest, 1979.

————. *Tossing and Turning.* New York: Knopf, 1977.

————. *Toward the End of Time.* New York: Knopf, 1997.

————. *Trust Me.* New York: Fawcett Crest, 1987.

————. "Why Rabbit Had to Go." *New York Times Book Review* (August 4, 1990): 1, 24.

————. *The Witches of Eastwick.* New York: Fawcett Crest, 1984.

————. Letter. *New York Times,* September 24, 1967.

Uphaus, Suzanne Henning. *John Updike.* New York: Frederick Ungar, 1980.

Vargo, Edward P. "Corn Chips, Catheters, Toyotas: The Making of History in *Rabbit at Rest.*" In *Rabbit Tales: Poetry and Politics in John Updike's Rabbit Novels,* edited by Lawrence Broer. Tuscaloosa: University of Alabama Press, 1998.

————. *Rainstorms and Fire: Ritual in the Novels of John Updike.* Port Washington, N.Y.: Kennikat Press, 1973.

"View from the Catacombs." *Time* (April 26, 1968): 66–75.

Waldmeir, Joseph J. "Only an Occasional Rutabaga: American Fiction since 1945." *Modern Fiction Studies* 15 (winter 1969/70): 467–81.

"The War Assayed by 259 Writers." *New York Times,* September 18, 1967.

Weisberger, Bernard A. *Cold War, Cold Peace.* Boston: Houghton Mifflin Company, 1984.

"Western Writers Appeal to Soviet." *New York Times,* February 1, 1966.

Whitfield, Stephen J. *The Culture of the Cold War.* Baltimore: Johns Hopkins University Press, 1991.

Woolf, Cecil, ed. *Authors Take Sides on Vietnam.* London: Owen, 1967.

"Writers Appeal on Soviet Jews." *New York Times,* May 21, 1967.

Wyatt, Bryant N. "John Updike: The Psychological Novel in Search of Structure." *Twentieth Century Literature* 13 (July 1967): 89-96.

"Yevtushenko Opens Tour of U.S." *New York Times,* November 7, 1966.

Yevtushenko, Yevgeny. *The Collected Poems 1952-1990.* Edited by Albert C. Todd. New York: Henry Holt, 1991.

Index